The Long Road to Methodist Union

THE SYMBOL OF UNION

Bishop Straughn, Bishop Hughes, Bishop Moore,
Uniting Conference, Kansas City, 1939

THE LONG ROAD TO METHODIST UNION

By
JOHN M. MOORE
A Bishop of The Methodist Church

With Forewords by
EDWIN HOLT HUGHES
JAMES H. STRAUGHN
Bishops of The Methodist Church

ABINGDON-COKESBURY PRESS
New York • Nashville

THE LONG ROAD TO METHODIST UNION
COPYRIGHT, MCMXLIII
BY WHITMORE & STONE

SET UP, PRINTED, AND BOUND BY THE
PARTHENON PRESS AT NASHVILLE, TEN-
NESSEE, UNITED STATES OF AMERICA

Dedicated to
The Memory and Honor of
All the Members of All the Commissions
Who Helped to Build
THE LONG ROAD
From Cape May to the Uniting Conference
by
One of Them

Foreword

BISHOP EDWIN HOLT HUGHES

I T IS THE AIM OF THIS INTRODUCTORY WORD TO TELL ABOUT THE writer rather than about the contents of the volume. The trite saying is applicable—the book "speaks for itself." For years to come those who are interested in a sad movement that made for separation, and in a glad movement that made for reunion, will find these pages the textbook for their research. It has been written by one who has made the subject a decade-by-decade study until, I may boldly affirm, no one in united Methodism could have made a record of more authority. Enthralled as I have been by the theme, so often discussed in my parsonages, first and second, and feeling myself well versed in the history involved, I have still fallen back often upon the larger information of my dear friend, Bishop Moore.

Strangely enough, the Chairmen of the three denominational Commissions that wrought for the making of the Plan finally adopted were changed in the very midst of the negotiations. Dr. John Calvin Broomfield, afterward Bishop, reached the expiration of his lovable term as President of the Methodist Protestant Conference, and was succeeded as Chairman by Dr. James H. Straughn, afterward Bishop. Each of these men did splendid service, each being especially adapted to the period for which he was designated.

Then one day Bishop Edwin D. Mouzon stepped suddenly out of this earthly life, after incalculable assistance in the great effort for union; and Bishop John M. Moore was chosen for the headship of the Southern Commission. Not long afterward Bishop William Fraser McDowell discovered that there was only one quick step between his earthly home and Heaven, and in a moment he changed countries. I shall never forget my own

sober feeling when I was made aware of the desire of my colleagues that I should head the Methodist Episcopal Commission.
Even before the formal election came, Bishop John W. Hamilton
said to me that in the providence of God I was to have a special
part in the achieving of Methodist union. His words of preview
sent me to prayer.

The final three Chairmen had one thing in common: they
were all sons of "the middle border"—the eastern shores of Maryland, Kentucky, and West Virginia. Bunyan shows us a doubt-
ful character named Mr. Facing-Both-Ways. In our cases the
name phrase could be glorified! We were obliged to look both
North and South. If we had glanced only in one of the two
directions, we would have disqualified ourselves. Other Commissioners did the one-way function finely. The High North
and the Deep South had efficient and kindly representations.
But our problem was to make a religious climate where pine and
palm would grow in the transformed Garden of the Lord. That
miracle was duly accomplished.

But among the men on the three Commissions, Bishop John
M. Moore had the pen of the "ready writer." I emphasize the
adjective. In most parliamentary gatherings the loss of time is
caused by the lack of penmanship. Desultory discussion has its
office, but results arrive only when big resolutions are actually
framed. In this respect Bishop Moore was our premier. His
pockets were labeled files. He had so long considered the in-
cidental issues, as well as the great principles, as to be really
ready. I suspect that he would admit that at times he had to
keep pieces of paper out of sight, lest men who headed other
committees might think him intrusive. Often I noticed that the
final action was based upon the wording of scraps of paper that
had been written by him in the night watches. He looked ahead,
saw the approaching turns of the Road, and was waiting there,
with signal lights and direction posts.

I must refer also to his spirit, and indeed to the spirit of all his
partners in negotiation. I know of no colossal thing that in its

last stages was carried on in more genuine harmony. I have at times tried to think of words that I would wish to have eliminated from our discussions. "The devil's advocate," so far as our work was concerned, would lose his position! I said frequently that if the attitudes and needs of the Commissions could be fully diffused throughout the three denominations the goal was fully assured. The three Chairmen are knit together by cords of love. The picture of our clasped hands, taken in the General Conference at Birmingham on the evening following the final vote of confirmation, is an utterly true one. You cannot break those hands apart by any word of severance. God joined us together; man cannot put us asunder.

I have no desire to overdo the personal tribute implied here. Doubtless, more than either of his two companions, Bishop Moore had to face difficulties. History had inevitably created a very sensitive Southland. The Northland has had little of troublesome aftermath following the consummation of union. Even still courts hear occasional echoes below Mason and Dixon's line. But the Judge of all the earth is following our efforts with a verdict of righteousness and peace. He has had no more faithful and efficient agent in this long crusade for the reunion of his people than the author of this volume. I close by reminding you again that the story herein written is the story of *the greatest reunion of Christ's people ever made in the nineteen hundred years of our faith.* And I hail as one of its chief heroes the man who rendered incalculable service in the sacred cause—

John Monroe Moore, God bless him!

Foreword

BISHOP JAMES H. STRAUGHN

METHODIST UNION BEGAN WITH METHODIST DIVISION. THAT WAS not known at the time, nor for many years afterward. It is not a point to be argued, needing only a testimony. The usual course of division is further and completer separation with the years, as each party to the division finds it necessary to explain and justify the division. Strong feelings existed in 1828 and 1844, but they were tempered with time, and when they were quieted we discovered that our essential loyalty to Methodism not only had not permitted a widening of the gap, but in fact had been a converging impulse. That was particularly true of the two major Churches in the matter of lay representation, which had been the divisive factor leading to the organization of the Methodist Protestant Church, and which by gradual legislation in the two major Churches had become an accepted principle in their polity. On the other hand, the individualism of the Methodist Protestants and the swing away from centralization of authority had melted down in the acceptance of completer supervision and control, in both Annual and General Conferences, as witness a full-time General Conference President for the first time in the belated year of 1920. Methodist union was easy after we got over our hurt feeling.

In these paragraphs I am of necessity writing from the standpoint of the Methodist Protestant Church and its part in the movement. What I have to say is intended only to bridge certain intervals of this book—that which came under my own personal observation. I was not a member of any of the Commissions on union until the death of President Albert Norman Ward in 1935, and at that time the Plan of Union had been

11

finished.   I came into the picture actively when elected President of the General Conference in 1936 and had in charge the submission of "The Plan" to the Annual Conferences for their decision.

To the Methodist Protestants, Methodist union became active in 1908 and again in 1930.   The initiating suggestion for the first movement started at the midwinter meeting, 1907-8, of the Methodist Social Union of Baltimore, a layman's organization, for the most part, of the Methodist Episcopal Church.   At that meeting several laymen and a few ministers began talking of the possibility of Methodist union.   Later conversations were held with a widening group.   In May, 1908, the General Conferences of the Northern Church (in Baltimore) and of the Protestant Church (in Pittsburgh) would be held.   There was an agreement that the two groups would exchange delegations, looking to the starting of a union movement.   To the meeting in Pittsburgh came Bishop H. W. Warren, Dr. John F. Goucher, and Senator J. P. Dolliver.   To the Baltimore meeting went Dr. T. H. Lewis (the new President of the General Conference), the Reverend A. L. Reynolds, and the Honorable J. W. Hering.

The speech of Dr. Lewis at Baltimore has become historic as setting fire to the union movement.   Later, in 1910, he visited the Southern General Conference at Asheville, North Carolina, where, as recorded in a Southern paper, he "struck twelve a second time."   All three bodies raised Commissions on union.   These Commissions met, as indicated in this volume, and submitted basic and tentative findings to succeeding General Conferences.   They were approved by all three bodies except, as recorded in Chapter VII, by action of the Southern Conference, the Methodist Protestant Church was omitted, and union from that time was considered between the two major Methodist bodies.   This later developed into a movement toward federation which defaulted, and Methodist union for the time being came to an end.   In the meanwhile, and certainly contributing to the omission of the Methodist Protestants from this latter movement, a plan of union had been started between the United Brethren Church and the Methodist Protestant Church before 1908, carrying through to 1912, when the Methodist Protestant General Conference, in addition to endorsing and continuing the Methodist movement, gave an imperative mandate for the conclusion of the union with the United Brethren Church. A plan of union was approved by these two commissions and at a special session of the Methodist Protestant Church in 1914 was adopted, but the union was never completed. The Methodist Protestants were then on the sideline awaiting developments of the other Methodist movement toward federation.

The second movement began also in an informal way, in Pittsburgh in 1929, when some Methodist Protestant ministers met with Bishop Welch to discuss the possibility of a union between the Methodist Episcopal and the Methodist Protestant Churches. These discussions were relayed to Bishop McDowell, Chairman of the Methodist Episcopal Commission, who in turn addressed a letter to the President of the Methodist Protestant General Conference, Dr. John C. Broomfield, suggesting a meeting of the two Commissions. Dr. Broomfield readily accepted the invitation and, until he relinquished his presidency in 1936, gave devoted and untiring leadership in his own Church to the cause of union. The first joint meeting was held in Pittsburgh, July 30. At that meeting regret was expressed that the Southern Church was not represented. Later it was discovered that that body had no commission empowered to act in this capacity. Several meetings of these two Commissions were held, looking to a union of the two Churches. In the January, 1932, meeting a resolution was adopted that no more meetings be held until another effort be made to bring in the Southern Church. A letter of invitation was written to Bishop McMurry, and on February 24, 1932, three members of each Church met in Washington. At that meeting Bishop McDowell offered a paper expressing an urgent desire for a perfect, not a partial union, and suggested that further efforts at union between the two Churches be postponed until the General Conference of the Southern body might have an opportunity to take action and authorize a commission. This decision was later approved by the Methodist Episcopal and the Methodist Protestant General Conferences in 1932. The Southern body at its 1934 General Conference entered heartily into the movement and raised up a Commission empowered to act; and from that time on the three Commissions speeded the process and were ready to report by the General Conferences of 1936. The later story is well set out in Bishop Moore's book.

The Methodist Protestant Church always realized that the major issues in union were between the major Churches, but felt at all times that it was making its own contribution to the union; that the movement which began in 1908 with the remarkable leadership and addresses of Dr. Lewis, while arrested from time to time, never altogether disappeared, and became basic to the final culmination. And, as Bishop Moore has so carefully traced herein, the Plan of Union as finally adopted was not the work of the last movement alone but an aggregate of all the previous efforts and sittings of the Commissions. Except for this back work, union could never have come as rapidly as it did. And even a cursory reading of what is herein printed must convince anyone of the tremendous contribution made by Bishop Moore in the development of the Plan. While I did not become an active participant in negotiations until late in the movement, yet from 1936 I came to see and highly appreciate his part in it. Not only this, but his great leadership within his own group will always be recognized.

I have followed with genuine interest and sympathy Bishop Moore's insistence on "union by reorganization." This Methodist Church is a new church, a fact which is not yet fully realized. For, North and South, there is the tendency to continue to do business as before. This is particularly true in those sections of the Church where there was little overlapping. The careful reading of the final chapter is the compelling testimony to the new order, however, and as a treatment of the question of the Jurisdictional Conference must be quite revealing and perhaps startling to some of our readers. Perhaps the main cause of criticism of the first Jurisdictional Conferences is to be based in a failure to understand their purpose. The tendency was simply to make little General Conferences of them, and they were accepted in a general way as making union possible by satisfying the Southern constituency. These bodies hereafter must organize and plan on other lines; perhaps, in addition to their specified responsibilities, to become great promotional agencies, and, to save the high contrast with the General Conference, to be separated from it by a longer period of time.

Many great compensations have come to me in Methodist union. Other than the supreme satisfaction of knowing we are together again in one family, one home, witnessing to earnest yearning for an obedience to that ancient prayer for the unity of Christ's people, and as a living witness before the world that these Methodists are one people, my most rewarding joy has been the association with the other two Chairmen, Bishop Moore and Bishop Hughes. I constantly thank my God for them, for every remembrance of them; no higher honor has ever come my way. Nor can I ever forget that amazing moment in Birmingham, 1938, that night after the most emphatic vote for union of the three groups! Union was assured. At last the uncertainty was over. The three Chairmen stood with clasped hands. Five thousand and more people surged forward in rejoicing as at a new Pentecost. Who can ever forget the moment at Kansas City of the Declaration of Union! With Bishop Hughes' ringing words upon our hearts, we stood there, bathed in tears, in happy realization that at last we were together again. Nor could I keep out of my mind the memory of the beloved Lewis crying out in 1908, in Baltimore, "But if it be required of us we bring all our treasure and lay all our identity upon the altar as a sacrifice; if we may but beat a drum or carry a flag, while Judah and Ephraim once more march on to the same music of peace, joyfully we will say, Amen, God wills it."

The Personal Word

LIFE BEGAN WITH THIS NARRATOR TWO YEARS AFTER THE CIVIL War, in the hill country of Kentucky about midway between the birthplaces of Abraham Lincoln on the east and Jefferson Davis on the west. His father was born in Virginia twelve miles from Appomattox, as were his grandfather and great-grandfather. His great-grandmother was Nancy Asbury, whose relations had something to do with the early Methodist ministry. His mother's father was English born, and her brothers fought in the Union army. His father's kin fought in the Confederate army. In his boyhood two reunions of the ex-soldiers were held annually in the community, and the picnic at each was the boy's delight. His father was a Southern Methodist steward, his father's brother was a Methodist Protestant steward, and some good neighbors were Northern Methodists. That was what might be called a mixed community, and a complex lineage. That is background enough to compel a man to think and practice union.

He was converted in a country meetinghouse under his mother's pastor, a beloved Cumberland Presbyterian minister. While in school in Ohio he joined the Northern Methodist Church. During the same year in Kentucky he was licensed to preach in the Southern Methodist Church. Five and a half years later, while a student in Yale, he was ordained a deacon by Bishop Charles H. Fowler in Brooklyn. In 1895 he was admitted into the itinerant ministry of the Methodist Episcopal Church, South, in which there has been much joy, congeniality, and satisfaction. All that helped to give the spirit of union a start.

In January, 1934, Bishop Charles B. Galloway, a great leader in the Church, South, addressed a convention of young people

17

in New Haven. He was delighted by the reception given him, and on his way to the midnight train he remarked that someday the two Churches would and should unite. That remark led to a passion to be used of God in promoting Methodist union which never died out.

In November, 1910, Dr. R. S. Hyer, a member of the Commission on Federation, and the first President of Southern Methodist University, asked "What would be your plan of union of the Northern and Southern Methodist Churches?" That question awoke to realization the fact that without a plan no union would be acceptable, and it also started a strenuous, continuous, and uninterrupted research, study, and writing that lasted three months. The outcome was an article of about a thousand words on "A Plan of Union," which was published March 3, 1911, in the *Christian Advocate* (Nashville), and which was more than an article to the writer. During the twenty-five years of negotiations confidence never diminished, much less failed, whatever the situation that might be developed, or the discussion that might be put forth, that union could be and would be eventually consummated upon the basis laid down in the article, and upon no other. This confidence proved to be well founded.

This autobiographical reference may be a bit improper, but it reveals the varied background and experience of the writer of this personal witnessing. The viewpoint of this book is meant to be not Southern, or Northern, or Eastern, or Western. It is too late for such writing. It is meant to be personal, and for that reason the author's background has probably some interest if not value to the reader.

The book is no mere narration, or recital of experiences. That alone would be of minor value. Something happened when these Churches broke away from each other; and something happened before and when they came back together. Those great Churches would not have stood apart for a century had there not been deep and grave issues that kept them separate. Only superficial thinking and meager information could have failed to realize the enormous obstacles to the restoration to unity. Unification was not to be simply a matter of allaying prejudices; it had to be a matter of finding, recognizing, and adjusting principles. What were the deeply dividing issues? How did they arise, and when? What were the various measures proposed, and what were finally adopted to remove the obstacles, and to satisfy the grave issues, and to provide guarantees against their recurring? To answer these questions is the purpose of this book.

In the last chapter some personal observations and suggestions have been added to the narrative. They may not be readily approved by some readers. But they may be helpful to those who have not acquainted themselves with certain principles that were basic in the separations, and which became fundamental in the policies of the uniting Churches, and which had to be embodied in any plan of union that was to be acceptable and permanent. It is hoped that they will be faithfully and sympathetically considered. The Plan of Union was not simply a device for bringing in union; it was more a structure for carrying unity and union on. This conviction is the apology for the emphasis in these wayside observations.

The Forewords by Bishop Edwin Holt Hughes and Bishop James H. Straughn were graciously contributed by the two Chairmen Colleagues upon the invitation of the author. These two highly esteemed associates in the Joint Commission assume no responsibility for what the author has written, and he in turn will take no responsibility for the eulogistic words which they have written. One of them boldly declared, "You are not allowed to change the personal estimate of your service which my conscience has led me to write." Profound appreciation for his gracious and generous words lies more deeply than language can express. The glow of them will make light and warmth for all the journey ahead.

Bishop Hughes in his Foreword speaks of Methodist union

as the greatest movement that has ever been consummated in American Protestantism or in the Christian Church. If his estimate is correct—and none can successfully gainsay it—then there is much need for a book that undertakes to give a succinct and accurate account of the many steps and long processes that were employed in its achievement, and also to impart some knowledge and understanding of the undergirding principles of the basic governmental structure of the new Church that has resulted from this union. This is the reason for this modest volume. "The Long Road to Methodist Union" is hereby opened to those who would know more perfectly the way in Methodist union. May those who take it have a profitable journey.

J. M. M.

Dallas, Texas
March 1, 1943

Contents

INTRODUCTION

Mᴇᴛʜᴏᴅɪsᴛ ᴜɴɪᴏɴ ғɪɴᴀʟʟʏ ᴀʀʀɪᴠᴇᴅ ᴀғᴛᴇʀ ᴀ ᴠᴇʀʏ ʟᴏɴɢ, ʜᴀʀᴅ journey. It started August 17, 1876, and came to a glorious destination on May 10, 1939, at 8:59 in the evening, a period of sixty-two years, eight months, and twenty-three days. At no time in this long period was this matter allowed to be entirely laid aside. Strong, conscientious men of high purpose, far vision, and righteous will kept before the Churches the lively hope that they could and would find their way into an honorable, effective, and substantial union. Processes were introduced and measures adopted from time to time which continued the Churches at work, through Commissions, upon the approaches that eventually led to unification. The history of those long and vital negotiations is exceedingly interesting, if not fascinating, and of such great importance that it should be widely known. Without the knowledge of the backgrounds lying in the sixty years of faithful, conscientious, and intelligent negotiations, the united Church in its future actions and movements could come to misfortune by its failure to observe those essential and directive principles by which union was agreed upon and consummated. For that reason it seems well that the story of the negotiations, the human elements involved, the principles recognized, the compact of agreement reached should be set forth in sketch and outline for those who may desire knowledge of this great movement in Methodism which brought into one body the Methodist Episcopal Church, the Methodist Episcopal Church, South, and the Methodist Protestant Church.

At the outset some interesting facts may be stated that will give some insight into the great strength and possibilities of Methodism in the United States and into its activities and service beyond this continent, and indicate its responsibility as a Christian force among the religious powers of the world. The facts may also aid in determining the future course of Methodism in consummating other processes of church union.

There are twenty-five million Methodists in the United States. Not all are church members. The church membership is about ten millions. Many persons hold the Methodist beliefs who have never become communicants in the Church. Children even if baptized do not become church members in The Methodist Church until they are old enough to understand the Church beliefs and assume the Church vows. But whether regarded as ten million communicants or as twenty-five million or more adherents, the Methodists form a very large religious group in the United States.

Methodism in the United States in 1938 had nineteen divisions, of which ten were entirely Negro. These Negro divisions alone had about 1,850,000 communicants and 5,000,000 adherents. The nine practically white divisions had about 8,000,000 communicants, of whom 325,000 were Negroes. Three of the Negro divisions had 95 per cent of the combined membership of all the Negro divisions and the other seven had only about 5 per cent. Three of the white or mixed divisions had 99 per cent, and the other six had only 1 per cent of the white membership. Of Negro Methodists 85 per cent were in the Negro divisions, and 15 per cent were in the white or mixed divisions.

The union of the Methodist Episcopal Church, the Methodist Episcopal Church, South, and the Methodist Protestant Church, declared May 10, 1939, brought into one Methodist Church 99 per cent of all the white Methodists in the United States. That the groups forming the other 1 per cent may find it religiously comfortable and desirable to come in the future, and at their will, into this one Church is to be earnestly hoped.

The African Methodist Episcopal Church has been an independent organization with its own General Conference, bishops, boards, and institutions since 1816; and the African Methodist

Episcopal Zion Church, since 1817. Their history has been highly honorable and their achievements noteworthy. The Colored Methodist Episcopal Church was organized in 1870 out of the Negro membership of the Methodist Episcopal Church, South, being set off and set up at their own request by the General Conference of the Methodist Episcopal Church, South. For seventy years they have made a splendid record and exhibited large capabilities for managing their own affairs. Originally the African Methodist Episcopal Church was altogether in the North, as was largely the Zion Church. After the emancipation of the slaves, these Churches came South and attached some of the emancipated people. The Colored Church was altogether in the South until the migration era which began about 1915 to 1920. It followed its people to the North and East. Now these three Churches are competitors in practically all the territory of the United States where the Negro people live. The unities of the race, of their religious life, and of ecclesiastical polity make such competition out of date.

The Negro Baptists of the United States soon after the opening of the century went into one organization, the National Baptist Convention. They have doubled in church membership since their merger. They had in 1938 about 3,500,000 communicants. In union they have found strength, inspiration, and zeal. During this period the Negro Methodist groups made only limited increase. They have been outstripped by their Baptist brethren.

The smaller Methodist groups will not be discounted because for conscience' sake they choose to live their Methodist lives in small sects. They are concerned for special emphasis on certain aspects of Methodist faith and religious experience. They believe they can get it best through the smaller groups. However, it must be recognized that the Methodism that feels its world-wide parochial responsibility must have a commensurate sweep. But the larger body has only love and good will for all who know the Aldersgate experience.

Methodist union and Methodist unity are now primary objectives in American Methodist life. They may not be the same thing, and that should be considered. Unity is always spiritual; union may be mechanical. Union is proper and desirable only when it leads to unity. A union that makes possible or even probable other divisions should not be contemplated, and if considered it should be postponed if not abandoned. The process of union—and genuine union is always a process—requires time for due consideration of all that is proposed, understanding of all issues and factors involved, patience with persons of confused if not conflicting and even opposing views, and courage to continue courses that will lead inevitably to just and proper goals in the spirit and way of substantial unity. The Methodist union that has been attained is undergirded with genuine unity, and it will grow in strength and power as that unity is jealously guarded and sacredly maintained. To that objective there should be unswerving devotion and loyalty.

The first and continuing task in attaining Methodist union was in finding and producing unity and the bases of unity. This search often uncovered also some disunities and caused disunity. These could not be ignored or pushed aside. They had to be brought into the open, examined, clarified, and thoroughly comprehended. By degrees they were finally dissolved, reduced, and removed through understanding, good will, and good procedure. Unity is nourished only by the truth and thrives only in the light of knowledge and reason. Methodist union is here today, and it relates to three Churches, because it has not been allowed to go forward faster than unity could open the way. This accounts for the long period of the negotiations through which the Churches patiently and persistently passed. Unity came, and union followed. So long as unity prevails union will endure, and not much longer. Any failure to preserve, promote, and perfect unity in the thought, purpose, spirit, activity, and life of the Church could eventuate in misfortune if not peril to union. If the measures and processes that brought about the sense and assurance of unity and built its bonds are lost sight of, union would soon suffer and gradually become less effective in its power, beauty, and blessedness. Unity is not a mere matter of sentiment and good intention, but of understanding, will, resolution, courage, and conscience in the face of the great realities of the Church's life, thought, and responsibility. If union is to be kept vital and vigorous, unity must be kept genuine and unmistakable.

Chapter One

THE DISRUPTION OF ONENESS

Methodist union is the end of a road of which disruption was the beginning. To reach the one it was necessary to start at the other. The greatest obstacle to the consummation of church union or reunion is the unwillingness of many persons to discover, appreciate, and appraise the causes which brought about and confirmed disunity and division. This is the field of unpleasant realities, and unpleasant realities are very disturbing to the placid mind and to persons who rely on others to deal with them and master them. Yet they frequently if not usually contain the roots of the very possibilities for which quest is being made. This is certainly true in the matter of Methodist union.

The man who wrote *Life Begins at Forty* could not write a complete biography of anyone worth writing about starting with his fortieth year. Emerson once said: "To make a man, one must begin a hundred years before he is born." To study developments and movements one must begin with the sources. The source book is the most important on the shelf.

The Plan of Methodist Union in reality did not come out of the last half of Methodist separation, but out of the first half. Great issues develop great principles, and great instruments for employing them. Struggles create strength. The human mind gets keen under stress. Pioneering is always path-making whether in an unsettled land or in an unsettled civilization. Methodism came to itself in both. The creative era of American Methodism is not the half century succeeding 1890, but that preceding. The platform of union had to be made of planks cut from the forests grown in that earlier period. No progress was made toward union or reunion until the factors that had to be embraced in the Plan were found and recognized. The security of union set up is with those who know, appreciate, and respect the underlying and undergirding principles of a triple-sided disunity. Those factors and principles now are the strength and grace of the new Methodist structure.

Union is assured so long as its bonds are unbroken, and no longer. It will be as strong as its bonds make it, and no stronger. Weakening or rupture of those bonds will lay open the possibility of a new disunity and disruption. The state of mind that has created and maintained a separation can be removed only by removing the factors and causes that produced it. The principle that has guided the efforts to produce an acceptable and satisfactory plan of union has been that of welding into a new unity, or bond, the forces that made the disunity and the division, and sealing that bond with a new confidence, trust, and respect. There is no element in the adopted Plan of Union that did not appear in suggestion, or advocacy, or incorporation in one or more of the three Churches previous to 1890. This fact gives importance to this period for the student of Methodist Union.

I

The Methodist Episcopal Church was organized at Christmas, 1784. In 1792 came the first disaffection and defection under James O'Kelly, taking away about 6,500 members. In 1816 came the second separation with the organization of the African Methodist Episcopal Church. In 1817 came the third in the organization of the African Methodist Episcopal Zion Church. In 1828 came the fourth with the withdrawal of the part of the Church that lay in Canada. In 1830 came the fifth with the organization of the Methodist Protestant Church. The second, third, and fourth involved no principles of doctrine or government, but the other two were due to a very decided divergence of views, and especially of administration and polity.

James O'Kelly of Virginia introduced in the General Conference of 1792 a resolution to the effect that "after the bishop appoints the preachers at Conference to their several circuits, if any one think himself injured by the appointment, he shall have liberty to appeal to the Conference and state his objections; and if the Conference approve his objection, the bishop shall appoint him to another circuit." He was strong against the authority and life-tenure of the bishops. He was supported by some of the strong men of the Church. On the final vote his proposition was defeated by a large majority. The O'Kellyites withdrew from the Church, but there were still left some who held the views which he advocated.

In 1820 Joshua Soule, of New York but a native of Maine, was elected Bishop. Just after his election the General Conference passed a law requiring the presiding elders to be elected by the Annual Conferences, upon the nomination of the bishop. Soule promptly notified the Conference that he regarded the action as violative of the constitution, and that he would not consent to ordination except with the understanding that he would not hold himself bound to obey the law. He was not ordained. The law was then suspended until the next General Conference in 1824. In 1824 it was declared null and void, and in 1828 it was rescinded. Soule was re-elected Bishop in 1824. But the thought of an elective presiding eldership remained in some minds.

Some very active and aggressive opposition to Methodist polity was developing in and around Baltimore and Philadelphia, led or supported by such men as Nicholas Snethen, Asa Shinn, Alexander McCaine, S. K. Jennings, and William S. Stockton. Stockton was a layman. In 1821 he established a paper called *Wesleyan Repository*. The principal plea was for lay participation in the government of the Church, but the attacks were also upon everything that had the appearance of exclusive clerical authority. McCaine, a former Secretary of the General Conference, issued a vicious attack on the episcopacy in a booklet entitled *History and Mystery of Methodist Episco-pacy*. The *Repository* became more and more aggressive in its utterances, and opposition to them was stirred. The name of the paper was changed to *The Mutual Rights of the Ministers and Members of the Methodist Episcopal Church*. Its circulation increased. "Union Societies" were formed to promote the cause of reform. Dennis P. Dorsey and William C. Pool of the Baltimore Conference were expelled for their activities for reform. Fifty women withdrew from the Church. The Reformers, as they were known, were most numerous in Baltimore, Philadelphia, New York, Pittsburgh, and Cincinnati. They were strongly opposed to the episcopacy and to the presiding eldership, and they strongly favored equal representation of the laity in the General and Annual Conferences. The "Union Societies" and *The Mutual Rights* were the agencies through which the "reforms" were vigorously advocated.

The General Conference of 1828 declined every appeal that was made by these Reformers. In November of that year a convention of the Reformers met in Baltimore, reaffirmed their positions, effected a provisional organization, and appointed an official convention for November, 1830. That convention met, adopted a constitution and discipline, and organized the Methodist Protestant Church; and it is known as the first General Conference of that Church. About 26,000 members went into the new organization from the Methodist Episcopal Church.

The Methodist Protestant Church arose in protest against the continued exclusion of all laymen from the legislative, executive, and judicial bodies of the mother Methodist Episcopal Church. This protest to exclusion of laymen was fundamental. However, the opposition to the episcopacy and the presiding eldership was acute and strong. Dr. Thomas H. Lewis, a very able man among all the leaders of that Church, says the constitution which was then adopted recognized Christ as the only Head of the Church, and all elders in the Church as equal, secured to every adult layman the right to vote and to be represented in every church meeting, and to every itinerant the right of appeal from an oppressive appointment and a vote upon his removal from a charge while in faithful discharge of his duty, until the expiration of his term. It made Church trials for matters of opinion impossible, and gave to every accused person the right to challenge his jurors and an appeal from their verdict. It refused the modern episcopacy and the presiding eldership as unnecessary. It guarded, as a necessary part of organic law, the rights and privileges of individual members and local churches as carefully as those of the Annual and General Conferences.

After one hundred years of history guided by these governmental principles the Methodist Protestant Church, under the inspiration given by Dr. Lewis and others for Methodist union, entered upon negotiations for union with the Methodist Episcopal Church and, four years later, with the Methodist Episcopal Church, South, both of which had retained the episcopacy intact and in force, as well as the appointive presiding eldership or district superintendency, and the final authority of the bishops to make the appointments of the preachers to their charges, but had adopted and applied the principles of lay representation in all the Conferences.

II

The bisection of the Methodist Episcopal Church in 1844 presents a very different situation from that of the separation in 1830. All the issues that produced the Methodist Protestant Church were ecclesiastical. Upon its consummation no serious aftereffects remained for either Church. But in 1844 the case was vastly different. The issue was not primarily ecclesiastical but social, and it permeated the entire nation. Not to understand this issue and what it developed is to miss the way to union.

A social creed is never disturbing until it becomes definite and demanding, and that is very seldom. Sociological thinking is excursionary and can never be brought to account because in it there is no standard of doctrine. But the social mind is always of enormous consequence in social action and in any action founded upon it. Church union must necessarily be more or less a social action if the original disruption was caused largely by a social issue. The unification of Northern and Southern Methodisms had to deal not merely with disrupted relations but with the states of mind and life that had resulted from that disruption.

Slavery was to the fore at the very opening of the General Conference of 1844. The atmosphere was charged with it. The slavery agitation had been coming on in the nation and in the Church for some years. The Southern people had slaves. In some states, like Georgia and Maryland, the laws would not allow the freeing of slaves. The ministers of the South, for the most part, defended slavery and slaveholding by their people. The ministers in the Northern states became more and more severe in their condemnation of slavery and slaveholding, and in their censure of ministers and people who upheld and defended slavery. In New England the demand for the abolition of slavery became very determined. The Methodist Episcopal Church embraced all these elements, and the state of mind was disturbed and divided.

The General Conference met with two very important cases to be considered. The Rev. Francis A. Harding had been suspended by resolution and without trial by the Baltimore Conference for holding slaves. In February, 1844, he had married a young woman who had inherited five slaves from her parents. They were held by her, and not by him. Under the Maryland law they could not be freed. The Baltimore Conference adopted the resolution: "Resolved that Brother Harding be suspended until the next Annual Conference, or until he assured the episcopacy that he had taken the necessary steps to secure the freedom of his slaves." Mr. Harding appealed his case to the General Conference, where it was vigorously

debated for five full days. The final vote stood 117 for to 57
against sustaining the action of the Baltimore Conference.

A week later an inquiry was ordered into the case of Bishop
James O. Andrew, who lived in Georgia. He wrote the Committee on Episcopacy saying an old lady bequeathed to him
a mulatto girl, to be kept until she was nineteen years old,
and then allowed to go to Liberia; if she refused to go then,
to keep her and make her as free as the laws of Georgia would
permit. The girl grew up, refused to go to Liberia, or to any
other state, and chose to remain his slave. He said: "In her
case I have been made a slaveholder legally, but not with my
own consent." His wife's mother bequeathed his wife a Negro
boy. At his wife's death, she leaving no will, the Negro boy
became his slave, and he could not free him under the Georgia
law. He later married a widow who had inherited slaves from
her first husband's estate. To prevent their becoming his
slaves, he secured them to her by deed of trust. This sets out
the case of Bishop Andrew.

What should be done? What could be done? Had the
General Conference the authority and power to do whatever
it might desire, and in whatever way it might choose? Those
were basic questions. They were then, and they have been
ever since. Is the General Conference supreme? Is a bishop
simply an officer of the General Conference, or is he an officer
of the Church, with such duties, rights, responsibilities, and
powers as have been constitutionally assigned and assured him?
These questions came to the front in the debates. They have
never been fully answered; neither have they been set at rest.
The unification negotiators found them on the board.

Bishop Andrew was held in esteem and affection throughout
the entire Church. He was a good, kind, gentle man. He
was legally a slaveholder, but morally he was not. He was
the guardian and keeper of some Negro persons who could not
under the law be given their freedom, and they would not go
where it would be theirs. Bishop Andrew was the victim of

a condition which he could not alter nor escape. But his relation to slaveholding had to be considered by the General Conference because of its constituency of divergent social convictions. The social issue became ecclesiastical.

The General Conference and the entire Church was greatly perplexed and profoundly stirred. Two weeks were given to the discussion of the procedure to be taken. Master men engaged in the debate. Finally the question took form in the following resolution:

Whereas the Discipline of our Church forbids the doing any thing calculated to destroy our itinerant general superintendency; and whereas Bishop Andrew has become connected with slavery by marriage and otherwise, and this act having drawn after it circumstances which in the estimation of the General Conference will greatly embarrass the exercise of his office as an itinerant general superintendent, if not in some places entirely prevent it; therefore,

Resolved, That it is the sense of this General Conference that he desist from the exercise of his office so long as this impediment remains.

The resolution was adopted by a vote of 111 to 69.

These two actions in the cases of Mr. Harding and Bishop Andrew, with the long and acrimonious debate covering in all about three weeks, uncovered and created great disunion and promoted daily an increasing demand for a sectional division of the Church. Two days later fifty-two delegates from Southern Conferences presented a declaration

that the continued agitation of the subject of slavery and abolition in a portion of the Church,—the frequent action on that subject in the General Conference,—and especially the extra-judicial proceedings against Bishop Andrew, which resulted, on Saturday last, in the virtual suspension of him from his office as superintendent,—must produce a state of things in the South which renders a continuance of the jurisdiction of that General Conference over these Conferences inconsistent with the success of the ministry in the slaveholding states.

The next day these Southern delegates, with Henry B. Bascom as their spokesman, delivered to the General Conference a forceful protest against the action taken against Bishop Andrew. It closed with the words:

And it is believed that, approaching the subject in this way, it will be found practicable to devise and adopt such measures and arrangements, present and prospective, as will secure an amicable division of the Church upon the broad principles of right and equity, and destined to result in the common good of the great body of ministers and members found on either side the line of separation.

By this time unity was in the throes of a raging fever, and union was hung with dark forebodings. The temper of the General Conference, and perhaps its judgment, made some new decisive action necessary. The Southern delegates contended that Bishop Andrew had been deposed, suspended, without the process of law, while some Northern delegates declared that his status had been left to his own decision. The Bishops asked for instructions regarding the publication of Bishop Andrew's name in the minutes, the hymnbook, and the Discipline, also regarding his support, and whether in any and what work he should be employed, and how he should be appointed to it. The situation required clarification. It was tense.

A committee of nine had been appointed to consider the declaration and protest of the Southern delegates. It was composed of Robert Paine, Nathan Bangs, L. L. Hamline, William Winans, Glezen Filmore, Peter Akers, Thomas Crowder, Thomas B. Sargent, James Porter. After the protest was delivered, this resolution offered by John B. McFerrin of Tennessee was adopted:

Resolved, That the committee appointed to take into consideration the communication of the delegates from the Southern Conferences be instructed, provided they cannot in their judgment devise a plan for an amicable adjustment of the difficulties now existing in the Church, on the subject of slavery, to devise, if possible, a constitutional plan for a mutual and friendly division of the Church.

The Committee in two days reported to the General Conference the following Plan of Separation, which was adopted by a vote of 135 to 15.

Whereas, a declaration has been presented to this General Conference, with the signatures of *fifty-one* delegates of the body from thirteen Annual Conferences in the slaveholding States, representing that, for various reasons enumerated, the objects and purposes of the Christian ministry and Church organization cannot be successfully accomplished by them under the jurisdiction of this General Conference as now constituted; and

Whereas, in the event of a separation, a contingency to which the declaration asks attention as not improbable, we esteem it the duty of this General Conference to meet the emergency with Christian kindness and the strictest equity; therefore,

Resolved, by the delegates of the several Annual Conferences in General Conference assembled,

1. That, should the Annual Conferences in the slaveholding States find it necessary to unite in a distinct ecclesiastical connection, the following rule shall be observed with regard to the Northern boundary of such connection:—All the societies, stations, and Conferences adhering to the Church in the South, by a vote of a majority of the members of said societies, stations, and Conferences, shall remain under the unmolested pastoral care of the Southern Church; and the ministers of the Methodist Episcopal Church shall in no wise attempt to organize Churches or societies within the limits of the Church South, nor shall they attempt to exercise any pastoral oversight therein; it being understood that the ministry of the South reciprocally observe the same rule in relation to stations, societies, and Conferences, adhering, by vote of a majority, to the Methodist Episcopal Church; provided also, that this rule shall apply only to societies, stations, and Conferences bordering on the line of division, and not to interior charges, which shall in all cases be left to the care of that Church within whose territory they are situated.

2. That ministers, local and traveling, of every grade and office in the Methodist Episcopal Church, may, as they prefer, remain in that Church, or, without blame, attach themselves to the Church South.

3. Resolved, by the delegates of all the Annual Conferences in General Conference assembled, That we recommend to all the Annual Conferences, at their first approaching sessions, to authorize a change of the sixth restrictive article, so that the first clause shall read thus: "They shall not appropriate the produce of the Book Concern, nor of the Chartered Fund, to any other purpose other than for the benefit of the traveling, supernumerary, superannuated, and worn-out preachers, their wives, widows, and children, and to such other purposes as may be determined upon by the vote of two-thirds of the members of the General Conference."

4. That whenever the Annual Conferences, by a vote of three-fourths of all their members voting on the third resolution, shall have concurred in the recommendation to alter the sixth restrictive article, the Agents at New York and Cincinnati shall, and they are hereby authorized and directed to deliver over to any authorized agent or appointee of the Church South, should one be organized, all notes and book accounts against the ministers, church members, or citizens, within its boundaries, with authority to collect the same for the sole use of the Southern Church, and that said Agents also convey to aforesaid agent or appointee of the South, all the real estate, and assign to him all the property, including presses, stock, and all right and interest connected with the printing establishments at Charleston, Richmond, and Nashville, which now belong to the Methodist Episcopal Church.

5. That when the Annual Conferences shall have approved the aforesaid change in the sixth restrictive article, there shall be transferred to the above agent for the Southern Church so much of the capital and produce of the Methodist Book Concern as will, with the notes, book accounts, presses, etc., mentioned in the last resolution, bear the same proportion to the whole property of said Concern that the traveling preachers in the Southern Church shall bear to all the traveling ministers of the Methodist Episcopal Church; the division to be made on the basis of the number of traveling preachers in the forthcoming Minutes.

6. That the above transfer shall be in the form of annual

payments of $25,000 per annum, and specifically in stock of the Book Concern, and in Southern notes and accounts due the establishment, and accruing after the first transfer mentioned above; and until the payments are made, the Southern Church shall share in all the net profits of the Book Concern, in the proportion that the amount due them, or in arrears, bears to all the property of the Concern.

7. That Nathan Bangs, George Peck, and James B. Finley be, and they are hereby appointed commissioners to act in concert with the same number of commissioners appointed by the Southern organization, (should one be formed,) to estimate the amount which will fall due to the South by the preceding rule, and to have full powers to carry into effect the whole arrangements proposed with regard to the division of property, should the separation take place. And if by any means a vacancy occurs in this board of commissioners, the Book Committee at New York shall fill said vacancy.

8. That whenever any agents of the Southern Church are clothed with legal authority or corporate power to act in the premises, the Agents at New York are hereby authorized and directed to act in concert with said Southern agents, so as to give the provisions of these resolutions a legally binding force.

9. That all the property of the Methodist Episcopal Church in meeting houses, parsonages, colleges, schools, Conference funds, cemeteries, and of every kind within the limits of the Southern organization, shall be forever free from any claim set up on the part of the Methodist Episcopal Church, so far as this resolution can be of force in the premises.

10. That the Church so formed in the South shall have a common right to use all the copy-rights in possession of the Book Concerns at New York and Cincinnati, at the time of the settlement by the commissioners.

11. That the Book Agents at New York be directed to make such compensation to the Conferences South, for their dividend from the Chartered Fund, as the commissioners above provided for shall agree upon.

12. That the Bishops be respectfully requested to lay that part of this report requiring the action of the Annual Conferences before them as soon as possible, beginning with the New York Conference.

A study of this famous document reveals certain facts:

1. The division of the Church was accomplished by this act of the General Conference—the adoption of the Plan of Separation—to become effective "should the Annual Conferences in the slaveholding States find it necessary to unite in a distinct ecclesiastical connection." The United States Supreme Court later rendered a decision to the effect that the General Conference acting alone divided the Church.

2. The Plan of Separation was adopted by a General Conference composed entirely of ministers. It was not submitted to the Annual Conferences of the Church as a whole, which were also composed entirely of ministers. It was not submitted to any laymen or to any local congregations for any vote of any kind.

3. The Annual Conferences in the slaveholding states did vote on the question of having an independent connection, but not on the adoption of the Plan. The Annual Conferences of the North did not vote on the question of the Plan or of an independent organization.

4. The Plan was devised and wrought out so as to establish a line of separation to be drawn through the border territory. On one side was to be one division, on the other side the other division.

5. "All the societies, stations, and Conferences adhering to the Church in the South, by a vote of a majority of the members of said societies, stations, and Conferences, shall remain under the unmolested pastoral care of the Southern Church; and the ministers of the Methodist Episcopal Church shall in no wise attempt to organize churches or societies within the limits of this Church South," and the Church South was to observe the same rule regarding the other side.

6. A change in the restrictive rule regarding the produce of the Book Concern was proposed to allow its division, and provisions were made in the proposal for dividing the property of the Book Concern.

The General Conference came to an end after sitting from May 3 to June 10. Great souls and great minds sought to master a great issue and save the Church from division, but division became inevitable. The cleavage at the beginning had become a chasm at the end. A great line, deep and dark, had been drawn. That line, strange as it may seem, was long the only hope of future unity in the Episcopal Methodism of America.

The framers and promoters of the Plan of Separation planned two divisions or jurisdictions of one Church, but swiftly moving events and the feelings and decisions resulting therefrom destroyed the sense and semblance of one Church and brought into competing existence two bodies that were more conscious of their antagonisms than of their unities. The two branches had no fraternal relations with each other for twenty-five years; and they shared in the sentiments, attitudes, and movements of the two respective sections of an unhappy country. This disruption of relations led to increased divergence in understanding and interpretation of the fundamental principles and the organic law that underlay the government of the Church. This was especially true in regard to the place and power of the General Conference, the basis and authority of the episcopacy, or general superintendency, and the basic power of the Annual Conference as the final authority in voicing the mind and will of the Church. The plan makers for Methodist union could not be given the power to decide all these issues, but they might meet them by setting up what the business and professional world calls checks and balances that would protect the Church from or in these divergences, ecclesiastical and social. That was their great task. The background for the Methodist union movement lay in the issues which produced the Methodist Protestant Church, and in those which the General Conference of 1844 uncovered and accentuated; and understanding of these is vital.

Chapter Two

DIVERGENCIES OF TWENTY-FIVE TURBULENT YEARS

THE GENERAL CONFERENCE ADJOURNED ITS DELIBERATIONS, BUT not its debates. It inaugurated a turbulent era in American Methodism and left it a rough and jagged road over which to travel. The suspension of Francis A. Harding, the command to Bishop Andrew to desist from the exercise of his office, the continuance of his salary, and the publication of his name in the Discipline, the vigorous if not bitter protest of the Southern delegates, the reply of the Northern delegates in like kind, and the general criticism on the one side and defense on the other of slavery and slaveholding, the assertion of General Conference supremacy, and the implication of Episcopal subserviency—all gave occasion for much discussion and even irritating rejoinders. The delegates soon found that the Plan of Separation offered no hope or highway for Methodist peace. It soon became a battleground for accusing contestants who inflamed the Methodist people in all sections. The delegates were soon disillusioned, discredited, saddened, and maddened by the reactions of their respective peoples. Disruption had brought jarring disunion and biting disunity. Turbulent years were on, and they made bitter the relations in American Methodism.

The black clouds of Civil War were rising in all the land. Differences were becoming bitter and accute, and the Church was in their midst. It was a time of accusations and denunciations, and the Church did not escape. Had there been no war with its turmoil, passions, engendered hates, ravages, and horrible, unforgettable clashes of section against section, the Separation of 1844 might have been early closed by the healing influence and power of the Holy Gospel and the common faith. But it did come in fury, and it left, as always, hurts which generated divisive principles, polities, and procedures that were all but irreconcilable. Dividing lines in Methodism were cut which decades could not remove. They may yet remain in considerable measure to be patiently and sympathetically brought together by the time-taking processes of life and love.

1. The Plan of Separation, often praised for its formulation, was not the product of Southern authorship, as is often supposed. It was framed by L. L. Hamline of Ohio, who was elected bishop at that Conference. Robert Paine, of Tennessee, the chairman of the Committee, and later elected a bishop of the Church South, was not favorable to separation, but wanted a division of territory with one Church. This information came from William Winans, of Mississippi, who was a member of the Committee. Five out of the nine members were from Northern Conferences. Dr. Charles Elliott of Ohio, who became later a strong partisan against separation, advocated the Plan on the floor of the General Conference. The unfavorable reaction to the Plan was almost entirely in the North, and there in many sections it was exceedingly strong. The Northern membership of the General Conference were later severely excoriated by their constituents for agreeing to the division of the Church.

2. The response of the Southern ministers and people was decidedly favorable to separation. They resented the treatment given Bishop Andrew, although they knew that he as a slaveholder, even though he never bought or sold a slave, was unacceptable as a bishop in the North, just as an abolitionist bishop would have been unacceptable in the South. The ministry and the Methodist Church in the South were intertwined with the social and economic life of the people, and it was constructed about the institution of slavery. It was all of one structure from which the Church could not be extricated, and the very issues of the General Conference struck at the central principles and forces

of Southern civilization. For the Southern representatives to
have yielded to the demands of the majority would have been
to have surrendered Methodism in the South. While they would
have preferred division of territory in one Church to disruption
into two Churches, yet they accepted separation as planned as
the only tolerable possibility open to them. In view of events
which followed, the procedure adopted saved Methodism in
the South as probably no other would have done.

3. The Southern delegates lost no time in putting the Plan
of Separation into operation. They met in New York at the
close of the General Conference to work out a procedure to be
offered their people. They proposed a Convention on organization to be held May 1, 1845. The Annual Conferences in the
slaveholding states at their fall meetings were prompt in giving
almost solid approval to the purpose and plan to form an independent connection, and they elected delegates to the convention.
In order to awaken enthusiasm, loyalty, and devotion to the new
Church, votes were taken in local congregations, especially in
the lower South. While this action had no legal value it stirred
up great fervor toward the new organization and at the same
time strong antagonism and even bitter animosity toward the
Church North. All the Annual Conferences in the South appointed special committees to prepare resolutions relative to the
treatment of Bishop Andrew and also on separation. These
resolutions, which had practically the same tenor, were usually
severe in their criticism of the Northern majority and strongly in
favor of an independent connection. Such votes in local congregations and such resolutions in Conferences linger in the
minds and spirits of the people so long as the generation that
participated is alive. The Convention had behind it the heated
approval of the Southern constituency, and with one mind it
proceeded to set up the Methodist Episcopal Church, South.

4. The Convention was in session in Louisville, Kentucky,
nineteen days. Bishop Joshua Soule, who was born in Maine,
and Bishop James O. Andrew aligned themselves with this

Church, and presided over the Convention. It set the first General Conference for May 1, 1846, to be held at Petersburg, Virginia. The one action taken which was a star of hope for those who sought a way of union when the sea was dark and turbulent is the following resolution:

Resolved, That while we cannot abandon or compromise the principles of action upon which we proceed to a separate organization in the South; nevertheless, cherishing a sincere desire to maintain Christian union and fraternal intercourse with the Church North, we shall always be ready, kindly, and respectfully to entertain, and duly and carefully consider, any composition or plan, having for its object the union of the two bodies, in the North and South, whether such proposal shall be *jurisdictional or connectional.*

That resolution had much significance, and it gave guidance in the negotiations for union over a quarter of a century.

5. The promptness and rapidity with which the Southern Conferences acted in establishing the new organization brought unanimity and solidarity to the South; but they brought criticism, opposition, and charges of illegality from the North. Members of the General Conference of 1844 in the North claimed that the power was not given to the Southern Conferences to organize a Church, that they had acted with precipitate haste, that the General Conference could not divide the Church, that the proposed amendment to the restrictive rule was a part of the Plan of Separation, that it was not adopted, and consequently the Plan was not adopted, and that the action of the Southern Conferences was a secession. The bitter discussions of these contentions and the answers to them filled the Church papers, and they were not kept from the pulpits in either section. The political discussions of slavery in Congress and out were continuous and gave fuel to the fires in the Church.

6. The General Conference of the Northern section of the Methodist Episcopal Church met in May, 1848, in Pittsburgh. Dr. Lovick Pierce had been appointed by the General Confer-

ence of the Methodist Episcopal Church, South, to bear fraternal greetings to the Pittsburgh General Conference. The General Conference refused to accept him as such because it refused to recognize the independent existence of the Methodist Episcopal Church, South. Dr. Pierce retired with this pronouncement:

You will therefore regard this communication as final on the part of the Methodist Episcopal Church, South. She can never renew the offer of fraternal relations between the two great bodies of Wesleyan Methodism in the United States. But the proposition can be renewed at any time, either now or hereafter, by the Methodist Episcopal Church. And if ever made upon the basis of the Plan of Separation, as adopted by the General Conference of 1844, the Church South will cordially entertain the proposition.

The two Churches went for twenty-five years with no semblance of fraternal relations, but with many unfortunate expressions of the very opposite. "Fraternal relations" were to be more than friendly relations, for they were to be "upon the basis of the Plan of Separation."

7. The General Conference in 1848 not only refused to recognize the Methodist Episcopal Church, South, but repudiated the Plan of Separation, and by a vote of 132 to 10 adopted a rescinding resolution. Two thirds of those who were in the General Conference of 1844, and voted for the Plan, failed of election to the General Conference of 1848. This act of repudiation made it necessary for the commissioners, appointed in 1844 for the purpose, to refuse to carry out the provisions in the Plan of Separation for the division of the assets and produce of the Book Concern.

The Commissioners of the Church South brought suit in the Federal District Court to compel division. The case went finally by appeal to the United States Supreme Court. That Court on April 25, 1854, rendered the final decision that the General Conference had the power to divide the Church; that it did divide the Church; that the Plan of Separation was legal; that the

Methodist Episcopal Church, South, had been legally organized under the plan; that the failure to change by the vote of the Annual Conferences the Sixth Restrictive Rule did not affect the validity of the Plan of Separation; that the Church having been divided by its own action the property rights of the South could not be jeopardized and destroyed by the refusal of the Annual Conferences to change the Restrictive Rule; and that therefore the Methodist Episcopal Church, South, was entitled to its proportionate share of the Book Concern and of the other property of the Church. This was a momentous decision. It quieted some contentions, but it did not give peace. In the South it brought jubilation, but in the North it brought questionings and resentment. The divergence was increased.

8. In 1854 Dr. Charles Elliott of Ohio, the Editor of the *Western Christian Advocate,* issued a book of 1,115 pages entitled *The Great Secession,* which in its very title was an offense and a red torch to Southern churchmen and partisans. It created a heavy quota of obstacles to any possible future union. Neither side was free of disquieting, accusing, and irritating outbursts.

The two Churches, although still of the same faith and order, polity and purpose, became unrelenting partisans of the two sides of the political, social, and economic thinking and action of the day as related to slavery; and they made the events and acts of 1844 the basis of their attitudes, positions, and philosophies. But secession was the only charge which the North would not relinquish and the one charge which the South would not admit. To admit secession was to deny the legality of the separation, which the General Conference had overwhelmingly authorized, and to vitiate the acts by which the Methodist Episcopal Church, South, had come into existence. It was to admit the ever-repeated contention of the existing Methodist Episcopal Church to be the mother church and not a sister church. The Church South never made that admission. Two sisters lived in the place of the common mother—this was the South's contention, and that position was indorsed by the Cape May Commission in 1876 and the ensuing General Conferences.

9. The war era very naturally deepened the chasm between the two Churches. The Church North, following a conquering army, took over occupied churches and held the property of the Church South and undertook to build up congregations. The entire era of reconstruction had tragic consequences for Methodism and Methodist relations. Memories of those days and events, full of tragedy and heartache, form backgrounds which cannot be ignored nor completely effaced. They have been handed down and will not be lightly regarded for many generations. But they have not been allowed by noble Christian men and women to defeat those ends to which loyalty to Christ and His Church leads and impels.

10. The war helped to create another condition which has brought its difficulties to those who have labored to bring about Methodist union. The Negro membership of the Methodist Episcopal Church in 1844 was almost entirely in the South and among the slaves. These went into the Church South upon the division. At the outbreak of the war the Church South had 207,766 Negro members, and in 1866 it had only 78,742. While a large share of these went to the two African Churches, a goodly number went to the Church North. From these there has been a slow growth that produced a constituency of about 315,000 in 1939, which became a factor in all discussions of union.

11. The Negro ministry and membership of the Church South in 1870 made request that they be set up as an independent church. This request was granted; and two ministers, upon their election, were ordained bishops by the bishops of the Church South. The Colored Methodist Episcopal Church had in 1939 nine bishops and a membership of 400,000 to 450,000. This Church and the Church South always maintained close relations; the Church South made annual contributions to the Colored Church for many years from its benevolence budget, and in addition many private contributions went from the white

members to the colored churches. This service was considered a privilege.

12. The two Churches had after 1870 different procedures in regard to passing on the constitutionality of the legislative acts of the General Conference. The Methodist Episcopal Church had in its General Conference a Committee on Judiciary to pass upon acts that were thought to affect the Constitution. The opinion of the Committee was usually accepted as final. Since the Committee was from the membership of the General Conference, the constitutionality of its own acts was passed upon by itself. In 1870 the College of Bishops was made the authoritative body to arrest, during the sitting of the General Conference only, any legislative acts of the General Conference which might affect the Constitution or any which the General Conference might refer to them, and their decision was final as to the constitutionality or unconstitutionality of the act. This law came by successive steps, as indicated here. The law of 1870 gave the College of Bishops no veto power as it did in the first instance, as its history shows.

The General Conference of the Church South in 1854 adopted the following resolution offered by Dr. William A. Smith:

Provided, that when any rule or regulation is adopted by the General Conference which, in the opinion of the Bishops, is unconstitutional, the said Bishops may present to the General Conference their objections to such rule or regulation, with the reasons thereof; and if, after hearing the objections and reasons of the Bishops, two thirds of the members of the Conference present shall vote in favor of the rule or regulation so objected to, it shall have the force of law—otherwise it shall be null and void.

Since it was adopted by the General Conference acting alone, and since it was meant to be part of a restrictive rule, its validity was called in question, and in 1866 an effort was made to alter it. In 1870 the Committee on Episcopacy declared that it was "not constitutionally a part of the Constitution." "It as-

sumes, first, that the right or power to veto an act of the General
Conference is inherent in the Episcopacy; and, second, that the
General Conference, in its own right, possesses the determining
of the constitutionality of its own acts."

These two assumptions were denied, and the denial was supported by strong arguments written by Leroy M. Lee. These
statements of the Committee became fundamental principles in
the Church South. The law of 1854 was altered by changing
the last words to read: "If the General Conference shall by a
two-thirds vote adhere to its action on said rule or regulation, it
shall then take the course prescribed for altering a restrictive
rule, and if thus passed upon affirmatively, the Bishops shall
announce that such rule or regulation takes effect from that
time." The members of the Annual Conferences gave the required majorities, and this became the law of the Church South,
to remain until 1934, when the Judicial Council was constitutionally established.

These twelve items contain facts, principles, and suggestions
which no commission on unification could ignore. They set out
the following summarized salient areas of conflict, social and
ecclesiastical, which had to be brought into reconciliation before
any union could be possible. The Southern Conferences accepted the Plan of Separation and all its provisions and acted
in accord therewith. The Northern General Conference in
1848 repudiated the Plan and all its provisions. It insisted that
the act of the Southern Conferences was a secession, while the
Church South contended that it was a legal, authorized separation. The Church South maintained that a line of division had
been established by the Plan beyond which neither Church was
at liberty to go, while the Church North contended that no line
had been established and none would be recognized. The
Church North held to the full supremacy of the General Conference in all things, while the Church South held that the
General Conference should not pass upon the constitutionality
of its own acts, and provided in the Bishops a body to arrest

legislation in process that they might deem unconstitutional. The Church North held to the policy of promoting Christianity and Methodism among the Negro people by a group within its own membership, while the Church South did this through a group without its membership. Each seemed satisfied with its own method, but neither Church had sufficient success with the Negro people, with either plan, to give it any particular pride. The Southern Conferences in their resolutions indorsing the Plan of Separation spoke continually and emphatically of the unwieldiness of a Church covering the entire country, and of the wisdom of jurisdictions; and the Convention even suggested that future union might be possible and practicable on the basis of jurisdictions. The Church North contended that it was and should be a national church without limits, with a centralized but representative government.

The two Churches at the end of twenty-five turbulent years found themselves with very divergent, if not contrary, viewpoints in attitude, polity, and purpose. This tragic period created and developed a state of mind that reduced consideration, confidence, respect, and regard to a low estate. The war had left its deep wounds which the two Churches were not in position to soothe or heal. Time had to be left alone to do its own blessed work. While the relations between them were wrecked, yet the two Churches remained and grew in their respective sections in power and influence. Separation had not been without its rewards.

To understand the principles and actions of the two Churches in this era it is very important, if not necessary, to be acquainted with the Stenographic Report of the Debates in the General Conference of 1844, especially in the case of Bishop Andrew; with the historic Protest of the Southern delegates written by Henry B. Bascom; with the memorable Reply to the Protest prepared by John P. Durbin, George Peck, and Charles Elliott; with the strong address by L. L. Hamline in the case of Bishop Andrew, in which he sets forth certain views of the Episcopacy and the relation of the General Conference to it; with Bascom's very forceful pamphlet on *Methodism and Slavery;* with Charles Elliott's great book, *The Great Secession;* with E. H. Myers' *The Disruption of the Methodist Episcopal Church;* with *The History of the Organization of the Methodist Episcopal Church, South* and *The Methodist Church Property Case;* with the report of the Committee on Episcopacy in the General Conference of the Methodist Episcopal Church, South, in 1870 on the veto of the Bishops written by Leroy M. Lee; and with the activities of the two Churches during this period as recorded in their histories.

Not to know these twenty-five turbulent years is to be poorly prepared to plan Methodist union or to sustain loyalty to that which was wrought out. They hold the history of the world's two greatest Methodisms in their making. In them they came to self-consciousness, self-determination, self-development, and self-assertion. The leaders of each, conscientious, courageous, capable, merit the esteem and honor of all today. They lost unity, but they saved Methodism.

Chapter Three

BUILDING THE APPROACHES

THE TWENTY-FIVE TURBULENT YEARS WERE FOLLOWED BY A PERIOD of forty years marked by gestures of good will, messages of mutual regard, and efforts at building bonds and foundations for closer relations, if not a new unified fellowship. The estrangement was so great and the divergences so extended that any movement made slow progress. The wounds were so deep and the lacerations so destructive of vital tissues that only religious patience and perseverance could have any assurance and hope of ultimate success.

The Northern General Conference in 1848, as said before, refused to enter into fraternal relations with the Church South. That cut deeply into the Southern people. In 1850 the General Conference of the Church South adopted this resolution in rejoinder:

Resolved, That we will steadfastly adhere to the ground taken in the last communication of our delegate to the General Conference of the Methodist Episcopal Church in Pittsburgh in May, 1848, to wit: that we cannot, under their act of rejection and refusal, renew our offer of fraternal relations and intercourse, but will, at all times, entertain any proposition coming from the Methodist Episcopal Church to us, whether it be by written communication or delegation, having for its object friendly relations, and predicated on the rights granted to us by the Plan of Separation adopted in New York in 1844.

This condition of recognition of the rights of the Church South under the Plan of Separation was never withdrawn or even reduced.

54

The New York East Annual Conference of the Methodist Episcopal Church, in session at Brooklyn in April, 1866, sent to the General Conference of the Methodist Episcopal Church, South, then in session at New Orleans, a lengthy telegram of salutations, and invited that General Conference to join that Annual Conference in observing the following Sunday, April 8, as a day of special prayer "for the peace and unity" of America, and "for the full restoration of Christian sympathy and love between the Churches, especially between the different branches of Methodism in this nation." The communication was received with great interest, and the Secretary of the General Conference was instructed to express to the New York East Conference "the cordial reciprocation of these Christian salutations and the cordial agreement to unite with the Conference" in observing the special day of prayer.

No movement toward establishing fraternal relations was made until May, 1869, and it was made then by the Bishops of the Methodist Episcopal Church. The Bishops of the Church South were in session in St. Louis. Bishop E. S. Janes and Bishop Matthew Simpson appeared before them, representing themselves and their colleagues in the following communication:

MEADVILLE, PA., April 23, 1869.

To the Reverends the Bishops of the Methodist Episcopal Church, South.

Dear Brethren: It seems to us that, as the division of those Churches of our country which are of like faith and order has been productive of evil, so the reunion of them would be productive of good.

As the main cause of the separation has been removed, so has the chief obstacle to the restoration.

It is fitting that the Methodist Church, which began the disunion, should not be the last to achieve the reunion; and it would be a reproach to the chief pastors of the separate bodies if they waited until their flocks prompted them to the union, which both the love of country and of religion invoke, and which the providence of God seems to render inevitable at no distant day.

We are aware that there are difficulties in the way, growing out of the controversies of the past and the tempers of the present.

We have, therefore, deputed our colleagues, Morris and Janes, to confer with you, alike as to propriety, practicability, and methods of reunion, hoping that they, having been elected to their high office by the Church before its severance, and endeared to all its parts by their apostolic labors, may live to see the severed parts united upon a foundation honorable to all, stable as truth, and harmonious with the fundamental law of our religion.

In behalf of the Bishops of the Methodist Episcopal Church, respectfully yours, etc.,

T. A. MORRIS, *President;*
D. W. CLARK, *Secretary.*

The two distinguished messengers presented their own personal communications, delivered felicitations, and retired.

The Southern Bishops sent the following reply to the one from the Northern Bishops:

To the Bishops of the Methodist Episcopal Church.

Reverend and Dear Brethren: It has afforded us pleasure to receive in person your respected colleagues, Bishops Janes and Simpson, deputed by you to confer with us, and we cannot forbear to express our regret that one of the delegation appointed by you to us—the venerable Bishop Morris—was not able to be present. We desired to see him again face to face, to enjoy his society, and to renew to him the assurances of our affection and regard. Our own senior Superintendent, Bishop Andrew, though in the city, was hindered by the feebleness and infirmities incident to age from being present at the reception of your colleagues, and enjoying with us the interview.

Your communication, together with that laid before us by your Commission, has been considered, and we entirely agree in your estimate of the responsibility in the premises resting on the chief pastors of the separated bodies of Methodism.

We would approach, dear brethren, the matter of your communication with the utmost candor and love, and so meet the advanced steps on your part that nothing shall be wanting on ours to bring about a better state of things, becoming and beneficial to us both. We deplore the unfortunate controversies and tempers that have prevailed, and still prevail, and our earnest desire and prayer to God is, that they may give place, and that speedily, to peace. In evidence of this we are ready not only to respond to, but to go further than your communication, and from our point of view to suggest what may help to remove the difficulties and obstacles that are in the way.

Permit us, then, to say, in regard to "reunion," that in our opinion there is another subject to be considered before that can be entertained, and necessarily in order to it—we mean the establishment of fraternal feelings and relations between the two Churches. They must be one in spirit before they can be one in organization. Concord must be achieved before any real union. Heart divisions must be cured before corporate divisions can be healed.

You will not consider it as unfriendly to the freest flow of Christian sympathy evoked by your overture if we remind you that we initiated the measure to effect fraternal relations some years ago; and as was declared then, and as we do now declare, in good faith and with most Christian purposes. Our General Conference sent one of its most honored elders to your General Conference to convey their Christian salutations, and through him to "offer to you the establishment of fraternal relations and intercourse." It pains us to refer to the fact, but it is matter of history that he was not received.

The closing words of Dr. Pierce to your General Conference, upon being notified of the failure of his mission, are in your possession:

"You will therefore regard this communication as final on the part of the Methodist Episcopal Church, South. She can never renew the offer of fraternal relations between the two great bodies of Wesleyan Methodism in the United States. But the proposition can be renewed at any time, either now or hereafter, by the Methodist Episcopal Church. And if ever made upon the basis of the Plan of Separation, as adopted by the General Conference of 1844, the Church South will cordially entertain the proposition."

His language to our General Conference in submitting this report was:

"Thus ended the well-intended Commission from your body. Upon this noble effort I verily believe the smile of Divine approbation will rest when the heavenly bodies themselves will have ceased to shine. We did affectionately endeavor to make and preserve peace, but our offer was rejected as of no deserving."

The evils that have followed this rejection we suffer in common with you. We lament them in common with you; and, notwithstanding all that has since occurred, we are ready, on terms honorable to all, to join heart and hand with you to stay and, as far as practicable, to remedy them. But you could not expect us to say less than this, that the words of our rejected delegate have been ever since, and still are, our words.

It may help to the more speedy and certain attainment of the ends we both desire to keep distinctly in mind our mutual positions, and to hold the facts involved in our common history in a clear light.

You say that "the great cause which led to the separation from us of both the Wesleyan Methodists of this country and of the Methodist Episcopal Church, South, has passed away." If we understand your reference, we so far differ from you in this opinion, that it may help any negotiations hereafter taking place to restate our position. Slavery was not, in any proper sense, the cause, but the occasion only of that separation, the necessity of which we regretted as much as you. But certain principles were developed in relation to the political aspects of that question, involving the right of ecclesiastical bodies to handle and determine matters lying outside of their proper jurisdiction, which we could not accept; and, in a case of arising, certain constructions of the constitutional powers and prerogatives of the General Conference were assumed and acted on, which we considered oppressive and destructive of the rights of the numerical minority represented in that highest judicatory of the Church. That which you are pleased to call, no doubt sincerely thinking it so, "the great cause" of separation, existed in the Church from its organization, and yet for sixty years there was no separation. But when those theories incidentally envolved in connection with it began to be put into practice, then the separation came.

We cannot think you mean to offend us when you speak of our having separated from you, and put us in the same category with a small body of schismatics who were always an acknowledged secession. Allow us, in all kindness, brethren, to remind you, and to keep the important fact of history prominent, that we separated from you in no sense in which you did not separate from us. The separation was by compact and mutual, and nearer approaches to each other can be conducted with hope of a successful issue only on this basis.

It is our opinion that the controversies and tempers which so disturb the Churches, and are so hurtful to the souls of those for whom Christ died, are due, in a large measure, to irritating causes which are not entirely beyond the control of the chief pastors of the separated bodies. To this end we invite your concurrence and co-operation.

And we take this occasion frankly to say that the conduct of some of your missionaries and agents who have been sent into that portion of our common country occupied by us, and their avowed purpose to disintegrate and absorb our societies, that otherwise dwelt quietly, have been very prejudicial to that charity which we desire our people to cultivate toward all Christians, and especially those who are called by the endeared name of Methodists; and their course in taking possession of some of our houses of worship has inflicted both grief and loss on us, and bears the appearance, to disinterested men of the world, of being not only a breach of charity, but an invasion of the plainest rights of property. Thus the adversary has had occasion to speak reproachfully, and the cause of our Master has been wounded by its professed friends.

Brethren, these things ought not so to be, and we propose, until some action more formal and authoritative, and advanced in this direction can be taken by our highest judicatories, to unite with you in preventing them. We do not say that our own people have been, in every instance of these unhappy controversies and tempers, without blame as toward you; but this we say, if any offenses against the law of love, committed by those under our appointment; any aggressions upon your just privileges and rights are properly represented to us, the representation will be respectfully considered, and we shall stand ready, by all the authority and influence we have, to restrain and correct them.

These are our views, and we are sure that we represent the sentiments of our ministers and people. We have no authority to determine any thing as to the "propriety, practicability, and methods" of reunion of the Churches represented by you and ourselves.

With sentiments of Christian regard, we are, dear brethren, very truly yours,

R. PAINE, *Chairman;*
H. N. McTYEIRE, *Secretary.*

ST. LOUIS, MO., May 11, 1869.

The General Conference of the Church North in May, 1868, authorized a Commission composed of the six bishops and eight ministers, whom the Bishops would appoint, with the instruction, "That the Commission confer with a like Commission from the African Methodist Episcopal Zion Church to arrange for the union of that body with our own, be also empowered to treat with a similar Commission from any other Methodist Church that may desire a like union." The Commission came to the Southern General Conference in 1870 with the statement, "The fact that the General Conference of the Methodist Episcopal Church appointed this Commission shows that in the judgment of that body there are now no sufficient reasons why a union may not be effected on terms equally honorable to all, and that the realization of such union is very important and desirable." It can be easily seen that the instructions to the Commissions were not expressed in a way to appeal to the Church South, and the response of the Southern General Conference was to the effect that it understood that the Commission was not constituted to establish fraternal relations, and to negotiate on union. The Conference expressed its gratification at the visit of the Commission as indicative of "the return of proper sentiments and relations between the two branches of Northern and Southern Methodism." But it went further and said, "Moreover, that if this distinguished Commission were fully clothed with authority to treat with us for union, it is the judgment of the Conference that the two interests of the Church of Christ require and demand the maintenance of our separation and distinct organizations."

In tendering to Bishop Janes and Dr. W. L. Harris high regards, it added: "We express our sincere desire that the day may soon come when proper Christian sentiments and fraternal relations between the two great branches of Northern and Southern Methodism shall be permanently established."

The year 1872 did, however, see the beginning of the exchange of fraternal messages to the General Conferences. The General

Conference of the Methodist Episcopal Church instructed the Bishops to send messengers to the Southern General Conference to be held in Louisville in May, 1874. Dr. A. S. Hunt, Dr. C. H. Fowler (later a bishop), and General Clinton B. Fisk came. It was a great day when they spoke. Their addresses stirred Methodist enthusiasm and brought warmth to Methodist hearts. However, their official attendance called forth an expression of much importance through a Committee composed of Alpheus W. Wilson, Linus Parker, A. L. Green, Robert Alexander, C. W. Miller, R. W. Jones, S. Bobo, J. L. de Yampert, and D. K. Pittman, men of high distinction in the Southern Church. They said, among other things:

Organic union is not involved in fraternity. In our view of the subject the reasons for the separate existence of these two branches of Methodism are such as to make corporate union undesirable and impracticable. The events and experiences of the last thirty years have confirmed us in the conviction that such a consummation is demanded by neither reason nor charity. We believe that each Church can do its work and fulfill its mission most effectively by maintaining an independent organization. The causes which led to the division in 1844 upon a Plan of Separation mutually agreed upon have not disappeared. Some of them exist in their original form and force, and others have been modified but not diminished.

One of the obstacles, according to their view, was the size of the General Conference, which upon any proper basis of representation would be unwieldy. The chief obstacle, however, was the difference in the conception of the powers of the General Conference.

The Northern members (General Conference of 1844), who were a controlling majority, claimed for it prerogatives which seemed to us both dangerous and unconstitutional. In their view the General Conference was supreme. Although restricted in the exercise of its power by a constitution, it was the judge of the restrictions, and is thus practically unlimited. In our view it is a body of limited powers. It cannot absorb the functions of other and co-ordinate branches of Church government; and there are methods by which all constitutional questions may be brought to a satisfactory issue.

While the Conference authorized the appointment of the fraternal messengers to the General Conference of 1876, and Dr. Lovick Pierce of Georgia, Dr. James A. Duncan of Virginia, and Chancellor Landon C. Garland of Vanderbilt University, were appointed, there was another matter of great importance. The Church North had built up a membership of 300,000 in the South. Friction had resulted in many communities. They said:

Measures preparatory to formal fraternity would be defective that leave out of view questions in dispute between the Methodist Episcopal Church and ourselves. These questions relate to the course pursued by some of their accredited agents while prosecuting their work in the South, and to property which has been taken and held by them to this day against our protest and remonstrance. Although feeling ourselves aggrieved in these things, we stand ready to meet our brethren of the Methodist Episcopal Church in the spirit of Christian candor, and to compose all differences upon the principles of justice and equity.

The report closed with the authorization of the appointment of a Commission of three ministers and two laymen by the College of Bishops, as called for in a resolution offered by Dr. Alpheus W. Wilson, to act with a like Commission from the Methodist Episcopal Church. This proved to be the most significant and far-reaching act taken since 1844.

The Northern General Conference of 1876 gave most gracious and generous welcome to the fraternal delegates from the South. The venerable Dr. Lovick Pierce was too feeble to be present, but he sent a very forceful letter in which he said, "We protest against any longer use of the popular phrase 'two Methodisms.' There is but one Episcopal Methodism in the United States of America, and you and we together make up this one Methodism." President Duncan, of Randolph-Macon College, was introduced by Dr. Cyrus D. Foss, and Chancellor Garland by Dr. John P.

Newman. Dr. Foss and Dr. Newman later became bishops. Dr. Duncan delivered a very eloquent suggestive address on fraternity and its proper and adequate basis.

The address of Chancellor Garland, simple in statement but profound in thought, was a remarkable contribution to the development of Christian relations. He said among other things:

In the Conference of 1844 the Northern and Southern delegates found themselves surrounded by a complication of difficulties out of which they saw no way of escape. They came to this conclusion reluctantly, and were forced by necessity into positions which they respectfully assumed. Neither party could have receded from its position without infidelity to the section it represented. Methodism would have been seriously damaged, if not totally destroyed, in one section or the other, had any other policy been adopted.

He said further:

We do sincerely desire the restoration of good feeling between the two Churches upon a basis derogatory to neither. If I know my own people, they do not expect, much less do they demand of you, any sacrifice of right of duty or of honor, in adjusting the difficulties between us; and we will not believe that you will demand any such sacrifice of us.

Chancellor Garland's address produced a very salutary impression upon the General Conference and upon his own people of the South, and it was a genuine contribution to the restoration of proper relations between the two Churches.

The General Conference in identical words authorized the appointment of a Commission of five to meet the similar Commission from the Church South "in order to remove all obstacles to formal fraternity between the two Churches."

THE CAPE MAY COMMISSION

The Bishops of the Church South appointed as its commissioners Dr. E. H. Myers of Georgia, Dr. R. K. Hargrove (later Bish-

op) of Tennessee, Dr. Thomas M. Finney of Missouri, the Hon.
Trusten Pope, and the Hon. David Clopton. Upon the death
of Mr. Pope, in April, 1876, the Hon. Robert B. Vance of North
Carolina was appointed his successor. The Bishops of the North
appointed Dr. Morris D'C. Crawford, the Hon. Enoch L.
Fancher, Dr. Erasmus Q. Fuller, General Clinton B. Fisk, and
Dr. John P. Newman (later Bishop). Cape May, New Jersey,
was the meeting place of this historic Commission, and the time
was August 17-23, 1876. Its task was to remove all obstacles to
formal fraternity between the two commissions by "adjusting
all existing difficulties." That was a large task, the full consummation of which was hardly to be expected. However, the
results achieved were most gratifying to both sides and made a
permanent basis for future relationships.

The Southern Commissioners met on August 16 and formulated a letter to the Northern Commissioners, and that afternoon
the Northern Commissioners met and formulated a reply. The
subject was not the adjustment of certain property conflicts, but
the basis of fraternity. The Southern Commissioners quoted Dr.
Lovick Pierce's statement in his fraternal address to the recent
General Conference: "There is but one Episcopal Methodism in
the United States, and you and we together make up this Methodism, our two General Conference jurisdictions being each
rightfully and historically integral parts of the original Methodist Episcopal Church constituted in 1784." They made it
clear that the first and foremost objective was, in the language
of Dr. Pierce, "the official recognition of the Methodist Episcopal
Church, South, as a legitimate organization of the Methodist
Episcopal Church into a second General Conference jurisdiction,
as provided for in 1844 by the last ecumenical General Conference of the Methodist Episcopal Church." This matter lay
heavily upon the Southern Commissioners, as it had for thirty
years on the Church South.

The Northern Commissioners replied in the most conciliatory
speech and fraternal spirit, and while not accepting all the

positions of the Southern Commissioners, they offered a remarkable and even magnanimous formula which became the basis of the final declaration.

The first business transacted next day was the adoption of the following historic declaration and basis of fraternity:

Each of said Churches is a legitimate branch of Episcopal Methodism in the United States, having a common origin in the Methodist Episcopal Church organized in 1784.

Since the organization of the Methodist Episcopal Church, South, was consummated in 1845 by the voluntary exercise of the right of the Southern Annual Conferences, ministers and members, to adhere to that communion, it has been an Evangelical Church, reared on Scriptural foundations, and her ministers and members, with those of the Methodist Episcopal Church, have constituted one Methodist family, though in distinct ecclesiastical connections.

The Commission considered a large number of conflicting property claims and made adjustments in most of them. Before adjournment it adopted rules for the settlement of claims in the future.

Both Commissions reported their work to their respective General Conferences, and both General Conferences heartily approved their action and emphatically accepted it as final. Some question arose in the General Conference of the Methodist Episcopal Church in 1880, but the following resolution offered by Dr. J. M. Buckley closed the matter:

Resolved, That we regard the action of the Commission on Fraternity, appointed by the bishops by the order of the last General Conference, as final.

This declaration, adopted by both Churches, that each is a legitimate branch of the original Methodist Episcopal Church and each is equal to the other in succession to the original, that the two are twin Sisters in Episcopal Methodism, was the answer to thirty years of questions, contentions, disputes, and conflicts.

It removed from the Church South the stigma of "secession." It supported the position of the Federal Court that the General Conference of 1844 was competent to divide the Church and that it did divide it. It recognized the independent and legitimate standing of the Church South. It was the most epoch-making utterance and action in Methodist history since 1844, and even for the succeeding half century and more. It put the two bodies upon a plane of equality, fraternity, and liberty that made possible a new common life. Its importance, influence, and effect cannot be overestimated. It is the golden milestone at the head of the highway that leads to unity and union in American Methodism.

The declaration that each was a legitimate branch of Episcopal Methodism met the approval of the great body of leaders and members of the Methodist Episcopal Church, but there were some who strongly denied that affirmation. Bishop Thomas B. Neely in his book published as late as 1916 on *American Methodism—Its Divisions and Unification* said:

This idea of both Churches being branches of the original Church founded in 1784 is an evident error. Both are not branches from the same original stock. In an accommodated sense it may be said that both are parts of Episcopal Methodism, but not that both are branches of the same original trunk. The Methodist Episcopal Church of 1784 is the Methodist Episcopal Church of this present time. One of the Churches branched from the Methodist Episcopal Church, and that one was the Methodist Episcopal Church, South. That is the branch. The other is the original trunk.

The fact should have been recognized and emphasized that the bishops and leaders of the Church North from 1869 showed great magnanimity by the aggressiveness, concessions, and abounding co-operation in their endeavors to adjust the fraternal relations between the two Churches. That spirit contributed greatly to the later approaches to unity and union.

The long journey to Methodist Union began on the ever-memorable day of August 17, 1876. The Cape May Commission unlocked the blockade to any possibilities of union of any kind. It stabilized thirty years of Methodist history and removed distressing accumulations of irritating obstacles from the highway of formal Methodist fraternity. The two Churches henceforth stood on the same level, and they faced together the common religious responsibilities of their communions.

FEDERATION OF METHODISM

The conflicting interpretations of the act of 1844 opened the way for competing activities of the two branches of Methodism in much of the border territory and even in places that should have been left free of competitions. The success of the Union armies was interpreted by some zealous partisans as license to occupy places which the South thought should have been left unmolested and unentered. These activities and the very natural claims by which they were sustained created much friction, hard feelings, unfriendly attitudes, and bitter criticisms. The Church South entered California, the Northwest, and Illinois. The divisions were often pitiable and not infrequently disastrous.

In some cases the disputes over property became acute. The Cape May Commission was appointed to settle as many of these difficulties as possible and to provide a formula for future action. Many special cases were settled, and rules for adjustment were adopted, but they were largely advisory. The general situation, however, was not greatly changed. The "altar against altar" condition prevailed all through the border territory, and the unhappy state did not improve. Methodism by its competing activities, willing accusations, conflicting claims, and divided spirit contributed to the continuance of the passions and attitudes of the unfortunate tragic era. It was evident that some movement to alter this condition should be inaugurated.

Fraternal messages eloquent and religious, highly commendatory of the common Methodism and its historic beginning, and complimentary of each other upon successes achieved, were exchanged with the successive General Conferences. But rivalry, competition, criticism, and conflict continued. Underneath it all was a spirit of a broken household, the attitude of estranged brothers, and actions that betokened lost consideration, disrupted confidence, and reduced regard. This went on for several years. Ever and anon someone suggested union, or organic unity, or reunion; but the response was not encouraging or reassuring. Such a person usually had little understanding of the depths that such an action would have to fathom. Before union was possible many things were necessary. Union was a long time coming, but it was not substantially possible any sooner. Union was not made; it grew.

In 1888 the General Conference of the Methodist Episcopal Church appointed a commission on Interecclesiastical Relations and made it their duty "to hold themselves ready to enter into brotherly conference with all or any Christian bodies seeking the restoration of the organic unity of the Church or the increase of Christian and Church fraternity." This was a worthy gesture, but it got no visible results.

The time had come when many felt that something should be done to bring the two Churches into closer affiliation and to remove irritating activities. In 1894, in the General Conference of the Methodist Episcopal Church, South, Rev. David W. Carter, a distinguished missionary to Mexico, moved that a Committee on Federation of Methodism be appointed by the College of Bishops. That motion became historic. The Committee, after some days of deliberation, recommended that a Commission on Federation of Methodism, composed of three bishops, three ministers, and three laymen, be appointed to act with a similar Commission of the Methodist Episcopal Church, if and when appointed, with a view to abating hurtful competitions and the waste of men and money in home and foreign fields; and report to the next General Conference any proposals or arrangements.

The General Conference of the Methodist Episcopal Church in 1896 approved the movement and appointed Commissioners.

The Church South appointed Bishop John C. Granbery, Bishop
R. K. Hargrove, Bishop W. W. Duncan, the Rev. E. E. Hoss,
the Rev. George G. N. MacDonell, the Rev. J. H. Dye, Judge
Walter Clark, Major R. W. Jones, and Asa Holt, Esq. The
Methodist Episcopal Church appointed Bishop S. M. Merrill,
Bishop W. X. Ninde, Bishop J. N. FitzGerald, the Rev. John
F. Goucher, the Rev. R. J. Cooke, the Rev. L. B. Wilson, Robert
T. Miller, Esq., T. B. Sweet, and Thomas H. Murray, Esq. This
was the beginning of the building of approaches that eventually
led to Methodist Union.

The Joint Commission met in Washington, D. C., January
7-8, 1898. All the Southern members were present. Bishop
John F. Hurst was substituted for Bishop FitzGerald and Rev.
L. B. Wilson (later a bishop) for Dr. John F. Goucher. Questions relating to property were not considered, but rather measures that would bring the two Methodisms into closer fellowship,
and some provision that would allay and prevent friction in
local communities. It recommended "the taking of prompt
steps for the preparation of a common catechism, a common
hymnbook, and a common order of worship"; and "in our
educational work in Eastern Asia the adoption of measures,
looking to the harmonious co-operation of our missions." They
adopted the following important resolution:

Resolved, That we recommend the respective General Conferences to enact provisions to the effect that where either Church
is doing the work expected of Methodism the other Church shall
not organize a society nor erect a church building until the
bishop having jurisdiction in the case of the work proposed
shall be consulted and his approval obtained.

The Southern General Conference in the following May approved and adopted the acts of the Joint Commission and
authorized the College of Bishops to execute the measures if
and when adopted by the Methodist Episcopal Church. The
Commission with its personnel unchanged was continued for the

ensuing quadrennium. The Northern General Conference received the report and referred it to a Committee, which reported back late in the session, and the General Conference adjourned without taking action. The Committee altered the item regarding new churches to read, "The question of the organization of new societies or the building of new churches shall be left to the decision of the presiding elders and the preacher in charge, subject to the approval of the bishop having jurisdiction." The Commission was continued. In 1904 the General Conference adopted the report made by the Joint Commission in 1900 in the exact language used by the Southern General Conference in 1898.

The Bishops appointed joint commissions on the preparation of a common hymnal, common catechism, and a common order of worship, and that work was duly and promptly finished. The mission work in Brazil and Cuba was all allocated to the Southern Church and that in Puerto Rico and the Philippines to the Northern Church. A common publishing house was established and built in China. In 1907 the two Churches and the Methodist Church of Canada united in the setting up of the Methodist Church of Japan. All these joint actions contributed greatly to the sense of brotherhood and companionship in service. The unities in church life through the order of worship, the catechism, and the hymnal were highly salutary. The common hymnal had a very great influence. The *Hymnal* was the best hymnbook which either Church had ever had, and it received worthy praise generally from ministers and church leaders in both denominations. That praise always brought forth reference to its being used by Methodists in all sections. It carried the common order of worship, which had been intelligently prepared. These were two bonds of unity that promoted the cause of union.

To be sure, the friction in border territory did not diminish. The Joint Commissions were not able to find a formula that produced any large results. The Church South was in the far

Northwest and on the Pacific Coast doing its utmost to keep up Southern sentiment, Southern prejudices, and Southern interests; and the Church North was in the South ministering to Northern people in small groups largely by ministers who were of Northern birth or Northern feelings. Home missions in the Northern Church were sustained and promoted by pleas based upon the deplorable condition of certain Southern groups, and in the Southern Church upon the neglected masses in the Northwest. All of it was competitive and not complementary, and created antagonisms in the various sections that outweigh the benefits of the service rendered. But in it all the sentiment for adjustment between the two Churches grew slowly apace.

The Commission on Federation appointed in 1902 by the Church South was composed of Bishop A. W. Wilson, Bishop W. W. Duncan, Bishop E. E. Hoss, the Rev. George G. N. MacDonell, the Rev. J. H. Dye, the Rev. James Atkins, Major R. W. Jones, Prof. E. B. Prettyman, and Prof. R. S. Hyer. In 1906 it was Bishop Wilson, Bishop Hoss, Bishop Atkins, the Rev. J. H. Dye, the Rev. W. L. Nelms, the Rev. Frank M. Thomas, Professor Jones, Professor Prettyman, and Judge Samuel B. Adams. The Northern Church in 1908 appointed Bishop John M. Walden, Bishop Earl Cranston, Bishop L. B. Wilson, the Rev. John F. Goucher, the Rev. G. A. Reeder, the Rev. W. W. Evans, R. T. Miller of Cincinnati, Hanford Crawford of St. Louis, and John A. Patten of Chattanooga. The labors of these strong and capable men are worthy of highest commendation and praise.

They sought to adjust difficulties in local communities, to produce methods for reducing friction, and to set up measures that would produce fellowship and good will. Their achievements were far beyond what appeared on the surface. The working together of great leaders created bonds of deep fraternity. The same was true of the joint commissions that produced the common hymnal, catechism, and orders of worship. Great approaches to union in this period of Federation were in the building.

The Joint Commission on Federation at its meeting in Baltimore, April 18, 1906, made provision for the organization of the Federal Council of Methodism. This provision was adopted by the General Conference of the Church South in 1906 and by the General Conference of the Church North in 1908.

Chapter Four

PROPRIETY, PRACTICABILITY,
AND METHODS

IT MAY APPEAR BY THIS TIME IN THIS HISTORICAL REVIEW WHY
union was slow in coming to Methodism. Union became
entangled, if not identified, with reunion, and reunion was
never a remote possibility. Reunion carried the implication of
a return, a coming back, the establishment of the former and
original status; and the Church South and its constituency never
entertained for one moment such a purpose or desire. Organic
unity came to mean a merger in the old molds, and those molds
had been superseded and put away. Reunion and organic unity
acquired through the proposals and discussions, meanings which
set them off as unacceptable. Union could not come unless and
until a new governmental structure could be produced. That
was the attitude and requirement of the leaders of the Church
South for sixty to seventy years; and these could not be ignored,
discounted, or set aside, for their people stood with them. On
the other hand, the leaders of the Church North held to the
idea, the desire, the purpose of a restoration of the original
status. Thus two diverse conceptions of union and a plan of
union for over three quarters of a century held sway, and
neither was conceivable and acceptable to the other side. That
is why union was slow in coming, and seemingly unreasonably
and inexcusably delayed. This state of things has not always
been understood, and it may not be thoroughly understood and
appreciated in some places yet.

Just twenty-five years after the disruption of the Church in
1844 the Bishops of the Methodist Episcopal Church wrote to

the Bishops of the Methodist Episcopal Church, South: "As the main cause of the separation has been removed . . . . we have, therefore, deputed our colleagues, Morris and Janes, to confer with you alike as to the propriety, practicability, and methods of reunion." The spirit and purpose of the communication were most fraternal and highly Christian, but the Southern Bishops did not agree that the main cause of separation had been removed. The words "propriety, practicability, and methods" were well and wisely chosen. They were guiding and controlling words in the discussion of union and the plan of union for the ensuing sixty years. They should even yet be deeply thought upon and regarded in completing the process of union. Propriety and practicability may well characterize any methods of procedure that may be adopted at any time.

The Southern Bishops in their answer declared that there were other causes of separation than slavery; that slavery was the occasion, but not the cause, of the division of the Church; and that consequently its removal did not open the way to reunion. Ever after that time that position was vigorously maintained by many very able leaders of the Church South. Whether or not this point of view is accepted it must be recognized in any survey of the facts relating to the issue under consideration.

It is true there had been in the Church for sixty years the question of slavery. It is also true that the demand for its abolition in the country had grown very strong, and it had made acute the matter of a Methodist slaveholding bishop. No one has ever claimed that had there been no slaveholding bishops separation would have been proposed and effected. There were other questions, to be sure, that brought out other differences, but none of them were acute and none of them of such vital importance that they would have called forth division. On the other hand, had no division come in 1844, or 1848 or 1852, it can scarcely be imagined that a separation necessity would not have arisen by 1856 or 1860. Slavery had possessed the South economically, socially, and politically; and the Church, whether

Methodist, Presbyterian, Baptist, or Episcopal, had become intricately involved. This is not said to the discredit of any one of them. Slavery divided the United States and brought on a terrible war between the sections, and why may we not see that it was a fundamental cause of dividing the Methodist Episcopal Church, as it was in dividing other churches?

The institution of slavery, the attack on it by the Northern citizenship, the terrible war, the tragic era that followed, created and developed to a high state a regional consciousness and solidarity in the South which reigned over a half century, and which has in reality never passed entirely away. That should be recognized and duly regarded. The South was then, and is now, more than a piece of geography. The "solid South" is not a mere political block. Its homogeneity socially, economically, culturally, religiously, is the precious product of ethnic unity, of outside pressure, and of inside inclinations as well. There has been created through the years a Southern mind, a Southern soul, and a Southern spirit. They are not intentionally selfishly sectional, but they are sectionally protectional and promotional of a Southern civilization and viewpoint. This interpretation of the South has not always been accepted, nor is it now fully appreciated; but it is a vital factor in the understanding of the Southern viewpoint.

The question inevitably arises, if slavery was only the occasion and not the cause of the separation, as the Southern Bishops claimed, what was the cause of the separation? Evidently that cause had not been removed, and it had made reunion impracticable. It was primarily the supreme General Conference. To the Southern Methodist leaders an absolutely supreme General Conference, with its large majority in the North, made reunion look uninviting. From it had come the suspension of a bishop without a trial. Such a General Conference could make any law, pass upon the constitutionality of its own acts, dispose of any property anywhere, create or destroy any boards, elect bishops and administrative officers as the majority saw fit. So the South regarded it. An independent Church, as the Church South was, handling its own affairs in its own way and with great success, ability, and influence, would scarcely welcome or accept a union, or reunion, that put under possible restraint or into jeopardy the control of its own interests. The liberty of self-expression could not be surrendered for any reunion under a supreme General Conference. The supreme General Conference was therefore problem number one thereafter in all discussions of union, and in all efforts for the production of an acceptable plan of union of the two Churches. That problem had to be solved before any plan of union could be possible.

After the Cape May Commission in 1876 declared that each Church was a legitimate branch of the original Church organized in 1784, ease came to the Church South, and the discussion of union increased. Dr. D. H. McAnally, the keen-minded Editor of the *St. Louis Christian Advocate,* became a strong advocate of union by some kind of jurisdictional system. The Southern Convention in 1846 closed its declaration with the words, "We shall always be ready, kindly and respectfully to entertain, and duly and carefully consider, any proposition or plan having for its object the union of the two great bodies, in the North and South, whether such proposed union be jurisdictional or connectional." Note the word "jurisdictional." This concept, while never expressed in definite terms, never passed out of the Southern mind as the essential ground of acceptable union. It became basic in all the thinking of those who eventually worked out the plan of union.

Dr. W. P. Harrison, the Book Editor of the Church South, and a highly respected thinker and leader, in the eighties, said: "There are many reasons why the Church South should remain independent. We are as nearly unanimous today as in 1844. As far into the future as it has been given us to see, the interests and welfare of our Southern Methodism imperatively demand the jurisdictional independence of the Methodist Episcopal Church, South." Jurisdictional independence!

Dr. Harrison in a book on *Methodist Union* published in 1891 offered the following interesting and illuminating suggestions:

The subject of organic union of all the Episcopal Methodist bodies possesses a charm for many persons. But there are so many difficulties in the way of such a consummation that it is useless to discuss the question in any proposition that looks to the absorption of ecclesiastical government under one General Conference. Here is however a more excellent way. Let there be one Methodist Episcopal Church in America under four General Conference Jurisdictions: (1) The Methodist Episcopal Church, North, comprising New England and the Central States to the Mississippi River, (2) the Methodist Episcopal Church, South, comprising the territory of the slaveholding states as they existed in 1860, or, if preferred, the boundary established by the Plan of Separation in 1844; (3) the Methodist Episcopal Church, West, comprising all the territory west of the Mississippi River; (4) the Colored Methodist Episcopal Church, comprising the African, the African Zion, and the Colored Methodist Episcopal Churches. These four divisions would be held in one church organization by a nexus of a Methodist Church Council meeting once in four years. The Council is to have no legislative or judicial functions, but to be an advisory body only.

These were the suggestions also of Dr. McAnally and other Southern leaders.

Bishop S. M. Merrill, of the Methodist Episcopal Church, who was recognized as one of the ablest interpreters of Methodist law and a leader of great influence, in 1891 published a book on *Organic Union* in which he advocated the reunion of the two Churches. He said: "There is little probability that organic union with the Methodist Episcopal Church, South, will ever be consummated without a pretty thorough sifting of the old issues." He proceeded to do some sifting. He said: "Slavery by its arrogance rendered the agitation unavoidable. Slavery was therefore both the 'cause' and the 'occasion,' and the action of the General Conference in the case of Bishop Andrew was the occasion of that sad event—the separation."

Bishop Merrill said further:

The famous so-called Plan of Separation was not a plan of separation at all. It had no such purpose. There is little doubt that our Southern brethren will differ from this statement most radically. The history they have made demands it. What they assert has been heard and considered, and it is in the face of all they have said, or can say, that this position is taken. The General Conference of 1844 neither divided the Church, nor authorized its division. It made one great mistake, but it did not do the dreadful thing so often attributed to it. Its mistake consisted in making any official recognition of the probability or possibility of a subsequent division or rupture, which was threatened. It heard the intimations and sought to avert the calamity, if possible; and if not possible, then to reduce the disaster to the minimum by working out a way to avoid all possible friction. With this in view, it adopted the report of the Committee, which is the famous Plan. It was simply an outline of concessions to be made in the event the Southern Conferences should resort to the extreme act of separation. It did not induce the act, nor authorize it, and sought to provide against its evils.

He maintained that the Plan contained a proposal to alter a Restrictive Rule which was never adopted, and that failure defeated the adoption of the Plan. He took issue strongly against the decision of the United States Supreme Court in which it was held that the General Conference divided the Church.

He said also:

That Plan, which was from its inception unconstitutional, tentative, conditional, and never legalized, contained a provision for dividing the territory of the country so that the jurisdiction of the new Church, if one should be formed, would be confined to such Annual Conferences in the slaveholding States as would prefer to leave the jurisdiction of the Methodist Episcopal Church. According to the wording of the Plan, it is evident that the line was to be a fixed boundary over which neither Church was to pass.

Bishop Merrill from this viewpoint urged the union of the Methodist Churches, and especially of the two Episcopal Methodisms. Union was indeed to be a reunion, a return of the withdrawn group to the original body and under the government of a supreme General Conference. His contentions and brilliant arguments never converted a single Southern Methodist to his way of thinking. Another hundred years of that line of argument would have produced no results in the South. To the Southern leaders, his advocacy of union, notwithstanding their high admiration of him, was only another appeal to return quickly to the "old Mother Church," and they would not return. Never again would they go under, or stay under, a supreme General Conference, a centralized power, that even passed upon the constitutionality of its own acts, and that was independent in action, and even defiant, of the ministry and membership of the Church. Henceforth they wanted a government of distributed power with checks and balances, and only a union on that basis would ever be acceptable. How that could ever be developed no one at that time saw. Dr. Harrison's plan provided a distribution of power, but it failed to create an actual union. It received the approval of Southern leaders, but they well knew it would not be acceptable to the North, where it was rightly regarded as a plan of division of the Methodist Episcopal Church rather than a means of unification.

The entire period from 1890 to 1910 was filled with discussions of need and desirability of union. Bishop Randolph S. Foster, an able theologian and a profound philosophical thinker, published a book in 1892 entitled *Union of Episcopal Methodism* in which he made a strong plea for union. Dr. John H. Brunner, of the Holston Conference, in a border territory where altar stood against altar, published a book *The Union of the Churches* in which he deplored the sectional feelings and border competitions, and pleaded for union on some basis that might be found. Fraternal messengers from the North to the Southern Conferences all spoke strongly of the desirability of union, while those from the South to the North reciprocated with warm fraternal assurances. They could not speak of union, because they knew that the South would not accept reunion and they had no basis to propose which the North would accept, and without a plan of union no union could be had. Many persons who had expressed strong union sentiments seemed never to have recognized that fact. The younger men were more and more insistent on some movement looking to the removal of church competition and friction and the establishment of practical unity. The General Conference of the Methodist Episcopal Church at Baltimore, May 11, 1908, adopted the following resolution, which inaugurated a movement toward union:

Such has been the growth of the Methodist Episcopal Church and of the Methodist Protestant Church along the lines of their individual development, each gradually modifying its policy and practice to meet the enlarging demands confronting it, that providentially the radical differences of policy which occasioned their separation have been so nearly eliminated that many of the most godly in both Churches are convinced that there is no longer sufficient cause for the maintenance of two distinct ecclesiastical organizations. Having a common origin, holding a common faith, possessing so much of the discipline and policy in common, and, above all, the deep-rooted and growing conviction that the union of the various Methodisms would strengthen the local churches, secure economy of resource, make for aggressive evangelism and hasten the kingdom of our Lord, they earnestly desire that the Methodist Protestant and the Methodist Episcopal Churches shall become organically one.

That the Methodist Episcopal Church in General Conference assembled, hereby most cordially invites the Methodist Protestant Church to unite with the Methodist Episcopal Church in order that, as one great Methodist body, they and we may fulfill the better our individual commissions by preventing the waste of rivalry and exalting the God of peace.

That inasmuch as the General Conference of the Methodist Protestant Church is about to convene in Pittsburgh, Pennsylvania, we hereby request our Board of Bishops to appoint a fraternal deputation to consist of one Bishop, one Minister, and one Layman, to convey to the Methodist Protestant Church through its General Conference this invitation together with the most cordial greetings of the Methodist Episcopal Church.

In accordance therewith the following fraternal deputation was duly appointed: Bishop Henry S. Warren, D.D., LL.D., the Rev. John F. Goucher, D.D., Senator John P. Dolliver.

The General Conference of the Methodist Protestant Church replied to the resolution of the Methodist Episcopal Church:

That we respond heartily to the proposal of the Methodist Episcopal Church, not unmindful of the difficulties to be over-come before a satisfactory conclusion can be reached, but ready to go as far and as rapidly in consummating a universal Methodism as the interests and integrity of our own denomination will permit; and to pray continually for the full realization of their and our hope.

That a commission, consisting of nine members, be appointed by this Conference for the purpose of meeting with a like commission of the Methodist Episcopal Church, of the Methodist Episcopal Church, South, and of other Methodist churches in this country, to promote and complete so far as may be possible the reunion of Methodists in America.

The nine Commissioners appointed were: Dr. Thomas. H. Lewis, the President, the Rev. M. L. Jennings of Ohio, the Rev. George Shaffer of Pittsburgh, the Rev. D. H. Helwick of West Virginia, the Rev. C. D. Sinkinson of New Jersey, Mr. S. R. Harris of North Carolina, Mr. J. E. Peterson of Iowa, Mr. W. N. Swift of Michigan, and Mr. J. J. Barge of Georgia.

Dr. Thomas H. Lewis in 1910 came to the General Conference of the Methodist Episcopal Church, South, as the fraternal messenger from the Methodist Protestant Church. He delivered a remarkably eloquent, stirring, effective address on Methodist union. The General Conference was deeply moved, and with enthusiasm ordered ten thousand copies of the address printed in pamphlet form for general distribution. Unity had grown enormously. Time had softened the attitudes of the senior leaders on both sides and the day of action seemed to be at the dawning. The general feeling was that the Churches should explore the possibilities. Had feeling and sentiment been sufficient for the purpose, union could have taken place by acclamation. But union is not a mere sentimental affair; it is living, laboring, and serving together, and the togetherness must be structural to be and to continue vital and abiding. To produce that structure was to create a Plan of Union.

FEDERAL COUNCIL OF METHODISM

The Commission on Federation had done remarkable service in getting a common hymnal, a common catechism, a common order of worship, a common publishing house in China, a common united Methodism in Japan, and an acceptable distribution of fields in Latin America; but it had not achieved any outstanding results in removing the irritating rivalries and competitions in the home fields. Here and there exchanges of small village and rural churches had been made, but none of large districts, areas, and sections. On both sides loyalty to the ecclesiastical body was made and kept strong by ecclesiastical promoters, ecclesiastical administrators, and ecclesiastical beneficence; and it held fast against all pleas, economic, social, and religious. Mission money and church extension funds built and maintained many an altar, and there seemed to be nothing that could be done about it. This may be illustrated by a resolution, offered in 1896 in the General Conference of the Methodist Episcopal Church by the Rev. Daniel Stevenson of the Kentucky Conference:

Resolved, That the Commission which this Conference has ordered to be appointed to meet the Commission appointed by the General Conference of the Methodist Episcopal Church, South, on Federation, be instructed, when appointed, to come to no agreement with the Methodist Episcopal Church, South, whereby any ground which we now hold in the South shall be abandoned, or the right which we now possess of establishing and maintaining churches in any part of the South where the people may wish to unite with us shall be relinquished, or the hands of our ministers and members in the South be weakened.

After facing this attitude, more or less strong in certain sections of both Churches, the Commission on Federation in April, 1906, decided to ask for the creation of a Federal Council of Methodism with increased power with which to meet the situations. The Southern General Conference a month later approved the plan of a Federal Council, "which without interfering with the autonomy of the respective churches, and having no legislative functions, shall yet be invested with advisory powers in regard to world-wide missions, Christian education, the evangelization of the unchurched masses, and the charitable and brotherly adjustment of all conflicts and misunderstandings that may arise between the different branches of Methodism." The General Conference of the Methodist Episcopal Church in 1908 approved the plan and added in regard to the uniting of local churches: "Such union shall be consummated with the approval" of the respective bishops of the Conferences concerned.

In 1910 the Council was given "full power to hear and finally determine, without appeal from its decisions, all cases of conflict or misunderstanding between the two branches of Methodism." Annual Conferences were given authority to appoint commissions on federation to meet similar commissions of the other Church, and "to hear and determine cases of local irritation and conflict. Said local commissions shall have advisory power. All cases which fail of settlement shall be carried to the Federal Council for final adjudication." The Federal Council was composed of three bishops, three ministers, and three laymen from each of the two Churches, with the vacancies to be filled by the respective groups of Commissioners.

Thus was set up the strongest possible joint body for the settlement of conflicts, misunderstandings, and irritating rivalries and competitions. It was thought that by this method "altar against altar" could be and would be removed. It was hoped that each Church would move to exchange territory with the other. It was supposed that many federated Methodist Churches would result, with agreements for the division of benevolences.

But this did not occur, except in a very limited number of cases. The Council was composed of capable, far-seeing, judicial, sympathetic men. It continued its efforts until 1916. In important cases the Council would divide along the respective church lines. This was all but inevitable. Each side in the case would appeal personally to the Commissioners of its own side and make vivid what was involved from that side. Sessions in such cases could not make for improved fraternity nor lead to finer, broader fellowship. A more difficult task did not fall to any group than these of the Federal Council. This disappointment, the siren voices from many sources advocating union, and the new appreciation of the leaders of each side for those of the other side impelled the Commissioners to undertake the exploration of the problems and possibilities of Methodist union.

The members of the Federal Council in 1910 from the Methodist Episcopal Church were Bishop John M. Walden, Bishop Earl Cranston, Bishop L. B. Wilson, President John F. Goucher of Goucher College, Dr. Richard J. Cooke, the Rev. G. A. Reeder, Mr. R. T. Miller of Cincinnati, Mr. John A. Patten of Chattanooga, Mr. Hanford Crawford of St. Louis. The members from the Methodist Episcopal Church, South, were Bishop A. W. Wilson, Bishop E. E. Hoss, Bishop Collins Denny, Dr. C. M. Bishop, Dr. W. J. Young, Dr. Frank M. Thomas, Judge M. L. Walton of Woodstock, Virginia, President R. S. Hyer of Southwestern University, and later of Southern Methodist University in Texas, and Mr. W. B. Stubbs of Savannah, Georgia.

Chapter Five

A TURN IN THE ROAD

HERE STARTS THE HIGHWAY. LITTLE DID THE THIRTY-SIX MEMBERS of the Joint Commission on Federation that undertook to explore the possibility of Methodist union realize that they were setting out on a journey that would take twenty-nine years to complete, and that only two of them would be alive when the final benediction was said. Those two are Bishop Collins Denny and the Rev. C. M. Bishop, D.D. Uniting a Church may be also the uniting of the sections of a country. When the two Episcopal Methodisms undertook to get together, their representatives found that the obstacles were fundamentally as social and civil as they were ecclesiastical and religious. The obstacles that were ecclesiastical had been developed because of the social and the civil. There had been more than the disruption of a church organization. The evidences of that were many and unmistakable as late as 1910, and the negotiations for union could go no faster than the restoration of social and spiritual unity. Building a plan of union was to be the production of a governmental structure that would ever maintain and secure unity. But union at bottom was a normal state for the two Churches, and disunion was a distinct abnormality. Time was on the side of union, and it was already making itself felt.

The Joint Commission on Federation met in December, 1910, in Baltimore, Maryland. The Commission of the Methodist Episcopal Church at the opening presented the following very important statement:

During the session of our General Conference held in this city in 1908 a Commission was appointed, with our senior bishop as Chairman, to visit the General Conference of the Methodist Protestant Church, then in session at Pittsburgh, bearing a cordial invitation to that body to unite with the Methodist Episcopal Church. The Commission was graciously welcomed, and a delegation was sent in return to make reply to the overtures which had been so cordially forwarded. Subsequently the General Conference of the Methodist Episcopal Church directed its Commission on Federation to invite the Evangelical Association, the United Brethren, and such other branches of Methodism as it might believe to be sympathetic, to confer through similar Commissions concerning federation or organic union as in the judgment of the said Churches, respectively, might be most desirable, and to report to the General Conference of 1912.

Our Commission is persuaded that the Methodist Episcopal Church, South, would have been included by name in this invitation as to organic union had the General Conference been satisfied that such action would not in any way have embarrassed our brethren of that Church.

We are unanimous also in the opinion that the phrase "other branches of Methodism believed to be sympathetic" was intended in the most delicate way possible to include that body should it see fit to respond.

The next step of record which seems to be significant was the official appearance at a meeting of the Commission of the Methodist Episcopal Church and the Methodist Episcopal Church, South, held at Ocean Grove on July 6, 1910, of Dr. T. H. Lewis, Chairman of the Commission appointed by the Methodist Protestant Church. The reception of Dr. Lewis in that capacity, acting under instructions looking to organic union; the consequent agreement to the effect that a joint meeting of the three Commissions should be held in the city of Baltimore, beginning November 30th (in which meeting we are now assembled) ; the call for this meeting by the chairmen of the three Commissions, acting conjointly, and the publishing therewith of the authorizations and instructions given to the several Commissions by their respective General Conferences—all proceeding from the later initiative taken by the Methodist Protestant Commission, seemed to us to distinctively indicate that the subject of organic union would occupy our attention here, which conclusion was further warranted by the fact that no proposals of federation merely had been advanced by either that Church or our own, doubtless because there had appeared so little need of the same.

While this seems to be the status as developed by the several actions and facts recited, we have no desire whatever to press upon the attention of the Joint Commission any unwelcome issue and, least of all, to force a discussion of organic union that might appear to either of our sister Churches ill-timed or likely to produce greater confusion where we are seeking harmony. Nevertheless, in view of the sentiment existing in our own Church growing out of our protracted and only partially successful efforts in federated co-operation with our brethren of the Methodist Episcopal Church, South, we feel that it will be for the general welfare of our Churches and of the kingdom of our Lord, first, to have it distinctly understood that we are ready to take up with our brethren of the other Churches the question of organic union, which for the reasons stated above we have been led to regard as the paramount object of this meeting.

It is our conviction that the time has come when it is due to our people as well as to an interested public that the desirability and practicability of organic union shall be discussed between us; and if the preponderance of judgment be found against either the desirability or practicability of organic union, that the reasons be clearly set before our Churches in order that, being informed as to the same, they may the more intelligently judge the work of their Commissions and conform their own utterances and actions to the conditions as thus developed. We believe they have a right to this knowledge and that we owe it to them to give them this opportunity to measure the difficulties and, as far as possible, to remove them or adjust themselves to actual conditions.

The other action of our General Conference, touching federation with the Methodist Episcopal Church, South, and providing for a Federal Council, we regard as not contradictory to the general provision concerning organic union with other bodies of Methodists, but rather intended to co-ordinate with it and to make provision for continued fraternal relations pending any consideration which might ensue under the general instructions touching organic union.

With this explanation of the reasons by which we are moved, we hereby tender a brotherly invitation to the Commissions of the respective Churches to consider with us at this time the desirability and practicability of organic union.

This statement of the Commission of the Methodist Episcopal Church really started the negotiations that never ceased until union was consummated. It was a call to action. It was a challenge to a desirous effort. The Commission of the Methodist Episcopal Church, South, was not confident of its authority to conduct negotiations looking toward union; but since the last General Conference had given specific instruction "to further, as far as is consistent and practicable, a closer relation between ourselves and the Methodist Episcopal Church, the Methodist Protestant Church, and other Methodist bodies," it was decided to proceed. The paper presented by the Northern Commission was given long and searching consideration through five sessions. At the close the following statement was adopted:

In response to the designation of our respective General Conferences and the provisions of the call for this joint meeting, we have felt it incumbent upon us to give very careful consideration to the existing situation in each of our Churches and especially to inquire in regard to their mutual relations to each other.

We are mutually agreed that the Churches represented by us are equally apostolic in faith and purpose and have a common origin, the Methodist Episcopal Church, organized in 1784; that they are joint heirs of the traditions and doctrinal standards of the fathers; and that they have proved their loyalty to the evangelical faith and evangelical spirit which characterized early Methodists.

We are mutually agreed that our fathers settled the issues of the past conscientiously for themselves, respectively, and separated regretfully, believing that only such action could insure their continued access to the people they were called to serve.

The benefits of fraternal efforts on the part of two of the Churches we represent and the exchange of fraternal messengers between all of them must be recognized in substantial results achieved within our own country and abroad and in the manifest improved feeling existing between these communions.

Our efforts to give sympathetic recognition to every interest involved, taken with the common obligations so to plan the work of the Church as to make the wisest use of the resources of the kingdom, coupled with the plain fact that such unnecessary competition and rivalry still exist among Methodist bodies while unchurched masses hunger for our ministry, compel us to admit that, while we rejoice in all that has been achieved by fraternal efforts up to this time, these results do not in every way meet the demand of the times nor the expectations of our people.

It therefore appears to be our imperative duty earnestly to consider the expediency and practicability of some form of unification that will further allay hurtful competition and conserve all vital interests without in the meantime interfering with the work of the Federal Council of Methodism.

In the presence of these important issues and the clear evidence of the desire of the members of our Churches to be divinely guided in the prosecution of the work to be done by these people of one spiritual ancestry, one faith and one doctrine we feel constrained to give further earnest consideration to the great interests brought to our attention by our respective Churches, and therefore agree:

1. That a joint committee of nine, three from each Commission here represented, be appointed to consider the causes which produce friction and waste and injury rather than promote the common cause—namely, the spreading of Scriptural holiness through these and other lands—and, if found practicable, to bring to this joint Commission a plan for submission to the General Conferences and people of the respective Churches, said plan to provide for such unification, through reorganization of the Methodist Churches concerned, as shall insure unity of purpose, administration, evangelistic effort, and all other functions for which our Methodism has stood from the beginning.

The Committee of Nine as thus agreed upon was appointed as follows: Bishop Earl Cranston, Dr. John F. Goucher, and Mr. R. T. Miller of the Methodist Episcopal Church; Bishop E. E. Hoss, Dr. Frank M. Thomas, and Judge M. L. Walton of the Church South; Dr. Thomas H. Lewis, the Rev. M. L. Jennings, and the Hon. S. R. Harris of the Methodist Protestant Church. Dr. Goucher was abroad and Bishop Walden took his place; Judge Walton was engaged in court and Judge W. G. M. Thomas of Chattanooga took his place. The Committee met in Cincinnati, January 18-20, 1911.

I

Various suggestions were presented in papers to the Commission at Cincinnati. One of much significance was from a group of ministers and laymen in the Chattanooga territory and of the two Churches. That paper is as follows:

THE CHATTANOOGA PROPOSAL

1. Our observation of the situation in East Tennessee convinces us that, during these past years, but for the presence of both denominations in this territory many would have been lost to Methodism. The radical differences in sentiment responsible for this situation have been gradually modified, the spirit of fraternity has grown, and in spite of the competition which has necessarily arisen the two Churches are generally laboring together in peace and harmony. Under these conditions one Church could now clearly best serve the interests of Methodism. The people in both Churches, while unswervingly loyal to their respective denominations, would, we believe, welcome reunion. Practical experience has demonstrated the difficulty, if not impossibility, of securing the removal of one Church from a given community where it is once established, even though all concerned recognizes that one society would serve that particular community more effectively than would two. A federation commission with full power to remove one denomination would still cause friction where that Church—the Church of the choice of many people—would be represented in the general section. For these and other reasons we favor the complete unification of the Methodist Episcopal Church, the Methodist Episcopal Church, South, and the Methodist Protestant Church through reorganization into The Methodist Church.

2. The purposes sought in this reorganization should be the elimination of existing competition and unnecessary duplication in all local fields, and the development of such unity of spirit in American Methodism as a whole as will most effectively advance the cause of evangelism at home and abroad, of education, and of civic righteousness.

3. For purposes of local administration group the Annual Conferences in the United States into four districts of approximately equal membership. To secure the largest benefit to all concerned through the intermingling of the officials and people of the different sections, the lines of division should preferably be

longitudinal, having care in the interest of fairness that the divisions are so arranged that the present membership of each of the larger Churches predominates in one or more of the sections.

4. The year before the meeting of the General Conference a delegated conference should be held in each of these four General Conference districts with as large authority in local government as is consistent with actual denominational unity. We suggest consideration by these Conferences of petitions and memorials before the same are sent to the General Conference for final action.

5. The General Conference should meet quadrennially, as now, with the same powers as at present except in so far as such powers have been given to the General District Conferences.

6. The Annual Conferences will elect delegates to the General Conference at their session preceding the General District Conference sessions, said delegates also to be delegates to the District Conference, additional District Conference delegates to be chosen following the election of those chosen to serve at both Conferences.

7. The General Superintendents to be elected by the General Conference in equal numbers from each district. Nominations for General Superintendents are to be made by the General District Conferences, and the General Conferences must elect from those so nominated, two to be nominated for each bishop to be elected. Delegates from Annual Conferences in each of the General Conference Districts may make nominations by meeting at the General Conference if vacancies occur in the list of nominations prepared by their General District Conferences.

8. The colored Methodists would best be served through a union of all the colored Churches and members with the active financial and personal interests of the unified Church. One great advantage of this union of Methodism would be that Christian men from all sections could unite on a basis entirely free from embarrassment in advancing the cause of Negro evangelization and education. If the union of all colored Churches cannot be secured, try to plan for the union of the Colored Methodist Episcopal Church and the colored membership of the Methodist Episcopal Church. If that is not practicable, make another General Conference District for the colored membership, giving them the additional power to elect their bishops (with authority limited to their own district), and, as a fair offset, their delegates would not have voting power in the General Conference.

II

Bishop Hoss presented a paper by himself, Dr. Thomas, and Judge Thomas. It was later withdrawn and they substituted the following:

1. We suggest, as a plan of reorganization, the merging of the Methodist Episcopal Church, the Methodist Protestant Church, and the Methodist Episcopal Church, South, into one Church, to be known as the Methodist Episcopal Church in America or the Methodist Church in America.

2. We suggest that this Church shall have throughout common Articles of Faith, common conditions of membership, a common hymnal, a common catechism, and a common ritual.

3. We suggest that this Church be organized under the jurisdiction of a General Conference, meeting every five years, and four Quadrennial Conferences.

4. We suggest that this General Conference be composed of equal numbers of ministerial and lay delegates, to be elected in equal proportions from the four jurisdictions.

5. We suggest that the General Conference shall have exclusive jurisdiction, legislative and administrative, over all matters of a purely connectional character.

6. We suggest that the Quadrennial Conferences shall name their own bishops and other officers and be vested with all powers not expressly granted to the General Conference.

7. We suggest, in order to protect the rights and interests of the entire Church and at the same time prevent the development of undue diversities, that both the General Conference and the Quadrennial Conferences be limited in their functions by the express restrictions of a written constitution.

8. We suggest, in order to safeguard the Constitution, that there must be lodged somewhere outside of the General Conference and the Quadrennial Conferences the power to arrest unconstitutional legislation.

In the first paper they suggested that the "Church be organized under the jurisdiction of a Methodist Council and four General Conferences," and that the "Council be constituted of two houses, the first house to be composed of all the bishops, and the second of two hundred delegates, fifty from each of the General Con-

ference divisions," and that the "Council have exclusive jurisdiction, legislative and administrative, over foreign missions,
church extension in foreign lands, educational and publishing
interests, and all other matters of a purely connectional character."

Bishop Cranston presented the following paper for the subcommittee of his Church:

1. We recommend that the Plan of Reorganization shall provide for five ecclesiastical jurisdictions, constructed, as far as
possible, with reference to harmonious internal administration,
and all to be represented in and under the direction of one
General Conference. It is our judgment that one of these jurisdictions should include the negro membership now related to
our several existing organizations.

2. We would allow to each jurisdiction the right to suggest
legislative action, to nominate its *pro rata* representation in the
Board of Bishops, and to manage its own internal affairs in all
matters not committed constitutionally or by the book of Discipline (as finally constructed) to the General Conference for
determination.

3. We would recommend that the bishops be eligible for administrative duty and service throughout the entire connection.

4. In order to secure legislative recognition and protection to
the minority Churches participating in this movement, we recommend that the General Conference be composed of two houses
—one to be chosen on the basis of ministerial and lay membership within the several Annual Conferences, and the other to be
selected by the several jurisdictions, an equal number from each
—the two houses to deliberate separately, but their concurrent
vote to be required for passing any measure involving a change
of Discipline or a declaration of principles.

5. We recommend that there be a Judicial Council constituted by nominations in equal numbers from each of the recognized jurisdictions and confirmed by the General Conference,
to which Council all appeals shall be referred for final decision,
and which Council shall also have power to pass upon the constitutionality of all legislation, its decisions to be reversible only
by a two-thirds vote of the Annual Conference.

6. We recommend that at least two nominations for every

office thus far named be sent by each nominating body to the General Conference.

III

Dr. Thomas H. Lewis, Dr. M. L. Jennings, and the Hon. S. R. Harris presented the following observations:

1. Two papers have been presented to the committee by those representing the Methodist Episcopal Church, South, and the Methodist Episcopal Church, respectively, in which the views of the character of the union proposed are quite different. There is perhaps no third view, for it seems that the legislative assembly of the Church must be one or more than one, central or distributed. As between these two views, we incline to the opinion that it will be better to have the new Church distributed into several legislative units and incorporated into one national unit to conserve national affairs.

2. We think it would be wise to call the new organization the Methodist Church in America. This would describe us all, and it would be a visible and outward sign that something has come into existence that did not exist before—viz., the union of three different Methodist Churches. The concession by the other two Churches would be inconsiderable, since while they would lose a part of their distinctive name they would retain the substance of their system, and it would retain a name sufficiently descriptive and historically exact.

3. We think that in writing the Constitution it ought to be accepted as a basic principle that the Church is composed of the ministry and laity, of equal responsibility each in their sphere, and entitled to equal recognition and honor. This is not intended to assert that laymen should be put everywhere as now obtains in the General Conference, but wherever they belong and can help.

4. The principle of autonomy having been maintained with reference to the legislative assembly, we think it would be consistent and wise to carry it into the Annual Conferences to some extent. The united Church once resolved to make the presiding eldership elective. Might not the reunited Church do well to give the Annual Conference some participation in filling an office so closely related to the vital concerns of the ministers and Churches?

IV

Bishop Cranston later in the session presented for his subcommittee the following supplemental statement:

1. While we would prefer the name under which our Churches at the outset had existence, we accept the name proposed by the representatives of the Methodist Episcopal Church, South, The Methodist Episcopal Church in America.

2. Yielding our preference for one General Conference, in which should be lodged all legislative power, we agree to the suggestions that the governing power of the reorganized Church shall be vested in one General Conference and three or four Quadrennial Conferences, both General and Quadrennial Conferences to exercise their powers under constitutional provisions and restrictions, the General Conference to have full legislative power over all matters distinctively connectional, and the Quadrennial Conferences to have full legislative power over all distinctively local affairs. (In legislation affecting directly both connectional and local interests concurrent action shall be required.)

3. The General Conference shall meet every sixth year. It shall consist of two houses—one house composed of the bishops and ministerial and lay delegates, as many of each class at least as there are bishops; and one house composed of an equal number of ministerial and lay delegates. All legislation altering or amending the Discipline shall require the concurrent action of the two houses. The delegates in the first house shall be apportioned equally among the quadrennial Conferences and elected under equitable rules provided therefor by the General Conference. The ministerial delegates in the second house shall be elected by the ministerial members of the Annual Conferences, and the lay delegates by the laity within the Annual Conferences, under equitable rules provided therefor, each Annual Conference to have at least one ministerial and one lay delegate, the larger Conferences to have one ministerial and one lay delegate for every ninety ministerial members of the Conference, also an additional ministerial and lay delegate where there is an excess of two-thirds of the fixed ratio of representation.

4. In order to perpetuate the itinerant General Superintendency as a cardinal feature of Church polity, we still prefer that bishops shall be nominated by the Quadrennial Conference and confirmed by the General Conference.

5. We propose that there shall be a Connectional Judicial Conference, which shall hold sessions at such times and places and with such powers and functions as shall be determined by the Constitution of the Church.

V

The Commission, with these five papers before them, after four days of careful consideration and frank, forceful discussion unanimously agreed upon the following suggestions to be reported to the Joint Commission:

1. We suggest, as a plan of reorganization, the merging of the Methodist Episcopal Church, the Methodist Protestant Church, the Methodist Episcopal Church, South, into one Church, to be known as the Methodist Episcopal Church in America or the Methodist Church in America.

2. We suggest that this Church shall have throughout common Articles of Faith, common conditions of membership, a common hymnal, a common catechism, and a common ritual.

3. We suggest that the governing power of the reorganized Church shall be vested in one General Conference and three or four Quadrennial Conferences, both General and Quadrennial Conferences to exercise their powers under constitutional provisions and restrictions, the General Conference to have full legislative power over all matters distinctively connectional, and the Quadrennial Conferences to have full legislative power over distinctively local affairs.

4. We suggest that the General Conference shall consist of two houses, each house to be composed of equal numbers of ministerial and lay delegates. The delegates in the first house shall be apportioned equally among the Quadrennial Conferences and elected under equitable rules to be provided therefor. The ministerial delegates in the second house shall be elected by the ministerial members of the Annual Conferences, and the lay delegates by the laity within the Annual Conferences under equitable rules provided therefor. Each Annual Conference shall have at least one ministerial and one lay delegate. The larger Conferences shall each have one additional ministerial and one additional lay delegate for every —— ministerial members of the Conference, also an additional ministerial and lay delegate where there is an excess of two-thirds of the fixed rate of repre-

sentation. All legislation of the General Conference shall require the concurrent action of the two houses.

5. We suggest that the Quadrennial Conferences shall name the bishops from their several jurisdictions, the same to be confirmed by the first house of the General Conference. We suggest that the Quadrennial Conferences shall be composed of an equal number of ministerial and lay delegates to be chosen by the several Annual Conferences within their several jurisdictions according to an equitable plan to be provided for.

6. We suggest that the Annual Conferences, whose boundaries shall be fixed by the Quadrennial Conferences, be composed of all traveling, supernumerary, and superannuated preachers within their prescribed boundaries, and that the principle of lay representation in the Annual Conferences be recognized.

7. We suggest that neither the General Conference nor any of the Quadrennial Conferences be invested with final authority to interpret the constitutionality of its own actions.

VI

The Joint Commission met in Chattanooga, Tennessee, May 10, 1911, to consider the report of the Committee of Nine. The session continued three days. Bishop Charles W. Smith served as the substitute for Dr. Goucher. The discussions were frank and full. The speeches were stenographically received and later printed. The chief discussion related to the powers of the General and the Quadrennial Conferences. In these debates the distinguishing viewpoints of the two Episcopal Methodist Churches were presented, interpreted, and advocated. The speakers were Bishop A. W. Wilson, Bishop Cranston, Bishop Walden, Bishop Denny, Bishop Smith, the Rev. R. J. Cooke, the Rev. Frank M. Thomas, the Rev. C. M. Bishop, Mr. R. T. Miller, Dr. Thomas H. Lewis, and Mr. J. A. Patten.

At the risk of seeming to reproduce old controversial attitudes which under other circumstances might be left unsaid, the occasion is here taken to insert certain speeches and excerpts from various Commissioners. This is done that the various points of view and attitudes may make clear to the modern reader exactly what the negotiators for union had to face in 1910 and even during later years.

Bishop A. W. Wilson

We can move in the lines proposed in this report without detriment to any Church. I very gravely doubt whether it will be accepted by any of the three Churches involved. It may be; but I shall not be sorry if it shall not be. Prejudice, as you call it, prevails to a large extent among the ordinary people. There are multitudes of people everywhere who do not know anything of the issues involved. When you talk of incorporating them with any other Church, they feel very much as if they were being surrendered hand and foot to their enemies. You cannot get that feeling out of them. I have no doubt, if you should adopt a plan of organic union such as is proposed here, there are five hundred thousand Methodists in the Methodist Episcopal Church, South, who would either go to other communions or organize an independent Methodist Church. I do not want any such results. I do not want to lose our people. I want them to remain in perfect sympathy with us in all our work, and feel that what we have done has been done for their advantage and for the best interests of the Kingdom of God. If anything can produce that sort of feeling among them, it will save them from disaffection. There might possibly be a plan worked out of actual federation with four or five sections united in their general interests and bound together by a general council. I am not particular about names. We must look below the surface of things and prejudice and special church connections and separate organizations. We pride ourselves upon them. The Methodist Episcopal Church has done a momentous work. Our own Church has done a work not surpassed in Protestant history. The Methodist Protestant Church deserves credit for its Methodist faith and practice. But, after all, the main question lies beyond all this. What do the best interests of the Kingdom of God require? Will any of them or all of them be made better by change? If not, we had better revert to the old situation and work along as best we can with all the difficulties incident to it. If we are going to improve the condition of things by the plan proposed, then all right, and we should thank God for the opportunity given us. I am very much of a conservative and progressive at the same time. I hold to the past with all the energy of my nature. I have talked with the fathers and have known some of them personally that could go back to the days of Asbury. I cherish the memory of them and their great heritage. I glory in the past of the Church. It has been a powerful history. Methodism has had and continues to have a powerful influence upon the nations of the earth. At the same time I know that we cannot reproduce the race of the fathers. We cannot bring up a generation of that sort again. We may bring up men with a great grasp upon the various phases of the Kingdom of God. We may bring up men more experienced in managing the material interests of the Kingdom of God. We may bring up a class of men representing higher scholarship. But I say, and I do not say it unhappily, we cannot reproduce those old men with their solid faith in God and with their mighty determination and their great devotion to Christ and their ability to point out the way of conquest of the world. We can carry along their work and possibly upon higher lines.

Sometimes we are led to be boastful of our gains. Would to God that we were "a thousand times so many more as we are," and that our people were men and women of solid faith and true piety, and not people who have simply taken upon themselves the Methodist name and then dishonored it by an utter disregard of Christ and his Gospel.

I am saying by way of personal allusion that it was a sore thing for me to break away from the old connections back in the sixties. The warmest friends I had were on your side of the line. Some of them were exceedingly bitter in their views and utterances. But I thank God the day came when the old affection was restored. I do not think a man of them was lost to me. They have been in my fellowship and affection in the course of a score of years. We consulted together as the evening shades came on and our hearts became tender to old-time friends, and it was delightful to enter into this old-time fellowship. It was hard for me to part from such friends. I believe that I did the only thing possible for the salvation of our Methodist Church in the times and territory with which we had to do. By our action we have saved tens of thousands of Methodists to the Kingdom of God who otherwise would have wandered away and been lost. In all that time I have never put a stone in the way of my brethren of the other Church. I have not hindered them and have simply done the work I was forced to do by the conditions under which I was placed. I have done no proselyting. No member of your

Church has been won away by any solicitation of mine. The end of my journey is not far off. This whole thing, when it goes through, will be sung in requiem over my grave, but I shall have no part in the final result. I have no concern about that, but I am concerned about the churches. I do not want any failure on the part of either of them. It would be hard for me to know that any part of our Methodism had failed to spread Scriptural holiness through the lands of the earth.

We need not fear to consider this report. If we come to an agreement, we can thank God for that much of unity among Methodists, and can report to our respective General Conferences, and they will not take final action in this matter without first presenting it to the church as a whole—our laymen and laywomen, our Annual Conferences. The whole business will have to be submitted to the judgment and conscience of every member of the Church. Whenever this proposed union shall have been effected, whatever it shall be, and the consensus of opinion throughout the entire Church shall be back of it, I predict it will be the best product of ecclesiastical statesmanship and of personal and denominational religion ever known. We have had bitter quarrels and bitter antagonisms and we have come out of them all, and we sit here together before God and exchange greetings and fellowship and nobody is hurt after all. But be cautious. Remember that you are to deal with people who do not know the situation and cannot know it. This matter must be put into such shape that all our people shall appreciate it and come to work at it heartily. I pray God may guide you in all your deliberations and cause the work of this Commission to add glory to his name and effectiveness to our beloved Methodism.

BISHOP E. E. HOSS

The minority Methodist bodies going into this proposed organization surrender more than the larger bodies. That cannot be questioned. The larger body will necessarily have, and ought to have, more influence in the reorganized Church than either of the other bodies. It is only a fair principle that numbers should count. On the other hand, it is an equally fair principle that there should be ample protection and guarantee for the rights of the minority. We are surrendering ourselves by this scheme of reorganization into the hands of our brethren of the Methodist Episcopal Church. It is a great surrender. It is not an easy thing. It is a great act of faith and trust on our part, much greater than you are called upon to exercise in uniting with us. You are two to our one. What we wish to know is, how much we are going to surrender to this supreme General Conference so that it cannot be misunderstood. The authority of the General Conference has been a great issue in all our history. It was a great thing in 1844 and at subsequent times. Some of you believe that the General Conference is supreme, absolutely. But there are some of us who cannot accept that doctrine concerning the General Conference. We are willing to give it all the powers it ought to have in order to make it a vital governing body of Methodism, and we want these powers to be under constitutional restrictions and limitations. We want to know what we are surrendering, and everything else we want to keep in our own hands. The question settled by the Civil War was that the State cannot withdraw from the Union of States, but inside of its limitations the State is just as supreme as ever. Now we are not willing just to pass up everything we have into the hands of the General Conference without any limitation, clearly defined, with regard to its powers. We are willing to sit down and consider with you what specific power it ought to have and as to the reach, extent, and measure of its authority; and when we come to a conclusion on that point we want to write it down and never have it questioned in the future as to what we have surrendered to the General Conference. I am sure that I know the belief of our great body of Methodist people on this point. Our people seem to think that they are being swallowed up. When we go into a partnership with a partner twice as strong as ourselves and the making of laws depends upon the counting of heads, we want protection, and this we can have only by imposing limitations upon the powers of the General Conference. I am not willing to trust the keeping of the rights of my Church into the hands of any body of men. In making this statement I express no distrust whatever of my brethren. I insist upon the strict definition and limitation of the rights and powers of the General Conference, expressly reserving everything else into the hands of these Quadrennial Conferences.

I mean that the legislative functions of the General Conference shall be strictly defined and that these functions shall be definite and that all other legislative functions shall be left in the hands of the Quadrennial Conferences. I would not at this time state what these limits should be. All I insist upon is that there should be definitions and limitation of them. I am willing to go the full length of making this body one of real power and authority. The Senate and House of Representatives have very real legislative powers, but they are very sharply defined by constitutional limitations. They cannot trespass upon the reserved rights of the States. If they were to do so, they would be arrested by the Supreme Court of the United States. We enumerate not the functions of the Quadrennial Conferences but the General Conference with the understanding that all functions not enumerated as belonging to the General Conference are reserved to the Quadrennial Conferences. All I insist upon is that there shall be a fixed limitation of these functions—fixed, definite, and immovable, beyond which the General Conference cannot go. I oppose the idea that the General Conference is a supreme body in executive, judicial, and legislative spheres. I am heartily opposed to leaving the matter open so that the General Conference may proceed to do anything it wants to do without limitation in any direction.

Bishop John M. Walden

Brethren, it is a time when we should speak frankly and fully. This proposition of having three or four distinct Conferences is not new. It originated in the South and has been suggested in the North many times. Perhaps there is nothing in the whole proposition that will create such strong and general discussion in the Church I represent as this feature of the paper now before us. Now, we have gone a long way in conceding these four districts. We have made a concession that you brethren cannot understand. This is what we must meet when it shall be presented to our constituency of more than three million members living on American soil. I did not believe that it would be possible for me ever to consent to a united Methodism divided into four districts. But when I heard the brethren in the subcommittee I thought I saw some justification for it. When the question of majorities and minorities was presented, and I am American enough to know that constitutions are made to protect minorities, I was then willing to make the concession that has been made in the report now before us. Who has been making larger concessions in the matter before us? If we are to have the support of three-fifths of the entire Methodism involved in this question, I do not believe it is wise to ask us to go beyond the concessions we have made; that is, to have these Quadrennial Conferences and to have them so organized that they will represent four distinct Conferences correlated in a general body the powers of which are not yet defined. The term "General Conference" employed in the discussion has a historical setting. Methodism, if it is to be a great body in this country, must be a connectional Methodism, and there are two things especially identified with that proposition. The one is the General Conference. You speak of the General Conference—at once every trained Methodist recognizes the dominant and controlling power of the Church. If we are to have a united Methodism, it must have a controlling power, and therefore we should not in these divisions give that name and function that will lead our people to believe they represent any trace of the great General Conference as we know it.

Bishop Collins Denny

There are one or two general remarks which I should like to submit at this time. In the first place I do not think any man should be regarded as offensive because he gives expression to the views of the Church he represents. We are here for that purpose. If we are going into a movement of this kind with any prospect of success, everybody must make concessions. No matter whether the number is few or many, they cannot expect to have things as they had them before. Things we have held quite dear may have to be surrendered. As I understand it, the irreducible minimum of the Methodist Episcopal Church, South, is succinctly stated, that no part of the Church shall make the Discipline for the other part. There is not to be for this Church one Discipline. Each General Conference is to make its own Discipline. We must elect our own officers. We cannot be subjected to others. Our people will not stand it, even at the expense of the plan of union, either in the matter of Discipline, or government, or supervision by men who are elected by some other body than themselves.

We must determine as to the benefit to be attained by going into this union, whether what we receive will outweigh what we yield. Here we have in view the unification of the three Methodist Churches in this country. If that end is to be more to us than the things which are holding us apart, then we can come together. If, however, the things that hold us apart are more to us than the things that bring us together, then we have to go along as we have been going till some better day.

We cannot expect you to carry to your people a scheme that

will wreck itself upon their opinions. Nor can we do that. If I know anything as to the position of our people in the South, it is perfectly clear that we are not willing to go into any union of any kind that will put into the hands of the other Methodists of this country to make the Discipline that will govern us. Nor are we willing to go into a union that will make it possible to bring us under the domination of a Negro Bishop. It is stated that Bishops elected by the Quadrennial Conferences should circulate throughout the Church. I object to that. If one of the Conferences should elect a Negro Bishop to preside over the whole Church, there would be no Methodism in the South for him to preside over. We cannot possibly subject our people to that possibility. They will not be willing to yield the point that you shall select our officers for us. We must select our own officers. As I understand this amendment, it prescribes limitations to the powers of the General Conference. The General Conference can have no powers whatever in the election of officers if this plan is to go through with us. I think this is the sentiment of our delegation and of our Church. There can be no officers for the reorganized Church if one is to be a Negro. On that point we might as well part company at once. If our willingness to yield to that point is necessary to union, then there can be no union.

BISHOP EARL CRANSTON

We never would consider four General Conferences. We never can think of four Methodisms in place of what we have now. That would not be unification, but quadrification. We have been sent here to unify something. Our people have heard of that plan for a long time and they would never be willing to consider a divisive proposition for a moment. The first thing they would ask us would be whether we were going to make four churches instead of one. If so, we might as well drop this whole business. We would say, No, we do not propose to do that, but we intend to have one General Conference that shall be supreme over the entire body. Well, they will say, If that is true, all right. But they will inquire, What are these Quadrennial Conferences? We might say in justification of what we were willing to agree to tentatively as a basis, that those will be simple matters, having only local bearing, which will be administered under the power given to the Quadrennial Conferences. But frankly, brethren, I do not know what these things are which are to be confided to the Quadrennial Conferences. We must know that. If the Quadrennial Conference is to be a subordinate body, I do not mean by that, to wear a yoke, but under constitutional restrictions so that there shall be no impingement between it and the supreme body, I can understand that. But if these carefully worded restrictions are to be imposed upon the General Conference, and everything not thus specifically confided to it is to be left within the jurisdiction of the Quadrennial Conferences, our people will prefer an affliction unendurable rather than to have that. From our standpoint the discretionary power should be in the General Conference and the restrictions should be laid upon the Quadrennial Conferences instead of the reverse. We agreed to the wording of the paper presented by the Committee of Nine. We had made the concession on one General Conference and the Quadrennial Conference arrangement, not forgetting that we would be one of these subordinate bodies under such a General Conference.

Another concession we made was this: We believed in one General Conference with all its embarrassments. We did not consider seriously two houses, though we realized the difficulties in the way of one house with so large a body of delegates. But we agreed, in order to reach a certain basis of negotiation for a reunion, to an upper house, to be made up of equal representation from each of the Quadrennial Conferences. It should correspond with the United States Senate and House of Representatives so that no law can be passed without the concurrence of both houses.

Now, I do claim that the people we represent are a magnanimous, true hearted people. At Cincinnati we said that in nothing that might transpire in our discussion of the questions between us, and in our efforts to bring to fruition the hopes some of us entertain, should any word of reproach ever be uttered on either side. But we further declared that we did not ask our brethren of the South to leave behind them one memory that was precious to them nor to repudiate, to the point of a letter, any action which had been taken by any of their spiritual fathers. We put ourselves on the platform of Christian men as starting from today and looking out into the future to be guided by the spirit of today and not looking backward over things concerning which we had no power. We threw aside at Baltimore considerations which were valuable to us. We put away all superiority in numbers and financial resources, and we came into your presence risking criticism at the hands of our brethren because of what we had agreed to confer about. We do not want you to go into an organization where you will feel that you are wearing a yoke. We would not impose a single duty or requirement that would be burdensome. We do long for the day when everything between us will be so shaped that every consideration of Christianity will bind us into one great brotherhood for righteousness.

BISHOP CHARLES W. SMITH

A very considerable part of the heat that has been engendered here tonight has arisen out of lack of agreement to the terms used. Controversies very often arise out of misapprehension of terms and definitions. The word "supreme" has been used as though it meant "unlimited." Bishop Hoss himself spoke of the supreme General Conference. There never was but one such General Conference, and that existed from 1784 to 1808. There never has been one since. I think I shall have to say that the question of 1844 was not as to a supreme General Conference. Everybody admitted that the General Conference was under a constitution. The question was one of construction and not as to whether the General Conference was supreme. There was a wide difference of opinion at that time. I do not accept the extreme view of Bishop Hamline, nor does our Church.

This paper says that the General Conference and the Quadrennial Conferences shall operate under certain constitutional provisions. Therefore they cannot be supreme. We have all agreed on that. The constitution ought to define what the powers of these respective Conferences are. They are constitutional bodies and cannot exercise any powers beyond constitutional limitations. There need be no misunderstanding. If we are speaking of an absolute General Conference, there is no thought of that kind in any mind here. The point of real difference is as to how much of legislative power shall be put into the hands of the General Conference and how much into the hands of the Quadrennial Conferences. We cannot agree on that. We, of the Methodist Episcopal Church, might want to put more power in the General Conference than you of the other Churches would accept. I am willing to let that go to the representatives of the Churches when they come to settle the checks and balances which shall exist between these two classes of Conferences.

Dr. Thomas H. Lewis

At the first meeting of the Commission held in Baltimore last December, representatives of the two Episcopal Methodisms spoke at length in explanation of the difficulties in the way of the nearer approach of Methodists of the South and of the North. It was quite proper and was necessary that they should. These constitute by far the largest and the most important factors in this problem, and it isn't worth while to discuss a Methodist union that leaves either of them out. We all felt, I think, that a most happy ending of that meeting was reached when by unanimous agreement a Committee of Nine was appointed with specific instructions to report to the Commission at its next meeting, if possible, "a plan to provide for such unification through reorganization of the Methodist Churches concerned, as shall insure unity of purpose, administration, evangelistic effort, and all other functions for which our Methodism has stood from the beginning."

We, twenty-seven commissioners, are unanimously agreed, I believe, that whenever the time comes for the unification of Methodism it will have to come about through a reorganization of the Methodist Churches concerned. Hence, all consideration of the subject must proceed upon the assumption that, as a matter of course, every party to the union must be ready to make concessions. How many and how important those concessions will be must be determined finally by each denomination for itself; but it will be admitted, I presume, that it ought not to be entirely governed by the size of the denomination. If union between a large church and a small church is thought desirable, and there are differences to be harmonized, the large church might be magnanimous and give up more, or the small church might be eager and give up more; but a more rational way of procedure would seem to be to consider every concession on its merits, with reference to the great ends sought—viz., to bring about a union, and to make the new organization better than any of the old. Proceeding thus, some things would be conceded which might not be regarded as having superior value for one of these ends, but necessary for the other. To get union at all, the people to be united must be satisfied; and so some concessions must be made for no other reason than to satisfy one of the parties to the union. On the other hand, it is necessary to regard the efficiency of the new organization as one of the prime objects and to incorporate in it whatever will increase that efficiency, whether it comes by concession or not.

Now, speaking for myself alone, I hold the first of these ends to be of more practical importance than the second. So far as this Commission is concerned we would not be here at all if there were no desire or hope of bringing about a union. What we do, therefore, and what we refrain from doing, should be determined primarily by its effect upon that end. And, while our main business is not the production of an ideal form of church polity, yet, since we must, in fact, produce a new organization, we ought to seize the opportunity of making that organization as good as possible. All of us are convinced that our respective organizations are now reasonably effective; they are producing good results.

But over and above the consideration of the excellence and efficiency of our own Churches, the question of union has met us with its own peculiar and imperative claims. Denominational bigotry and sectional prejudices are simply out of date; and whatever fine names some people give them, they will no longer raise the dead nor inspire many of the living. Everybody who will open his eyes can see it written on the wall of Christendom, "One is your Master, even Christ; and all ye are brethren." This is the watchword of an awakened Church, and the greatest movements of Christian energy today are pulsing to that measure. It is not a conclusion of despair, "United we stand, divided we fall;" but the inspiration of greater things than we have yet seen; moving forward instead of standing, triumphing instead of enduring, and rising into the perfect fellowship of love instead of tolerating one another's peculiarities. It is great achievement we are looking forward to, animated by a great sentiment, and both inspired by our Lord's greatest desire. I know no more fitting expression of it as respects us than this sentence from Dr. Buckley: "To see Methodism in this great nation substantially united would be worth living for and sacrificing for through the toiling of long years; and were men to exert themselves to the point of impoverishment, if they lived to see the vision drawing near to realization, their joy would be such as to obliterate the memory of those sacrifices."

Now considering the details of this new organization, with constant reference to the two great ends in view—viz., to bring about a union, and to make the new organization better than any of the old—I desire to submit to your Christian judgment a few particulars which I believe would be gratifying to all Methodist Protestants and might resolve the hesitancy of those among us who now look upon this movement with scant favor.

They are:

1. Equal lay representation in the Annual Conference. The Committee of Nine has recommended that the principle of lay representation in the Annual Conference be recognized, but they have not expressed any opinion as to its extent. Logically it seems inevitable that the admission of laymen in the General Conference should lead to their admission in the Annual Conference; and I think it is safe to say that the laymen generally feel more concerned about the action of an Annual than a General Conference. The Methodist Episcopal Church, South, has already recognized this principle.

2. Some method by which Annual Conferences might participate in the selection of District Superintendents or Presiding Elders. This is a very old question in Methodist polity. The General Conference of 1820 passed a law making presiding elders elective, as is well known; and this action was suspended and finally indefinitely postponed on the protest of Bishop-elect Soule. But it is a live question yet, and is likely to be, because it concerns the autonomy of Annual Conferences. I believe they will not be satisfied until some concession of this principle is made.

3. Some provision for reviewing the plan of appointments. I should think such a change would be welcomed most of all by those who make the appointments. The General Conference of the Methodist Episcopal Church, South, in 1910, directed the Bishops to read the plan of appointments to the presiding elders before announcing it to the Conference, and I suppose this is a concession to the principle of review. At any rate, it would be but a step from this to some safe and sane provision for some sort of a Committee of Appeal which would relieve the itinerancy of a load it ought not to bear, involuntary oppression. Let me add that although our President has always made the plan of appointments quite after the fashion of a Bishop, and his plan is never voted on, yet I have never heard of but one church rejecting its pastor in the whole history of the Conference.

4. The election of all local church officers by the church membership. This is the final step in that representative democracy to which all Methodisms have committed themselves, and the legitimate outgrowth of that uplift of mind and heart

among lay people which Methodism has done so much to promote. It is no longer fitting to deal with full-grown Methodists as our fathers dealt with their children. The larger responsibility is already here; we should match it with the larger opportunity.

The Committee of Nine has submitted two names, "The Methodist Episcopal Church in America" and "The Methodist Church in America," for your consideration. For the first name suggested it is to be said that it was the name of the Church before any division came about, and the name under which Methodism was first organized in this country. Moreover, since it is expected that the new organization will continue the system of a general superintendency, this name will more fully and accurately describe the organization.

To adopt "The Methodist Church in America," as the name of the united Church, will first of all proclaim in the most literal and emphatic way that a union has taken place. There is no Church so designated now, and the name is simply what is left of our three names after all differentiating adjectives have been dropped, and "signifieth the removing of those things that are shaken, as of things that are made, that those things which cannot be shaken may remain." Again, it will bear the test of historical and ecclesiastical accuracy. Historically we were Methodists before we organized the Methodist Episcopal Church, and though some of us have ceased to be members of that Church we continue to be Methodists unto this day. Ecclesiastically, I maintain that the second name is more accurate than the first.

The Joint Commission, after three days of faithful consideration, approved the report of the Committee of Nine with two important additions. The one was made to Item 3: "We suggest that the colored membership of the Methodist Episcopal Church, the Methodist Protestant Church, and such organizations of colored Methodists as may enter into agreement with them, may be constituted and recognized as one of the Quadrennial or Jurisdictional Conferences of the proposed organization." The other became Item 5: "We suggest that the Quadrennial Conferences shall be composed of an equal number of ministerial and lay delegates to be chosen by the Annual Conferences within their several jurisdictions according to an equitable plan to be provided for."

Bishop Denny announced that he voted against all the items of the report, and before the adjournment he offered the following resolution, which was adopted:

Resolved, That at the close of our deliberations we emphasize the statement that the suggestions here outlined are only tentative, that in no sense are these suggestions a plan, but merely the result of our explorations in search of a basis of union. It has not been possible to think through even the questions that have come before us. Other questions not yet touched will need to be weighed, analyzed, and carefully stated.

Chapter Six

FACING THE ISSUE

THE GENERAL CONFERENCES OF THE METHODIST EPISCOPAL AND the Methodist Protestant Churches met in May, 1912. The Commission of the Methodist Protestant Church, in submitting the "Suggestions" of the Joint Commission on Federation, offered the following important resolution which was adopted by the General Conference:

1) The series of suggestions agreed upon by the Joint Commission are confessedly but a fragment, relating only to a small part of the organization of the new Church. And they are presented for the consideration principally of the two Episcopal Methodisms, since the first great problem with them is to discover a form of General Conference organization under which they can live harmoniously together. With this phase of the problem the Methodist Protestant Church has little immediate concern, having itself no sectional question, and its fundamental principle of equal lay representation being freely conceded in all the plans proposed. Your Commission does not deem it necessary, therefore, that this General Conference should express itself on the merits of these suggestions at this time.

2) The second suggestion of your Commission is that this General Conference continue this Commission, or appoint another for the purpose of carrying on to completion the negotiations so auspiciously begun, repeating our declaration of 1908 that we are "ready to go as far and as rapidly in consummating a universal Methodism as the interests and integrity of our own denomination will permit; and asserting as the fundamental condition of this movement that the two Episcopal Methodisms must come into agreement before we can go further than we have gone."

The statement in the first suggestion that "the first great

problem with them [the two Episcopal Methodisms] is to discover a form of General Conference organization under which they can live harmoniously together," and that in the second, "and asserting as the fundamental condition of this movement that the two Episcopal Methodisms must come into agreement before we can go further than we have gone," explain the absence of the Methodist Protestant Commission from the negotiations of the other two Churches for twenty years. The two Episcopal Methodisms had to find a basis of understanding and agreement before the three Commissions could together enter upon the production of a general Plan of Union.

The General Conference of the Methodist Episcopal Church received the report of their Commissioners, but they took no action on it. They seemed to have felt that they were not at liberty to act because of the resolution offered by Bishop Denny, and adopted by the Joint Commission on Federation, "that at the close of our deliberations we emphasize the statement that the suggestions here outlined are only tentative, that in no sense are the suggestions a plan, but merely the result of our explorations in search of a basis of union." The "Suggestions" were in such contradiction of what had been proposed by that Church in the way of "union" or "reunion" and in such opposition to their conception of a supreme General Conference that it is quite possible they were not ready to make an expression of any kind. The General Conference, however, declared: "We heartily approve the action of our Commission on Federation in proposing the question of organic union to the Commissioners in joint session at Baltimore, believing that the membership of the Methodist Episcopal Church would welcome a corporate reunion of the Methodisms of America." A Commission on Federation was appointed with full power and authority to continue negotiations concerning the "commendable purposes of advancing organic union or close federation."

The Joint Commission met in Washington, D. C., April 8

and 9, 1913. The Commissioners of the Methodist Episcopal Church, South, presented a paper containing these words:

Since the General Conference of the Methodist Episcopal Church, when the Suggestions were presented to it by its Commission in May, 1912, did not see fit to take action thereon, ... it seems useless to take any further action in that direction at the present time. But we desire as Commissioners of the Methodist Episcopal Church, South, to say that we stand on the same ground that we have occupied, and express our perfect willingness to continue negotiations on the general lines then laid down.

The Joint Commission then gave its attention to the task of perfecting a plan of procedure for the Federal Council of Methodism. The Council met for its first session in Nashville, Tennessee, January 21, 1914. It adjourned to meet in Put-in-Bay, Michigan, in June, 1914.

I

The General Conference of the Methodist Episcopal Church, South, at its meeting in Oklahoma City, in May, 1914, in view of the above statement of its Commissioners, was of a mind to say something notwithstanding the embargo of the Bishop Denny resolution. The "Suggestions" submitted in the report of the Joint Commission had been written largely by the Southern Commissioners. Not many favored a two-house General Conference, but the other "Suggestions" contained acceptable principles and provisions. The report of the Joint Commission went to the standing Committee on "Church Relations," of which Dr. Frank M. Thomas, of Kentucky, was Chairman, and Dr. R. H. Wynn, of Louisiana, was the Secretary. The Committee was strongly constituted. On it were W. N. Ainsworth, James Cannon, Jr., U. V. W. Darlington, W. F. Tillett, Stonewall Anderson, E. B. Mann, N. L. Linebaugh, S. H. C. Burgin, W. P. Few, R. S. Hyer, P. D. Maddin, M. E. Lawson, and others of prominence and ability. The report of the Commission went to a subcommittee composed of John M. Moore, C. H. Ireland of North Carolina, R. E. Wood of Louisville, and two others who never served. After due and diligent consideration of the "Suggestions" the subcommittee studiously prepared their report and submitted it to the full standing committee, and they accepted it without any change, except that, upon the motion of Thomas Whitehead and the Rev. James Cannon, Jr., of Virginia (later Bishop), the following was added to the second item:

However, we recommend that the colored membership of the various Methodist bodies be formed into an independent organization holding fraternal relations with the reorganized and united Church.

Dr. Thomas arranged to call up the report for action by the General Conference the day Bishop Hoss was presiding. Bishop Hoss was largely the author of the "Suggestions." Upon motion of W. N. Ainsworth, the Chair (Bishop Hoss) was requested to address the Conference on this subject in hand. He called Bishop Denny to the chair and proceeded to deliver a very able address upon unification by reorganization. The vote on the report was unanimous and enthusiastic. That was the great day of the General Conference.

The Declaration was adopted, and it is as follows:

1. The Methodist Episcopal Church, South, considers the plan outlined in the suggestions that were adopted by the Joint Commission representing the Methodist Episcopal Church, the Methodist Protestant Church, and the Methodist Episcopal Church, South, and reported to the General Conferences of their respective Churches, as tentative, but nevertheless containing the basic principles of a genuine unification of the Methodist bodies in the United States, and especially of the Methodist Episcopal Church and the Methodist Episcopal Church, South, by the method of reorganization.

2. The Methodist Episcopal Church, South, regards the unification of the Methodist Episcopal Church, the Methodist Protestant Church, and the Methodist Episcopal Church, South, by the plan proposed by the Joint Commission on Federation, as feasible and desirable, and hereby declares itself in favor of

the unification of the Methodist Episcopal Church and the Methodist Episcopal Church, South, in accordance with this general plan of reorganization, and in favor of the unification of all or any Methodist bodies who accept this proposed plan after it has been accepted by the Methodist Episcopal Church. However, we recommend that the colored membership of the various Methodist bodies be formed into an independent organization holding fraternal relations with the reorganized and united Church.

3. The representatives of the Methodist Episcopal Church, South, in the Federal Council of Methodism are hereby instructed and empowered to act as Commissioners with like Commissioners of the Methodist Episcopal Church, or with Commissioners of the Methodist Episcopal Church, the Methodist Protestant Church, and other Methodist bodies in the United States, in elaborating and perfecting the tentative plan that has been proposed and in carrying forward such negotiations as have for their purpose, and may result in, the consummation of the proposed unification in accordance with the basic principles enunciated in the Suggestions which were adopted by the Joint Commission and reported to the General Conferences. Should the General Conference of the Methodist Episcopal Church in 1916 declare itself in favor of unification through the proposed plan of reorganization and should it appoint a Commission on Unification, separate from the Federal Council of Methodism, the representatives of the Methodist Episcopal Church, South, are hereby instructed and empowered to appoint a similar Commission that shall serve until the meeting of the next General Conference. The representatives of this Church in the Federal Council of Methodism, or such Commission on Unification as may be appointed, shall report to the next General Conference the full details of the plan of unification which may be agreed upon by the Federal Council of Methodism, or the Joint Commission on Unification, for its consideration and final determination. The representatives of this Church are hereby instructed to say to the Joint Commission on Unification that the name preferred for the reorganized and united Church is the Methodist Church in America.

II

The Oklahoma pronouncement was not the adoption of a

plan, but the declaration of an attitude. It recognized the outline as tentative and yet "containing the basic principles of a genuine unification of the Methodist bodies in the United States and especially of the Methodist Episcopal Church and the Methodist Episcopal Church, South, by the method of reorganization." The word "reorganization" was well underscored. The General Conference went so far as to say that this unification is "feasible and desirable." After seventy years of separation this declaration was epoch-forming and history-making. "Unification by reorganization" was on the calendar, and it stayed there twenty-five years as the unfinished business of American Methodism, and until it was absolutely finished by the historic Uniting Conference.

The General Conference of the Methodist Episcopal Church in May, 1916, had back the report of the Joint Commission which it seemed wise four years before not to act upon, and also this stirring and challenging Oklahoma Declaration of the Southern General Conference. Of course the challenge was accepted freely and in practically the same language as that of the Southern declaration. That action did not mean that this General Conference or the Southern General Conference approved even the tentative terms of the plan. The "Suggestions" were simply accepted as the basis of further negotiations with the hope that an acceptable structure of government could be worked out for an adequate plan of union. A Commission on Unification was appointed consisting of Bishop Earl Cranston, Bishop John W. Hamilton, Bishop W. F. McDowell, Bishop F. D. Leete, Bishop R. J. Cooke, the Rev. Edgar Blake, the Rev. James R. Day, the Rev. David G. Downey, the Rev. John F. Goucher, the Rev. Robert E. Jones, the Rev. A. J. Nast, the Rev. Frank Neff, the Rev. E. M. Randall, the Rev. Claudius B. Spencer, the Rev. J. W. Van Cleve, Mr. George Warren Brown of St. Louis, the Hon. Charles W. Fairbanks, Dr. A. W. Harris, Mr. C. W. Kinne, Mr. I. Garland Penn, Judge I. E. Robinson, Judge Henry Wade Rogers, Mr. William Rule, Judge Alexander

Simpson, and Mr. Rolla V. Watt. Dr. Day resigned, and Dr. J. J. Wallace was appointed in his place. Alternates elected December 28, 1916, were Bishop L. B. Wilson, Dr. Charles M. Stuart, Dr. James R. Joy, and Judge C. A. Pollock; and on July 4, 1919, Dr. Frank Mason North and Elmer L. Kidney, Esq. The alternates attended all the sessions and frequently were seated. Vice-President Fairbanks died June 4, 1918, and Dr. Joy was seated as a principal.

The General Conference of the Methodist Episcopal Church, South, appointed nine persons as members of the Federal Council of Methodism with instructions that in case the Northern General Conference of 1916 should appoint a Commission of five bishops, ten ministers, and ten laymen, the nine were to add two bishops, seven ministers, and seven laymen to their number and the twenty-five were to be the Commission on Unification. The nine appointed by the General Conference were Bishop A. W. Wilson, Bishop E. E. Hoss, Bishop Collins Denny, the Rev. Frank M. Thomas, the Rev. W. J. Young, the Rev. John M. Moore, Judge M. L. Walton, Dr. H. N. Snyder, and the Hon. Percy D. Maddin. These nine met at Tate Springs, Tennessee, August 9, 1916, and added the following: Bishop Edwin D. Mouzon, Bishop Warren A. Candler, the Rev. C. M. Bishop, the Rev. E. B. Chappell, the Rev. T. N. Ivey, the Rev. A. F. Watkins, the Rev. H. M. Du Bose, the Rev. W. N. Ainsworth, the Rev. A. J. Lamar, Judge J. L. Kelley, the Hon. T. D. Samford, Mr. John R. Pepper, Colonel E. C. Reeves, Dr. R. S. Hyer, Dr. J. H. Reynolds, and Dr. R. E. Blackwell. Alternates added were: the Rev. W. Asbury Christian, the Rev. E. U. Regester, the Rev. C. H. Briggs, Judge H. H. White, Judge E. W. Hines, and Captain G. T. Fitzhugh.

The Declaration of the Oklahoma General Conference of the Church South stirred Methodism in the entire country. It was not expected, but it was welcomed. The union sentiment now had something very definite to gather about. The Church papers gave considerable space to the discussion and interpretation of the action, but much caution was exercised in passing judgment upon the proposal. The "tentativeness" of the "Suggestions" was strongly emphasized by the leaders in the two principal Churches. Strong expressions favorable and unfavorable duly appeared.

The Christian Advocate of New York said plainly:

Too many Methodists who honestly think they are in favor of union have really never conceived of a united Methodist Church which shall be anything else but the Methodist Episcopal Church on a large scale. It is because the other proposed elements in the union plainly see this that they are looking about for a plan of union in which the rights of the minority shall be safeguarded.

Bishop Earl Cranston, who had recently published a very forceful little volume on *Breaking Down the Walls*, speaking in Boston said:

Here is the crucial question: Is the Methodist Episcopal Church great enough to give to other divided communions which, like our Methodism, hold the essentials of unity, the inspiration of a great example, or will she insist that as a condition of union the other Methodist bodies, so often invited to consider terms, must, if they come, pass under the domination of her numerical majority?

Not all the leaders of the Church North looked with friendliness and favor upon "unification by reorganization" which was set forth in the "Suggestions" and in the Oklahoma Declaration. Some of them condemned it in the popular mind by simply calling it the Southern Plan, or the Scarritt Plan, which meant to them setting up autonomous sections in the Church with the practical preservation of the Church South intact. Bishop Joseph Hartzell spoke of it as a "scheme of the Church South to accomplish its old desire."

Bishop R. J. Cooke, writing in *Zion's Herald,* said:

The South in this plan will not trust the North. It consolidates itself, but cuts up the rest.   No section is to trust the other to make laws, rules, and regulations for the whole.   Each shall make its own laws.   In this plan the Supreme General Conference at bottom is nothing more than a clearing house for the Boards.   What spontaneity of thought or feeling is there in such a document?   It is a union by disruption.   Instead of the Union of Methodism, we have the disruption of Methodism. It is an impossible ultimatum, and could never be a finality. The Methodist Episcopal Church is invited to commit suicide.   It is to carve itself, under the guise of reorganization, into segments, fragments, divisions, each segment to think itself a unit, in itself independent and yet dependent, with about as much unity in a collective whole as there is in a scrap heap.

This reaction of Bishop Cooke to the principles in the "Suggestions" which the General Conference of the Church South had declared were basic to a genuine unification was not shared by all the leaders of his Church, but by very many.   It can be seen now that he woefully misinterpreted the Commission's plan and greatly misconstructed its provisions.

The writers and speakers of the Church North who opposed the suggested plan almost always referred to it as the plan proposed by the Church South.   Although this was in a sense true, yet the Joint Commission that reported it out had only nine representatives from the Church South in its total membership of twenty-seven.   The General Conference of the Church South did not change the plan in any way except to express its preference of the two names proposed for the united Church, and suggested that the Negro membership become a part of a United Negro Methodist Church.

The editors and leaders of the Church South had very little to say about the tentative plan involved in the "Suggestions" and the Declaration.   Very little attention was given to the "Suggestions," South or North, when they were published in 1911.   In fact, they were not regarded as having any immediate importance, since they were only "Suggestions" and not a completed plan, and since also the Commission itself by resolution had asked that they be not acted upon as a plan. In the second place, the Southern General Conference approved the "Declaration" unanimously, and criticism and opposition would be more or less out of order. In the third place, it was generally held that the next move was up to the Church North, and it was generally felt that since its General Conference did not act upon the report of the Commission in 1912 it would probably not do so in 1916, but would offer some substitute. It was therefore a time for waiting and watching with a close study of the reactions in the North. The Committee on Church Relations of the Oklahoma General Conference was really responsible for bringing the matter to the front. Yet it should be said here that while all was quiet in the South, not all was well. There was a large portion of the Southern membership that did not favor union even upon the basis contained in the "Suggestions," and they found a way, public and private, to let that be known.

One of the most important efforts made to get the mind of the two Churches, North and South, was what was called "A Working Conference on the Union of American Methodism," which was held in Evanston, Illinois, February 15-17, 1916, under the auspices of the John Richard Lindgren Foundation for the Promotion of International Peace and Christian Unity.

This conference was described as a "working conference" to indicate that it was not the controlling purpose of the gathering to adopt resolutions, to carry on negotiations, or to appeal to public sentiment; but that it was its purpose to gather into a clear, impartial, and scholarly statement the facts and considerations relating to union in the hope of helping to a wise decision those bodies and persons whose duty it will be to act officially. President Charles M. Stuart of Garrett Biblical Institute prepared the original outline of the program. The selection of those who presented papers was based upon wide advice, and was made without regard to personal views upon reunion.

So wrote Dr. Abram W. Harris, the Chairman of the Committee of Direction.

Thirty-four persons presented papers, and they were published in a most interesting and valuable volume. Their significance may be seen through the subjects discussed. The first three are "The History of the Various Separations" by Professor John A. Faulkner, "The History of the Agitations for Union" by Professor W. W. Sweet, "Methodist Union in Great Britain and Canada" by Superintendent S. D. Chown of Canada. Then Bishop Earl Cranston and Bishop Collins Denny gave "A Review of the Existing Situation." Dr. James W. Lee and Hanford Crawford of St. Louis discussed the problems of "Sectional Characteristics," Dr. W. Asbury Christian and Dr. David G. Downey that of "Church Polity," Dean Wilbur F. Tillett and Dr. J. W. E. Bowen that of "Doctrine and Ritual," Dr. Fitzgerald S. Parker, J. A. Johnson, and Bishop John W. Hamilton that of "Church Discipline," while the place of the Negro in Methodism was discussed by Bishop Robert E. Jones, Dr. Henry N. Snyder, Bishop Wilbur P. Thirkield, and Dr. T. J. Coppin. "The Work in Foreign Fields" was presented by Bishop Eugene R. Hendrix and Dr. John F. Goucher, and in the "Home Fields" by Dr. Claudius B. Spencer, Dr. Thomas N. Ivey, and I. Garland Penn. "Property Holdings" was discussed by Judge M. L. Walton and "Connectional Enterprises" by Bishop Thomas Nicholson.

The last three subjects were: "The Comparative Value of Federation and Church Union," discussed by Dr. Charles M. Bishop, Bishop C. H. Phillips, and Bishop Francis J. McConnell; "A Suggested Working Plan for Methodist Union," by John M. Moore, Bishop Alexander Walters, and Dr. Edgar Blake; "The Dynamic of a United Methodism," by Bishop G. W. Clinton, Dr. Thomas H. Lewis, and Dr. Frank M. Thomas.

This Conference brought great seriousness into the thinking on union among the leaders of the Methodist Churches of the United States. Light came from these many angles upon the problems that had been very perplexing to many persons. The discussions uncovered no impossible barriers. While there were obstructing obstacles, yet they were ceasing to seem unsurmountable. To be sure, the long-existing divergences in social attitudes and ecclesiastical interpretation were not considered and discussed. They were problems which no convention could solve or dissolve. However, the Working Conference at Evanston made a more valuable contribution to union than has been generally recognized. The possibility of an acceptable union became more and more impressive. The will to produce a plan of union that would be satisfactory to all was greatly strengthened.

Union and the desirability of union depended almost entirely upon the Plan of Union. Could a satisfactory plan of union be produced? Along what lines must it be laid out? Did the "Suggestions" of the Commission contain the principles and germ ideas of a feasible and desirable union and plan of union? Back of all the discussions at the Evanston Conference were these questions.

Dr. Edgar Blake, later a bishop, made a very straightforward, positive, affirmative address on a Plan of Union in which he took strong position for Sectional Conferences, or for what was later called Regional Conferences, or Jurisdictional Conferences, with the power to elect bishops, to supervise and promote the institutions and interests within the region, and to make such laws for the administration of regional matters as did not conflict with the laws made by the General Conference. His address laid the basis of what was eventually developed.

This author spoke with Dr. Blake on "A Working Plan of Methodist Union." His address was an elaboration of an article on "A Plan of Union" which he studiously had prepared in the early weeks of 1911 and published in *The Christian Advocate* (Nashville) on March 3, 1911, or two months before the Commission on Federation met and formulated the historic "Suggestions." This article contained the basic principles to which he adhered throughout all the negotiations of the Joint Commission on Unification. However, he suggested in the article that the Negro membership go into a united Negro

Methodist Church, or, in case that was not satisfactory, into a Synodical Conference like unto the five white Synodical Conferences. The following quotations from the article give his proposed basis of union:

Let there be one General Conference and five Synodical Conferences. The three Synodical Conferences east of the Mississippi River could be made to embrace more than one million members each; the two west of the River would have more than one million members between them, with fair prospects of large increase within the decade. The General Conference, made up of representatives of all the Annual Conferences, should have no electoral powers, but be a lawmaking body with exclusive rights to deal with doctrine and ritual.

The Synodical Conferences should have the power to make such laws as would not conflict with those made by the General Conference. Certain sections of the Church might need such legislation as would not be satisfactory or desirable to the entire Church. The Synodical Conference should have full electoral powers. It should elect its quota of bishops, which quota may be determined upon a basis of Church membership. It should elect the editor of the Synodical organ, or any officers which the General Conference should decide that it should have. It should elect its quota of the various General Boards. The General Boards thus constituted by the Synodical Conferences should elect their general secretary or administrative officer. The Book Committee should elect the Publishing Agent. Wherever a General Board required a synodical representative in its officiary, he should be elected by the Synodical Conference or its representatives in the General Board. Synodical Boards should probably also be created to carry out the policies of the General Boards, and carry on such work as could not be well done by the General Boards. The rules and regulations of such Boards would be determined by the General Conference. They would have their own administrative officers, who might be elected by the Synodical Conferences or the Boards.

Chapter Seven

CROSSING THE DIVIDE

THE CHURCHES ARE INCLINED TO THINK OF THE JOINT COMMISSION of 1934 to 1939 as having produced the Plan of Union that brought them union. No honor should be taken from these skillful negotiators for what they did, but they are not the originators of the Plan. That distinction belongs more largely to the Commissions of 1916 to 1920. The basic and comprehensive elements of the Plan came by the hard toil, the inventive genius, the conscientious faithfulness, and the marked ability of the early Commissions. The Church should ever hold them in high appreciation and unfading remembrance. Only a few of them lived to see the full fruit of their labors, but they all should be given a crown of honor.

To be sure, the Plan was a growth rather than a production, the outcome of continuing developments through many years. The jurisdictional or regional idea, which is central in the plan, had long existed in some form, as has been heretofore shown, however inadequately defined and unsatisfactorily presented. Then the discussion in the Churches and the votes in the Churches in 1924 to 1926 were of great value in bringing the people to realize that Methodist Church union was important, that it was inevitable, and that the jurisdictional system would give protection, promotion, and efficiency in administration, cultivation, and development to all sections and interests of a great nation-wide Church with world-wide relations and responsibilities. The membership and ministry of the three negotiating Churches were ready for a just, practical, and adequate plan of union.

The Commission of 1934 brought many necessary improvements to the Plan of 1920. The Plan of 1920 would probably not have been adopted even in the later period just as it was. It is also true that the Plan of 1935 would not have been adopted in 1920, because the temper and mind of the Churches were not ready. Fifteen years had brought remarkable alterations in the attitude and spirit of the people on both sides. Ninety-five years are a very long time to continue a separation occasioned by slavery that had been out of existence for seventy-five years. Thinking superficially, that is true; but the separation was far deeper than that, and it could not be closed by salutations, felicitations, and sentimental resolutions. That separation broke down a great structure, social, political, religious, and ecclesiastical; and the structure could not be returned, restored; it had to be rebuilt. Unification could come only by reorganization.

The General Conference of the Methodist Episcopal Church in 1916 at Saratoga Springs, when it declared itself "in favor of the unification of the Methodist Episcopal Church, South, and the Methodist Episcopal Church in accordance with this general plan of reorganization," altered completely the method of union which its great leaders had proposed and supported for fifty years. The idea of union by reunion, or merger, was forever laid aside. Unification by reorganization as proposed in the "Suggestions" of the Joint Commission on Federation was accepted. This was a remarkably generous and revolutionary action by this great Church, and it made possible the profound negotiations that led finally to union.

The Joint Commission on Unification, a great body, met December 29, 1916, to January 2, 1917, in Baltimore, the cradle of American Methodism. One session was held in the First Methodist Episcopal Church, the lineal descendant of Lovely Lane Meeting House, in which the Church was organized in 1784. A pilgrimage was made on Sunday afternoon to Mount Olivet Cemetery for a short memorial service at the graves of Francis Asbury, Robert Strawbridge, Jesse Lee, John Emory,

Beverly Waugh, and Enoch George. That night, watch-night services were held in Trinity Methodist Episcopal Church, South. All this contributed to the atmosphere of union.

The Commission was composed of men who had leadership in the two Churches. The two official chairmen were Bishop Earl Cranston and Bishop Warren A. Candler, one the fervent apostle of union and the other a constant and conscientious opponent of union. Bishop Cranston was seventy-six years old and retired. While he was not able to make any large contributions to the creation of a plan of union, yet his constant and devout appeals for union had large influence in the Churches and with the Commissioners. His small book entitled *Breaking Down the Walls* had much value with many people. He was indeed an apostle of union. Bishop Candler participated very little in the discussions of the Commission. He took the position that since he was opposed to union, he should have very little to do with creating a plan, and no one could criticize that attitude. He won the affectionate regard and high esteem of all members of the Commission by his affable and generous spirit.

Bishop William Fraser McDowell was very active and very valuable in all the work of the Commission. He was not creative in devising provisions of the plan, but he was highly effective in summarizing expressed opinions and out of them getting a unified result, and in proposing actions to be taken. His poise, mental alertness, generous spirit, and conspicuous ability gave him strong and accepted leadership in the Commission. Bishop John W. Hamilton, retired, had spent much of his life and service for the Negro membership of his Church. While he offered suggestions from time to time on the provisions proposed, yet his chief interest was in giving the Negro membership a satisfactory status in the new Church. He was always considerate of his Southern brethren. Bishop R. J. Cooke was born in Ireland. He had spent much time in service in East Tennessee. He had been Book Editor of his Church. He always spoke with effectiveness. Bishop Frederick D. Leete was one of the most valuable members of the Commission. He spoke always with directness and understanding, and his suggestions, motions, and decisions contributed greatly to working out the plan of union. By his long ministry in prominent pastorates in the North and his discerning Episcopal service in the Atlanta area, he had acquainted himself not only with the mind of his own Church but with the necessary position and requirements of the Church South. He set himself sympathetically and resolutely to that kind of "reorganization" which would bring out the most acceptable plan of union, and he never swerved one particle from it. He served on every Commission that dealt with union, and he served most effectively. He met the issues with deep insight, clear vision, broad churchmanship, calm courage and genuine statesmanship. Such men make and keep union.

The most creative, inventive, resourceful, and efficient member of the Commission in devising, formulating, perfecting, and adopting the provisions of the Plan of Union was the Rev. Edgar Blake, D.D., Secretary of the Sunday School Board of his Church, and later a Bishop. He early saw that union could not be achieved except by the distribution of ecclesiastical power through the Jurisdictional Conference and Judicial Council. The two Churches were wide apart in their conceptions of what these two bodies should be and what powers they should possess. Other adjustments could be made only after the Jurisdictional Conference and the Judicial Council had been brought out and agreed upon. These both cut into certain prevailing conceptions in his own Church of a supreme General Conference, its powers and prerogatives. In this area the inventive genius and large understanding of Dr. Blake made him an indispensable constructive leader.

Dr. David G. Downey, the Book Editor, was a very forceful, keen-minded, able man. He leaned strongly to the conceptions of union, common to his Church, that had centered in a supreme

General Conference. He came slowly to the Jurisdictional idea. Dr. John F. Goucher was well known in the South and highly esteemed by all its leaders. He was brotherly, conciliatory, and wise. He carried weight in his opinions. Dr. John J. Wallace, Editor of the *Pittsburgh Advocate,* who took the place of Chancellor James R. Day, spoke seldom, but always with insight and illustration. Dr. Robert E. Jones, Editor of the *Southwestern Advocate,* confined himself largely to provisions relating to the Negro membership. He was always considerate, reasonable, encouraging, and forceful. His fine spirit gave great aid in working out the status of the Negro membership. Dr. A. J. Nast represented the German membership of his Church, and he spoke only when it was involved. Dr. Claudius B. Spencer, Editor of the *Central Advocate,* had written a small book in which he had supported the "reunion" idea of union and opposed the Jurisdictional idea. He was affable in spirit. Dr. J. W. Van Cleve of Illinois, Dr. E. M. Randall of Washington State, and Dr. Frank Neff were exceedingly serviceable members of the Commission.

Among the Northern laymen were the Hon. Charles W. Fairbanks, former Vice-President of the United States; Judge Henry Wade Rogers of the Federal Circuit Court in New York, a highly influential member of the Commission; the Hon. Alexander Simpson, lawyer of Philadelphia, later Chief Justice of his State, a keen and capable Commissioner; Judge Ira E. Robinson, a Federal District Judge in West Virginia; George Warren Brown, head of the Brown Shoe Company in St. Louis; William Rule, publisher of the *Knoxville Journal;* Charles W. Kinne, a businessman of Jacksonville, Florida; Rolla V. Watt of San Francisco; Irvine G. Penn, Secretary of the Freedmen's Bureau; and Dr. A. W. Harris, Secretary of Education, who was one of the secretaries and one of the most influential members of the Commission. Dr. James R. Joy, the Editor of the *New York Advocate,* early took the place of Mr. Fairbanks and was the only layman of his Church who served on every Commission that dealt with the Plan of Union, and his service was of the first order. The other persons of that Church who served in all the negotiations were Bishops Mc-Dowell, Leete, and Jones. A stronger, finer group of laymen in any Church could scarcely be found.

Six members of the Southern Commission served on all the Commissions that dealt with union: Bishop Edwin D. Mouzon, Dr. H. N. Snyder, Dr. J. H. Reynolds, the Hon. P. D. Maddin, Judge H. H. White, and this author. Of the ten ministers of the Commission, six were connectional officers: Dr. A. J. Lamar, Publishing Agent; T. N. Ivey, Editor of *The Nashville Christian Advocate;* H. M. Du Bose, Editor of *The Methodist Review;* E. B. Chappell, Editor of Sunday School Literature; and John M. Moore, Secretary of Home Missions. Two were college presidents: President A. F. Watkins of Millsaps College, and President C. M. Bishop of Southwestern University. Two were pastors: Dr. W. N. Ainsworth of Georgia and Dr. F. M. Thomas of Kentucky. Dr. W. J. Young was Professor in Emory School of Theology in 1918. John M. Moore, H. M. Du Bose, and W. N. Ainsworth were elected bishops in 1918.

Of the ten laymen, one was a banker, Mr. John R. Pepper, of Memphis. Four were college presidents: President H. N. Snyder of Wofford, President R. S. Hyer of Southern Methodist University, President R. E. Blackwell of Randolph-Macon, and President J. H. Reynolds of Hendrix. Five were lawyers: P. D. Maddin, H. H. White, Colonel E. C. Reeves, M. R. Walton, and T. D. Samford.

These ministers and laymen were strong, representative men of the Church South and also of the mind and attitude of the people of the South. They were not of one mind regarding union, but whatever their views they made valuable contribution to the work of unification. Ministers and laymen, they were all capable, forceful, vigorous participants in all the negotiations.

Bishop A. W. Wilson, who was not favorable to union, died before the Commission met. Bishop Wilson was a man of great ability. His place was taken by Bishop W. B. Murrah, who seldom spoke and seldom voted in favor of union measures. Bishop E. E. Hoss was in feeble health and did not attend all the meetings. He died in 1919. He was a brilliant debater, a strong partisan of the South, and a vigorous advocate of a jurisdictional system of administration and of a constitutional check on the General Conference. Bishop Mouzon was an exceedingly forceful and effective member of the Commission. He labored untiringly to produce an acceptable plan of union. No man was his superior in advocating union. He died before his Church had acted on the final proposed plan, but his name stands high among those who brought it about. Bishop Collins Denny was never able to support any plan of union, and he stood in opposition to any measures that looked to union. He is a very able man, a man of very strong convictions, of superior intellect, and of deep devotion to the principles and feelings of the leaders that made the Church South.

These ministers and laymen of both Churches were all very strong men as would be indicated by the high places that they occupied in their Church and in their communities. They did not agree in their interpretations of the history of the past, nor in their conceptions of what should take place in the future. When the two Commissions faced each other on December 28, 1916, they knew that Greek had met Greek. It was to be a battle of vigorous intellects and mighty wills. They soon realized that they had on hand no tea party nor ecclesiastical rally. They looked at each other across a deep gulch cut sharp by the storms and torrents of many years. They were one people in faith, spirit, purpose, and religious life; but something very hard to understand had grown up between them. They were now in reality two peoples, and they could hope to come together, not on the basis of the distant past, but only upon a satisfactory structure for the approaching future.

With this early realization they conscientiously, diligently, sympathetically, and strenuously set about the task of devising and creating an adequate governmental structure. They had, before them scant sketches of a possible plan which the General Conferences had instructed them to observe. Five days were spent in speech-making, reciting history, defining attitudes, stating positions, and telling each other their doings—putting it mildly—and all in fine spirit and in entertaining statement.

Finally it was agreed to appoint four major committees to which the subjects could be assigned for study and for formulation and recommendations: (1) Committee on General and Jurisdictional Conferences; (2) Committee on Judicial Council (that name had been agreed upon by the motion of this author) ; (3) Committee on Status of the Negro Membership; (4) Committee on General Reference.

The appointees to these committees were: (1) Conferences, Bishop McDowell, Bishop Hoss, Dr. Blake, Dr. Chappell, Dr. Goucher, Dr. Du Bose, Mr. Simpson, Mr. Samford, Dr. Harris, and Dr. Hyer; (2) Judicial Council, Bishop Murrah, Bishop Cooke, Dr. Lamar, Dr. Downey, Dr. Thomas, Dr. Spencer, Mr. Walton, Mr. Fairbanks, Colonel Reeves, and Judge Robinson; (3) Status of Negro Membership, Bishop Cranston, Bishop Denny, Dr. Jones, Dr. Van Cleve, Dr. Wallace, Mr. Penn, Judge Rogers, Mr. Brown, Dr. Moore, Dr. Ainsworth, Dr. Young, Mr. White, Mr. Maddin, and Dr. Snyder; (4) Reference, Bishop Candler, Bishop Mouzon, Dr. Ivey, Dr. Bishop, Dr. Watkins, Mr. Pepper, Dr. Blackwell, Dr. Reynolds, Bishop Hamilton, Bishop Leete, Dr. Nast, Dr. Neff, Dr. Randall, Mr. Kinne, and Mr. Watt.

Some Commissioners expressed surprise and regret that after five days no conclusions had been reached and no agreements adopted in this first meeting that could be reported to the Churches. They did not realize the enormity of the task, the streams that had to be bridged, the mountainous obstacles to be tunneled, the deep cuts to be filled. Engineers of broad knowledge and deep insight, of accumulated skill and far vision, would be required to prepare the long rough road for the arrival of union. It took nearly twenty years to achieve that which was expected in a few days. The Joint Commission adjourned to meet June 27, 1917, in Traverse City, Michigan.

TRAVERSE CITY

The Traverse City meeting was one of the most important that was ever held. Its five days were taken up almost entirely with the report of the Committee on Conferences. Reports from the other Committees were presented, but consideration was postponed until the Savannah meeting, as the time was consumed upon the first report.

The two General Conferences based their declarations of 1914 and 1916 on the "Suggestions" of 1911 of the Joint Commission on Federation. One of these suggestions was that the General Conference should consist of two houses. That was voted out at once by the Joint Commission. The central suggestion was "that the governing power of the reorganized Church shall be vested in one General Conference and three or four Quadrennial Conferences," and that the Negro membership be constituted as one of the Quadrennial or Jurisdictional Conferences. Another suggestion was "that the Quadrennial Conferences shall name the bishops from their several jurisdictions, the same to be confirmed by the first house of the General Conference." Another was that "neither the General Conference nor any of the Quadrennial Conferences be invested with final authority to interpret the constitutionality of its own actions." The name suggested for the reorganized Church was the Methodist Episcopal Church in America or the Methodist Church in America. The two General Conferences had declared, that these "Suggestions" contain the basic principles of a genuine unification by the method of reorganization.

The Joint Commission now faced the fundamental and essential issues in the negotiations: (*a*) What powers shall the General Conference have? (*b*) What powers shall be assured to the Jurisdictional Conference? (*c*) How guarantee the itinerant general superintendency which may be jurisdictionally elected? The discussions for five days centered and revolved about those three questions.

In the committee of the whole the Northern Commission inquired if the Southern Commission would consent to consider the Episcopal Area as the Unit of Regional or Quadrennial Conference representation, with the understanding that bishops should be nominated by such regional areas. The Southern Commission responded:

We feel bound in this respect by our last General Conference, which approved the tentative plan, containing the following article: "We suggest that the governing power in the reorganized Church shall be vested in one General Conference and three or four Quadrennial Conferences, both General and Quadrennial Conferences to exercise their powers under constitutional provisions and restrictions, the General Conference to have full legislation over all matters distinctively connectional, and the Quadrennial Conferences to have full power over distinctively local affairs." We, therefore, are compelled to regard the Regional Conference as a basic principle of a genuine unification of our Methodist Bodies, and we cannot, in the light of the action of our General Conference, depart from this basic principle.

No Commission of the Church South, and no member of any Commission of that Church, ever departed from that basic principle. No union would come and no union would successfully remain without the complete and constant recognition of that basic principle. The powers of the General Conference should be limited and designated beyond which it may not speak with authority. Its duties are legislative within designated limits. The duties of the Jurisdictional Conference are administrative and promotional, and it must have legislative powers adequate to the discharge of its two chief responsibilities. With administration its duty, elections of administrative officers became its right, either separately or collectively through representatives. This provision would ensure protection of minorities and sections which in a supreme General Conference could be ignored or overridden, and furthermore it would give the electorate the opportunity for knowing the persons who were worthy to be considered for the office. Such were the views and arguments of the Southern Commissioners.

Some Northern Commissioners argued, on the other hand, that strong Jurisdictional Conferences, as suggested, would make separate Churches, that bishops elected by Jurisdictional Conferences would be diocesan, that the itinerant general superintendency would be destroyed, that connectional officers would have to be elected by the General Conference to have creditable church-wide standing. They wanted the Jurisdictional Conference to have very little power, and to be established only as an alleviating expedient. Others, however, became more and more inclined to the principles set forth and maintained by the Southern Commissioners.

The Committee on Conferences presented a fine full report defining the composition, rights, and powers of all Conferences, especially the General and Jurisdictional Conferences. Under the guidance of Dr. Blake, the secretary of the Committee, the report was considered carefully and critically, and tentatively agreed to. The discussions and addresses from all participants were incisive, forceful, able. It was not thought by anyone that the final conclusions had been reached, but a broad, substantial basis had been laid. With this the Joint Commission adjourned July 3, 1917, to meet January 23, 1918, in Savannah, Georgia. That progress had been made was quite evident.

SAVANNAH

The Savannah meeting lasted from January 23 to February 6, two weeks, the longest ever held. Dr. James R. Joy was seated permanently in the place of Mr. Fairbanks. He served on all Commissions thereafter. Bishop James Atkins was seated in the place of Bishop Hoss, who was ill. Dr. Charles M. Stuart, President of Garrett Biblical Institute, served as an alternate. The subjects considered during the meeting were the Judicial Council and the status of the Negro membership in the reorganized Church.

Two days were given to consideration of the report on the Judicial Council, and only minor changes were made.

The Judicial Council shall have full power to review, on appeal on constitutional grounds, the acts of the General and Quadrennial Conferences, the records and documents transmitted to it from Judicial Conferences, to hear and determine questions of law and all other appeals coming to it in course of lawful procedure from Annual Conferences, from Judicial and Quadrennial Conferences (hereafter to be provided), and from the General Conference. In all cases the decision of the Judicial Council shall be final; provided that if, on a constitutional question, there shall be a majority vote of the members of the General Conference, present and voting, disapproving a decision of the Judicial Council, the question involved shall be sent to the Annual Conferences for full decision as provided in the Constitution.

The membership of the Council was to be a minister and a layman from each Regional Conference, elected by the General Conference. The members would be ineligible for membership in the General or Quadrennial Conferences. The term of service was set at four years, but later changed to eight, with re-election possible. In this tentative draft, which was tentatively adopted, are some principles that became permanent.

It was widely feared and prophesied that union would fail because of irreconcilable views of the necessary status of the Negro membership in the reorganized Church. The Southern General Conference in 1914 declared: "However, we recommend that the colored membership of the various Methodist bodies be formed into an independent organization holding fraternal relations with the reorganized and united Church." The Northern General Conference in 1916 recommended, "That, conforming to the Suggestion of the Joint Commission, the colored membership of the reorganized Church be constituted into one or more Quadrennial or Jurisdictional Conferences." The two recommendations were radically different, and reconciliation seemed beyond the range of possibility.

The South and the Southern Commissioners were all but unanimous in the opinion that a united Negro Methodist Church in the United States, embracing the Negro constituency in the Methodist Episcopal Church, the Colored Methodist Episcopal Church, and the two African Methodist Episcopal Churches, should be the goal in the union movement. To that end they held that the Negro membership of 315,000 in the Methodist Episcopal Church could best be served, and could best serve the cause of union, through an independent organization of their own. The Northern Commissioners held that their Negro constituents could not be set up into an independent organization except by their own will and action and that they were unwilling to inaugurate such a movement. Their contacts had been almost entirely with the first ranks of the Negro race. They saw the situation from the standpoint of a mission board or an educational institution. There had been no Negroes in the Church South—except an occasional one—since 1870. Separation of the races in the South had become a well-established custom. The Southern people were fully convinced that this state of things was best for both races, and best for Southern civilization, and that it should continue. Any movement or trend that might change this condition was disturbing and was regarded with suspicion and opposition. This philosophy of race relations was deep-seated and stronger even than any church affiliations. The Southern Commissioners knew this, and wisdom dictated that their commitments should accord with their understanding.

The Committee on the Status of the Negro Membership brought to the Traverse City meeting a majority and a minority report, by a vote of seven to five, with one member, this author, not voting, as neither was acceptable to him. The majority recommended Associate General Conferences: one, "an African Associate General Conference, which would embrace within its jurisdictions all Annual Conferences, Mission Conferences, and Missions composed of persons of African descent in the United States and upon the continent of Africa," and others for Europe, Eastern Asia, Southern Asia, and Latin America. The minority asked that the recommendations of the majority be not adopted, "and that a separate organization should be set up for our colored brethren in which they would legislate for themselves and interpret their own legislation." These reports were not taken up by the Commission.

Following the Traverse City meeting, the Committee on the Negro appointed a subcommittee of two from each Commission to reformulate the report. This subcommittee reported at Savannah:

Your Committee have found it impossible to present their conclusions as to what should be the status of the Negro membership in the reorganized and unified Church without stating the same in a form which relates this subject to questions already reported upon or to be reported upon by co-ordinate committees and tentatively adopted by the Joint Commission. We present as our preferential report the following, which places the Negro membership in an Associate Regional Jurisdiction of the kind and powers herein indicated.

Then they reported:

We present as an alternative report the following, which places the Negro membership in an Associate General Conference which shall comprise within its jurisdiction the Negro membership of the Church in the United States and Africa, and which shall have complete legislative, judicial, and executive powers in the ecclesiastical government of said Negro membership in harmony with and subject to the Constitution of the unified Church. Said Associate General Conference shall have the power to elect the Bishops, constitute the boards, and elect their general administrative officers, for the Negro Conferences and membership and create its own Judicial Council.

The Joint Commission at Savannah faced this preferential and this alternative recommendation. Shall the Negro membership be given an Associate Regional Conference, such as would be given the Church in foreign lands, or shall it be given an Associate General Conference of its own with some representation in the General Conference and with constitutional relation to the unified Church? Or shall the Negro membership be given a full Regional Conference, as given to the white membership in the United States?

For eight days these questions were discussed. Thirty-six of the fifty Commissioners, equally divided, made major addresses lasting from fifteen to thirty minutes each, and they were all excellent. Nevertheless, a finer spirit never prevailed in a deliberative body. The line of cleavage was very clear. The Southern Commissioners strongly supported the Associate General Conference, while the Northern Commissioners supported the Associate Regional Conference, or a full Regional Conference. The report contained the provision, "Each Associate Regional Jurisdiction shall be entitled to be represented in the General Conference by five ministerial and five lay delegates, who shall be elected by the Associate Regional Conference by ballot." The Southern Commissioners did not approve this provision. Some of the Northern Commissioners did not approve this provision. Some of the Northern Commissioners held that this did not give the Negro membership proper representation in the General Conference.

After five days Judge Henry Wade Rogers presented for the subcommittee the following proposal: "When any [sub-Regional, Central, or Associate] Conference attains a membership of 600,000, its right to representation in the General Conference shall terminate, except as hereinafter provided, and it shall establish, unless by constitutional process it is otherwise ordered, an Associate General Conference which shall have complete legislative, judicial, and executive powers. . . . ." There was much discussion of the words "it shall establish," it being suggested that they be "it may establish."

A special Joint Committee of Eight was appointed to har-
monize as far as possible the several reports and the suggestions
on the status of the Negro membership and report back as early
as possible. The Committee was constituted as follows: John
M. Moore, Edgar Blake, H. M. Du Bose, J. J. Wallace, H. N.
Snyder, Alexander Simpson, Jr., R. S. Hyer, and George Warren
Brown.

The next day the Committee of Eight reported, providing for
five Associate Regional Conferences, one being the Afro-Ameri-
can, and each to be entitled to five ministerial and five lay
representatives in the General Conference, with the right to
speak, but not to vote. It provided further that

Any Associate Regional Conference by a majority of its members present and voting, with the concurrence of a majority of
the members of the several Annual Conferences, Mission Conferences, and Missions of its Jurisdiction, present and voting, and
with the approval of the General Conference, may become an
Associate General Conference, and when it has 600,000 Church
members in full connection shall become an Associate General
Conference with the privileges and powers herein provided.

This report was discussed for two days. The Northern Commission then reported its action as follows:

Resolved, That this Commission advise the Commissioners of
the Methodist Episcopal Church, South, that if the Southern
Commissioners, without committing themselves to all its provisions, will accept, in principle, the report of the Committee
of Eight, this Commission will likewise accept it; and that this
Commission recommends that when the Report shall have been
accepted by both Commissions, any member of the Joint Commission shall be at liberty to propose, by motion, in session of
the Joint Commission, any change he may desire.

The Southern Commission adopted the following resolution:

Resolved, That we approve the report of the Committee of
Eight as a basis for determining the Status of the Negro within
the reorganized Church.

The Southern Commission proposed this amendment:

Provided, That if the Colored Methodist Episcopal Church decide to become a part of the proposed organization, the colored members of the reorganized Church shall have and are hereby granted the privilege of organization into an Associate General Conference in accordance with the plan herein provided. In the event that the Colored Methodist Episcopal Church should not accept the invitation to join in the organization of an Associate General Conference, as provided above, the Regional Conferences within the territory predominantly Southern Methodist territory shall be allowed to direct their contributions for the colored work to the benefit of the Colored Methodist Episcopal Church.

The discussion of the report of the Committee of Eight continued for three days. Bishop McDowell proposed that "Associate Regional Conference" be changed to "Central Conference"; that there be five, for (1) colored people, (2) Latin America, (3) Europe, (4) Eastern Asia, (5) Southern Asia; that the colored have twelve representatives in the General Conference and the other four have eight each; that there be two additional representatives for each additional 100,000 members up to 600,000; that at 600,000 the Central Conference may choose to become an Associate General Conference.

At the end of fourteen days the Commission adjourned to meet in St. Louis.

St. Louis

The Joint Commission met in St. Louis on April 10, 1918. Bishop Candler and Bishop Atkins could not attend. Bishop Hoss was present for his last time, feeble in body but brilliant in mind. For twenty-five years he had served in the Commissions that sought to find ways to closer relations between the two Churches. He wanted union, but he had very definite convictions as to how it should come. He had seen the two Churches travel a long way toward each other.

Four days were given to the St. Louis meeting, and they were strenuously devoted to reviewing, revising, and adopting tentatively the reports of the Committees on Conferences, and on the Judicial Council, and of the Committee of Eight on the Status of the Negro Membership. The chief item of discussion in the report on Conferences related to the number of white Regional or Jurisdictional Conferences the united Church should have. The Committee, after much consideration, recommended six. Dr. Goucher suggested eight, Dr. Penn three, Dr. Spencer nine, and Bishop McDowell thought in higher numbers. Dr. Penn advocated dividing the territory of the United States into three sections, by lines running North and South. He received no support. The higher numbers were opposed by those who desired to support the deeper significance and broader power of the Jurisdictional Conference, which had not been fully recognized by all as an essential administrative and promotional unit in the reorganized Church. Dr. Goucher, however, said:

The aim and object of the Regional Conference, as I understand it, is to secure local representation. I do not believe in a union that is absolutely cast-iron and copper-riveted. In my judgment the best possible system of union is the federation which is represented by the United States Government. I deem it that we are wise in having the General Conference as a centralized power to legislate for all connectional interests, but to give the largest possible autonomy for local self-government in these Regional Conferences.

Bishop Hoss said:

I am opposed to making six or eight Regional Conferences, and then giving the General Conference at its own pleasure power to wipe them out. I am very much in favor of the Quadrennial Conferences as they were proposed in the original meetings of the Commission [on Federation], but they were very different things from the Regional Conferences proposed now.

That was true and had it not been true union would have halted. His view was influential with a very large group. The vote finally stood 31 to 16 in favor of six Regional Conferences. The other items in the report, with some alterations, were tentatively adopted. In the consideration of the restrictive rules it was emphatically expressed that a strong episcopacy should be maintained and that the Regional Conference system should not be allowed to reduce the itinerant general superintendency.

The report on the Judicial Council was tentatively adopted with few alterations. The report of the Committee of Eight on the Status of the Negro, with the amendment by Bishop McDowell, was considered for nearly two days. Dr. Penn offered an amendment that would increase the Negro representation in the General Conference from ten to fifty. The discussion showed clearly that an agreement was not possible.

It was brought out that the Northern Commission did not give a majority in favor of six Regional Conferences. In view of these facts, and the fact that the General Conference of the Methodist Episcopal Church, South, would meet in three weeks, the Joint Commission deemed it desirable to adjourn, but voted to meet again at the call of the two Chairmen. A Committee composed of Messrs. Thomas, Maddin, Chappell, Moore, McDowell, Goucher, Downey, and Harris was appointed to prepare for the General Conferences a report of what had been tentatively agreed upon by the Commission.

The Joint Commission at the end of four great meetings covering twenty-eight days with three sessions a day, and many other days in committee meetings, had not created a satisfactory and acceptable plan of union, but they had found the road to it. Such diligence and devotion, such conscientious effort and keen capability, have never been excelled in Church or State by men appointed to any task. Again and again they seemed face to face with the impassable and impossible. But they refused to accept defeat. Neither side would retire from its positions, but both sides kept the main goal above their own claims. They would toil on, looking for some new and unseen turn in the road. They usually reached it, and then in renewed courage they went on to the next lap. Explorers they were, of undaunted courage, of triumphant faith, of untiring effort, and of royal Christian spirit. At the end of the four meetings they looked back and found that they had made a very great journey, and all toward the destination of their high desires. They unanimously asked that the Joint Commission be continued.

Chapter Eight

GOING ON THROUGH

THE GENERAL CONFERENCE OF THE METHODIST EPISCOPAL CHURCH, South, met May 2-18, 1918, in Atlanta, Georgia. Bishop Candler, the Chairman, and Dr. Frank M. Thomas, the Secretary, delivered the report of the Commission on Unification, and it was received most cordially. They said:

The record shows that your Commissioners went as far as it seemed possible for them to go under the instructions of the General Conference by which the Commission was created. They were ever mindful of your specific pronouncements and the general instructions and the spirit thereof. They agreed to accept and to recommend to the General Conference, with minor modifications that should not affect the general principles included in them, the finally amended report on Conferences and the finally amended report on the Judicial Council, and also the report on the Status of the Negro in the United Church presented unanimously by a Committee of Eight members—four from each Commission. Your Commissioners kept in mind the recommendations of the last General Conference, "That the Colored membership of the various Methodist bodies be formed into an independent organization, holding fraternal relations with the reorganized and united Church." They did not construe this recommendation as an ultimatum, nor did they consider that by "independent organization" was necessarily meant an independent church. The proceedings will show that your Commissioners for the most part did advocate an independent church, but they, in accordance with their interpretation of the recommendation of the General Conference, were willing to accept for the Negroes an Associate General Conference under the general constitution of the Church, or for a time an Associate Regional Conference under the Common General Conference, by which

145

the Negro membership would be able to govern in large measure their own affairs.

Your Commissioners deeply regret that our negotiations with our brethren were not more fruitful in immediate results. At the same time we are sure that our labors were not in vain.

The General Conference expressed its high appreciation of the faithful and earnest efforts of the Commission, reaffirmed the action of the General Conference of 1914, recommended close co-operation of the two Churches in their various activities, endorsed the publication of the proceedings of the Joint Commission, and voted to continue the Commission. The personnel of the Commission was only slightly changed. Bishop John M. Moore and Bishop James Cannon, Jr., took the places of Bishop Hoss and Bishop Murrah. Dr. Paul H. Linn, Dr. Charles C. Selecman, and Dr. James E. Dickey took the places of John M. Moore, H. M. Du Bose, and W. N. Ainsworth, who had been elected to the episcopacy. Judge J. G. McGowan took the place of Colonel E. C. Reeves. Alternates appointed were Bishop H. M. Du Bose, Bishop W. N. Ainsworth, Dr. W. D. Bradfield, Dr. I. C. Jenkins, Dr. L. E. Todd, Dr. D. H. Kern, Judge E. W. Hines, Judge G. T. Fitzhugh, Judge C. M. Hay, and President W. P. Few. Bishop Mouzon was made chairman of the Commission. Bishop Cannon, Dr. Linn, and Dr. Selecman were very active and very valuable members of the Commission. Dr. Dickey and Judge McGowan were not favorable to union and the plan that was being produced.

The Joint Commission met in Cleveland, Ohio, July 7-10, 1919. The status of the Negro membership in the reorganized Church occupied the entire session. The Northern members of a Committee of Ten on Conferences proposed "that the colored membership of the Church shall be constituted and recognized as a Quadrennial or Regional Conference, with proportionate representation in the General Conference."

The Southern members proposed that there be Regional Conferences for the colored people, Latin America, Europe, Eastern Asia, and Southern Asia, and that these

shall have representation in the General Conference in proportion to their membership in full standing; provided that each of such Regional Conferences shall be entitled to at least five clerical and five lay delegates; provided, further, that the number of delegates from any one of these shall not exceed five per cent of the entire membership of the General Conference. . . . . Whenever the membership in full standing of any of these Regional Conferences shall exceed four hundred thousand, upon request of said Conference the General Conference shall organize the membership of said Conference into an Associate General Conference with the powers proposed for such Associate General Conference in the report of the Committee on Conferences at the Savannah meeting of the Joint Commission.

The discussion of three days brought no approach to agreement, but it revealed fundamental divergence as to what the status of the Negro membership should be. Dr. Van Cleve expressed the Northern position: "By a Colored Regional Conference we mean precisely the same thing as we do with reference to a White Regional Conference." The Southern Commissioners did not look with favor upon such a classification. They believed that the strength of the Church must and would be measured always by the strength and authority of its white membership in the United States. They believed that the spread of control would weaken the force and effectiveness of the denomination in itself and in its ministrations. This philosophy was basal in their thinking in the social, political, and ecclesiastical life and policy of the South, and they could not ignore it or lay it lightly aside.

The Southern Commission proposed a Joint Committee of Reference to take under consideration the whole matter of unification of American Methodism and report to the Joint Commission at such time as might be agreed upon. This was accepted. A Committee of Fourteen was appointed as follows: Bishop McDowell, Edgar Blake, David G. Downey, John J.

Wallace, James R. Joy, Elmer L. Kidney, and A. W. Harris;
Bishop Cannon, Frank M. Thomas, W. J. Young, Paul H. Linn,
Percy D. Maddin, R. S. Hyer, and H. H. White.

This Committee met November 7, 1919, in Richmond, Virginia, and by several days of very arduous and efficient labors produced a plan of union with all the features of a constitution for a reorganized Church. The document was presented to the Joint Commission at its meeting, January 15, 1920, in Louisville, Kentucky. Six days were given to its consideration and revision. No main provisions were changed, nor were any attitudes and positions. The Commissioners concluded that they could go no further, and that they should transmit to the General Conferences without endorsement or recommendation the plan of union which they had produced. Neither side was fully committed to what had been done, but the Southern Commission more nearly accepted the principles and provisions of the document than did the Northern Commission.

Here it should be said that the Regional Conference was accepted by the Northern Commissioners; but as Dr. Harris declared, they had no "consuming affection" for it. They regarded it as an expedient for securing union, but not as an essential element in the governmental structure of a nation-wide and world-wide Church. The Northern Church generally regarded it as divisive and not unifying. They had difficulty in endorsing the distribution of power which the Regional or Jurisdictional Conference and the Judicial Council necessitated, and were established to secure and maintain. The General Conference in their thinking, as in their history, held and should hold all controlling power. They looked upon centralization as vital to genuine unification. In the final analysis this principle and provision of distribution of power was the chief obstacle to union. The Southern Commissioners believed to the end that the Regional Conference was not only essential to union but also to any satisfactory and adequate administration of the Church and of the highest promotion of its work. The South in its governmental philosophy followed Thomas Jefferson rather than Alexander Hamilton. The states' rights in legislation and administration were supported. Regional life with its homogeneity and distinctive traits was regarded as contributory to the broader and finer expression of national thought and culture. The South for over a century had believed in the first-rank quality and worth of its white citizenship and had built and maintained its civilization on that belief. Backgrounds have much to do with what comes to the fore. The history of a people does something to them that enters into the blood of the veins and fiber of their minds and souls. It was so in the South and in the Church that encompassed the South; it was so in the North and in the Methodism of the North. Even Church union will not take it all away.

THE PLAN OF 1920

By the majority vote of each Commission, voting separately, the following action was taken:

We respectfully transmit to the General Conferences of the two Churches the following draft of a Constitution for the Methodist Church, together with recommendations for methods of procedure, as the best that we have been able to agree upon under the circumstances and under our instructions, and we submit the same for their consideration and decision.

Bishop Denny, Dr. Dickey, Judge T. D. Samford, and Judge J. G. McGowan asked to be recorded in opposition.

PREAMBLE

To the glory of God and for the advancement of his kingdom, we, the ministers and members of the Methodist Church, in accordance with the established methods of constitutional procedure, do hereby ordain and set forth this Constitution. In the name of the Father, the Son, and the Holy Ghost.

ARTICLE I. NAME

The name of the Church herein constituted shall be The Methodist Church.

ARTICLE II. PASTORAL CHARGES

The members of the Church shall be organized into local societies, one or more of which shall constitute a pastoral charge.

ARTICLE III. ANNUAL CONFERENCES

The Annual Conferences shall be composed of (1) the traveling preachers, including supernumerary and superannuated preachers, and (2) laymen, in such number as may be determined by the General Conference, which shall prescribe their qualifications and the method of their election.

The Annual Conferences shall have such powers and duties as are hereinafter provided for.

ARTICLE IV. REGIONAL CONFERENCES

SECTION 1. There shall be the following Regional Jurisdictions, each having its own Regional Conferences:

1) *White Membership in the United States*

Jurisdiction One.—Maine, New Hampshire, Vermont, Massachusetts, Rhode Island, Connecticut, New York, Pennsylvania, and New Jersey.

Jurisdiction Two.—Delaware, Maryland, District of Columbia, Virginia, West Virginia, Kentucky, North Carolina, and that part of Tennessee now embraced in the Holston Conferences of the Methodist Episcopal Church and the Methodist Episcopal Church, South.

Jurisdiction Three.—South Carolina, Georgia, Florida, Alabama, Mississippi, and that part of Tennessee not included in Regional Jurisdiction Two.

Jurisdiction Four.—Ohio, Indiana, Illinois, Michigan, and Wisconsin.

Jurisdiction Five.—Minnesota, Iowa, Kansas, Nebraska, South Dakota, North Dakota, Montana, Wyoming, Colorado, Utah, Nevada, Idaho, Washington, Oregon, California, Hawaii, and Alaska.

Jurisdiction Six.—Missouri, Arkansas, Louisiana, Oklahoma, Texas, New Mexico, and Arizona.

2) *Colored Membership in the United States*

Jurisdiction Seven.—The Annual Conferences, Mission Conferences, and Missions embracing the work among colored people in the United States.

3) *Membership in Foreign Countries*

The number and boundaries of the Regional Jurisdictions in foreign countries shall be determined by the General Conference.

Members

SEC. 2. (1) Each Regional Conference for white membership in the United States shall be composed of the ministerial and lay delegates elected to the General Conference by the Annual Conferences within the Jurisdiction of said Regional Conference.

2) The Regional Conference for colored membership in the United States shall be composed of one ministerial and one lay delegate from and elected by each Annual Conference, Mission Conference, and Mission of its Jurisdiction for each two thousand Church members in full connection, or fraction of two-thirds thereof; provided, that each Annual Conference, Mission Conference, and Mission shall be entitled to at least one ministerial and one lay delegate. The numerical basis of representation in said Regional Conference may be changed by said Regional Conference, subject to approval by the General Conference. The membership of said Regional Conference shall not exceed four hundred and shall be composed of ministers and laymen in equal number.

3) Each Regional Conference for membership in foreign countries shall be composed of one ministerial and one lay delegate from and elected by each Annual Conference, Mission Conference, and Mission of its Jurisdiction for each two thousand Church members in full connection, or fraction of two-thirds thereof; provided, that each Annual Conference, Mission Conference, and Mission shall be entitled to at least one ministerial and one lay delegate. The numerical basis of representation in any foreign Regional Conference may be changed by said Regional Conference, subject to approval by the General Conference. The membership of foreign Regional Conferences shall not exceed four hundred, and shall be composed of ministers and laymen in equal number.

Powers

SEC. 3. (1) Subject to the limitations and restrictions of this Constitution, each Regional Conference shall have full power over all distinctively Regional affairs within its Jurisdiction, including the power to fix the boundaries of Annual Conferences, Mission Conferences, and Missions, and to provide for the organization of the same; but no new Annual Conference shall be organized in the States of the United States with less than fourteen thousand Church members in full connection.

2) Each Regional Conference shall have power to receive, own, transfer, and control publishing, educational, benevolent, and charitable institutions of the Church within its Jurisdiction and not otherwise legally provided for, and shall have supervision of all such enterprises, except those which are owned, controlled, and supervised by some other organic agency of the Church.

3) Each Regional Conference shall have power to elect the number of bishops allotted to it by the General Conference, and said bishops shall be confirmed by the General Conference, and ordained by the bishops, unless two-thirds of the members of the General Conference, present and voting, shall object to their confirmation. The powers, duties, and privileges of a bishop elected by or for a colored or foreign Regional Conference shall be limited to the Regional Jurisdiction by or for which he is elected.

4) The powers and privileges of a foreign Regional Conference representing less than one hundred and fifty thousand Church members in full connection shall be determined by the General Conference.

5) No Regional Conference shall, in the exercise of the powers provided herein, make rules or regulations contrary to, or in conflict with, any rule or regulation made by the General Conference for the Government and control of the connectional affairs of the Church.

ARTICLE V. THE GENERAL CONFERENCE

Membership

SECTION 1. The General Conference shall consist of not less than six hundred and seventy nor more than eight hundred and fifty delegates, ministerial and lay in equal number, as the General Conference may determine, who shall be apportioned to the several Regional Jurisdictions according to a uniform rule to be established by the General Conference, subject to the further limitations and provisions of this Article. It shall be composed of:

1) Not less than one hundred delegates, ministerial and lay, in equal number, chosen in such manner as the General Con-

ference may determine, from each white Regional Jurisdiction in the United States; provided, that the number of delegates from any white Regional Jurisdiction shall not exceed twenty per cent of the total membership of the General Conference.

2) Not less than thirty nor more than forty-two delegates, ministerial and lay, in equal number, chosen in such manner as the General Conference may determine, from the colored Regional Jurisdiction in the United States; provided, that the number of delegates from said Regional Jurisdiction shall not exceed five per cent of the total membership of the General Conference.

3) Not less than ten or more than forty delegates, ministerial and lay, in equal number, chosen in such manner as the General Conference may determine, from each foreign Regional Jurisdiction; provided, that the number of delegates from any foreign Regional Jurisdiction shall not exceed five per cent of the total membership of the General Conference.

Provided, that the first General Conference shall be composed of four hundred delegates, ministerial and lay, in equal number, from the Methodist Episcopal Church, and of four hundred delegates, ministerial and lay, in equal number, from the Methodist Episcopal Church, South; chosen in such a manner as may be determined by their respective General Conferences.

Powers

Sec. 2. The General Conference shall have full legislative power over all matters distinctively connectional, subject to the limitations and restrictions of this Constitution.

In the exercise of said power it shall have authority as follows:

1) To define and fix the conditions, privileges, and duties of Church membership.

2) To define and fix the qualifications and duties of elders, deacons, local preachers, exhorters, and deaconesses.

3) To provide for District, Quarterly, and Church Conferences, and to define and fix their powers and duties.

4) To define and fix the powers and duties of Annual Conferences, Mission Conferences, and Missions.

5) To define and fix the powers and duties of those foreign Regional Conferences representing a membership of less than one hundred and fifty thousand in full connection, and to elect the bishops for such Jurisdictions.

6) To change the boundaries of Regional Jurisdictions; but it shall not take away territory from any Regional Jurisdiction

without its consent, except by the concurrent vote of two successive General Conferences; nor change the boundaries of a Regional Jurisdiction without its consent for a period of three quadrenniums succeeding the adoption of this Constitution; nor create any new Regional Jurisdiction in the United States with less than five hundred thousand members in full connection.

7) To define and fix the powers, duties, and privileges of the episcopacy; to fix the number of bishops to be elected by each of the several Regional Conferences; to confirm their election; by a general rule, to superannuate them upon reaching a determined age; to retire them for inefficiency or unacceptability after due notice and proper hearing, provided that it shall require a two-thirds vote to retire a bishop without the concurrence of the Regional Conference of the Jurisdiction in which his official residence is fixed.

A bishop shall be assigned by the General Conference for residential supervision to the Regional Jurisdiction by or for which he was elected; but any bishop, except as herein otherwise provided, may be assigned by the general superintendents to any Annual Conference for presidential supervision, if a majority of the resident bishops of the Jurisdiction to which he is assigned shall concur in said assignment; but such concurrence shall not be necessary in the case of assignment to a foreign Regional Jurisdiction.

The General Conference may assign a bishop to any Jurisdiction for residential supervision with the consent of the delegates of the Jurisdictions from which the bishop is to be taken and to which he is to be assigned. But the consent of the delegates of a foreign Regional Jurisdiction shall not be necessary to the assignment or transfer of a bishop to or from a foreign Regional Jurisdiction.

8) To alter and change the hymnal and the ritual of the Church, and to regulate all matters relating to the form and mode of worship.

9) To describe the method of acquisition, control, and disposition of the real and personal property of the Church and of all its branches.

10) To govern the judicial administration of the Church, except as herein otherwise provided.

11) To review the decisions of the Judicial Council on constitutional questions, provided that no decisions of the Judicial Council shall be reversed except by a concurrent vote of two-

thirds of the General Conference, present and voting, and three-fourths of the members of the several Annual Conferences, present and voting.

12) To control and direct all connectional publishing, missionary, benevolent, and educational enterprises of the Church.

13) To govern any and all other matters of a connectional character.

Restrictions

1) The General Conference shall not revoke, alter, nor change our Articles of Religion, nor establish any new standards or rules of doctrine contrary to our present existing and established standards of doctrine.

2) The General Conference shall not change or alter any part or rule of our government so as to do away with episcopacy, or to destroy our itinerant general superintendency.

3) The General Conference shall not revoke nor change the General Rules of our Church.

4) The General Conference shall not deprive our ministers of the right of trial by the Annual Conference, or by a selected number thereof, nor of an appeal; nor shall it deprive our members of the right of trial by a committee of members of our Church, nor of an appeal.

5) The General Conference shall not appropriate the produce of the Publishing House or Book Concern, nor of the Chartered Fund, to any purpose other than for the benefit of the traveling, supernumerary, and superannuated preachers, their wives, widows, and children.

SEC. 3. (1) The General Conference shall meet once in four years at such time and place as shall be fixed by the preceding General Conference, or by a commission to be appointed quadrennially by the General Conference; and the commission shall have power to change the time and place, a majority of the general superintendents concurring.

2) The general superintendents may, by a two-thirds vote, and shall, when requested by a majority of the Annual Conferences, call a special session of the General Conference.

The general superintendents, before the General Conference convenes, shall elect from their own number one bishop, or more, to preside during the session. The General Conference shall elect such other officers as shall be necessary.

SEC. 4. (1) The ministerial and lay delegates shall deliberate as one body, and, except as otherwise provided, shall vote as one body, but each delegate shall have the right to his vote, or refusal to vote, recorded by name in the journal.

2) One-fifth of either order of delegates, present and voting, may require a vote by orders, in which case it shall require the concurrence of the two orders to decide the matter under consideration, except that for changes in the Constitution a vote of two-thirds of the members of the General Conference, present and voting, shall be sufficient, as provided in Article VIII.

3) One-fifth of those present and voting may require that a yea and nay vote be taken.

4) Whenever a majority of each of two Regional delegations in the United States shall so request, a vote shall be taken on any pending motion or resolution, including amendments to the Constitution, by Regional delegations, and it shall require the concurrence of two-thirds of the Regional delegates in the United States, the members of each Regional delegation voting as one body, to adopt said motion or resolution; provided, however, that no motion or resolution shall be adopted that does not receive a majority vote of the members of the General Conference present and voting.

SEC. 5. Two-thirds of the members elected to the General Conference shall constitute a quorum, but a smaller number may adjourn from day to day, and at the final session may approve the journal, order and record the final roll call, and adjourn.

ARTICLE VI. ASSOCIATE GENERAL CONFERENCES

Whenever in any colored or foreign Regional Conference the membership in full connection shall exceed 400,000, upon request of said Conference, the General Conference shall organize the membership of said Conference into an Associate General Conference, with privileges and powers herein provided.

The relation of an Associate General Conference may be granted to other Churches through the constitutional process.

An Associate General Conference shall be represented in the General Conference by ten ministerial and ten lay delegates, who shall have the right to speak and vote on all matters affecting the interests of its Jurisdiction. The General Conference may be represented in any Associate General Conference by ten ministerial and ten lay delegates.

SECTION 1. An Associate General Conference shall be composed of an equal number of ministers and laymen to be chosen in such number and manner as said Associate General Conference may determine.

SEC. 2. Subject to the restrictions and limitations of this Constitution, each Associate General Conference shall, so far as relates to its Jurisdiction, have powers of the General Conference, legislative, executive, and judicial, except as herein otherwise provided.

An Associate General Conference shall not prescribe conditions, privileges, or duties of Church membership contrary to, or in conflict with, those prescribed by the General Conference, nor shall it define and fix powers, duties, or privileges of the episcopacy contrary to, or in conflict with, the powers, duties, and privileges of the episcopacy as defined and fixed by the General Conference.

SEC. 3. An Associate General Conference shall be entitled:

1) To have such representation as the General Conference may determine in the connectional boards and societies in which its interests are directly involved.

2) To have such share as the General Conference may determine in the produce of the Book Concern and Publishing House.

SEC. 4. An Associate General Conference shall meet quadrennially, and at such other times, and at such places as it may determine. It shall be governed by such rules of procedure as it may prescribe.

ARTICLE VII. THE JUDICIAL COUNCIL

SECTION 1. There shall be, and hereby is, established a Judicial Council, whose decisions shall be final, except as herein otherwise provided.

SEC. 2. The Judicial Council shall be composed of fifteen members, ministers and laymen, to be nominated by the general superintendents by a two-thirds vote and elected by the General Conference.

SEC. 3. Members of the Judicial Council shall serve for eight years, or until their successors are elected, and shall be eligible for re-election. The term of each member, except as provided in Section 9 of this Article, shall expire at the close of the second General Conference succeeding that at which he was elected, except that seven members of the first Judicial Council shall be elected for four years, and thereafter their successors for eight years.

SEC. 4. Members of the Judicial Council shall not be eligible to membership in the General or Regional Conferences, nor shall they hold any other connectional office, nor serve on any connectional board during their term. After the first election no member of the General Conference or of a Regional Conference shall, during his term of service, be eligible to membership in the Judicial Council. No member of the Judicial Council shall hear, review, or determine any case before the Judicial Council to which he may be in any way related, nor shall he sit in the Council while such case is being examined.

SEC. 5. The members of the Judicial Council shall convene at the close of each General Conference and shall organize by choosing from their number, by ballot, a president and a secretary; provided, that the members of the first Judicial Council shall organize immediately upon their election. The secretary shall keep a record of all proceedings, together with the records and documents in each case, with the decision and reasons for the same, and shall report such decisions to the parties involved and also to the succeeding General Conference. All decisions of the Judicial Council shall be in writing.

SEC. 6. (1) The Judicial Council shall have full power to review upon appeal on constitutional grounds the acts of the General Conference, the Associate General Conferences, the Regional Conferences, and Annual Conferences; to hear and determine all other appeals and matters coming to it in course of lawful procedure; provided that no appeal by any Conference shall be entertained unless the same has been taken by at least one-fifth of said Conference, present and voting.

2) The Judicial Council shall have access to all records and documents which it may call for, or which may be transmitted to it from any Conference.

3) The Judicial Council shall also have power to arrest an action of a connectional board or other connectional body when such action is brought before it by appeal by one-fifth of the members of said body, present and voting, or by the general superintendents.

4) In all cases the decision of the Judicial Council shall be final, except as provided in Article V, Section 2, subsection (11).

SEC. 7. The Judicial Council shall prescribe rules and regulations for its government and methods of procedure for the hearing and disposition of appeals, which rules and methods shall be printed in the Discipline, and shall not be changed or altered during the quadrennium, without due notice.

SEC. 8. Two-thirds of the Judicial Council shall constitute a quorum. Constitutional matters shall be decided by a majority vote of the entire Judicial Council. All other appeals shall be decided by a majority of those present and voting.

SEC. 9. The Judicial Council shall meet at the same time and place as the General Conference and shall continue in session until the final adjournment of the General Conference; provided, that if during the session of a General Conference the appeal of a bishop is pending, the Judicial Council shall defer its time of adjournment until it disposes of said appeal.

The Judicial Council shall convene during each quadrennium at such times and places as it may deem necessary to hear and determine appeals.

SEC. 10. Vacancies in its membership shall be filled by the Judicial Council from the same order, lay or ministerial, in which the vacancy occurs, until the next meeting of the General Conference, which may then fill the vacancy for the remainder of the unexpired term.

ARTICLE VIII. AMENDMENTS

SECTION 1. The recommendation of three-fourths of all the members of the several Annual Conferences, present and voting, shall suffice to authorize the next ensuing General Conference, by a two-thirds vote of those members present and voting, to alter or amend any of the provisions of this Constitution; and also whenever such alteration or amendment shall have been first recommended by a General Conference, by a two-thirds vote of those members present and voting, then so soon as three-fourths of all the members of the several Annual Conferences present and voting shall have concurred therein, provided that such concurrence shall take place previous to the meeting of the next ensuing General Conference, such alteration or amendment shall take effect; and the result of the vote shall be announced by the general superintendents.

RECOMMENDATION

We recommend that the General Conference make an equitable provision for the financial support of the Colored Methodist Episcopal Church by setting apart a designated amount or a fixed percentage of the total annual offerings of the reorganized Church for the support of work among colored people.

PROCEDURE

The Joint Commission provided for a First General Conference to be composed of four hundred delegates, ministerial and lay in equal numbers, from each of the two Churches "chosen in such manner as may be determined by their respective General Conferences" and to be held within eighteen months after the final approval and adoption of the proposed Constitution of the united Church. Pending the meeting of the first General Conference each Church was to be governed by the rules and regulations of its own *Discipline*.

Chapter Nine

DETOURING

THE GENERAL CONFERENCE OF THE METHODIST EPISCOPAL CHURCH met in May, 1920, in Des Moines, Iowa. The common greeting from day to day was, "What shall be done about unification?" The proposed plan from the Joint Commission was presented May 3 and referred to a special committee of one hundred and three carefully selected members. They labored arduously and faithfully until May 20, holding five regular meetings each week, two hours or more in length. No group of men ever worked harder or more conscientiously to come to a just and proper conclusion. On that day they came to a unanimous agreement, which the General Conference on May 24 unanimously approved.

They prefaced the report with the statement, "There appear to be in each Church considerable numbers who are not entirely satisfied with the plan suggested for consideration." That was very true. One Southern leader had declared that in his opinion 500,000 members in the South would leave the Church were the plan adopted. That estimate was generally considered extravagant, but there was strong opposition in the South. In the North the Regional Conference met widespread antagonism. That the plan had imperfections even its best friends admitted. However, it had virtues and values which could not be put into discard, and this General Conference recognized that fact by its action.

We therefore propose, if agreeable to the Methodist Episcopal Church, South, that a Joint General Convention be called, to be composed of a total membership of not less than two hundred nor more than four hundred members, ministers and laymen in equal numbers, from each of the two Churches, chosen in such manner as each General Conference may determine, to which shall be committed the plan submitted by the Joint Commission, and any other plan or plans that may be proposed.

It was that proposal upon which the Northern General Conference agreed. To this proposal was attached this affirmation:

We affirm our deep conviction that the Methodist Episcopal Church and the Methodist Episcopal Church, South, should be reunited into one Church. And so earnestly do we desire such a reunion that we declare ourselves ready to accept any equitable plan of union that shall be mutually satisfactory to the membership of both Churches.

The actions of that Church during the ensuing sixteen years fully corroborated this affirmation.

But that proposal made little or no appeal to the leaders of the Church South. They knew the issues, and the obstacles in the way of union, and the attitudes of both sides. It was their view that if fifty able, far-visioned, constructive men, such as had constituted the Joint Commission, could not produce an acceptable plan of union, neither could two hundred, or four hundred. The trouble lay with the constituencies and not with the Commissioners. Until there was a change in the underlying and undergirding attitudes, convictions, and principles of the two constituencies, the Commissioners were estopped in their labor of formulation. The South interpreted the proposal as an inability or refusal of the Church North to go any further along the way of the Regional Conference and the consequent distribution of power. All over the South it was said, "The Northern General Conference turned down unification." This was not true, as was abundantly shown afterwards. The opponents of union saw in it the end of the unification movement and rejoiced, while the friends of union were afraid it was the end. But unification was being saved and not destroyed, as we now know. The chief engineers were disappointed, but not defeated, and they went at once to the task of working out a redeeming detour.

The General Conference of the Methodist Episcopal Church, South, met in May, 1922, in Hot Springs, Arkansas. Careful consideration was given to the report of the Joint Commission, to the action and proposal of the Northern General Conference, and to memorials asking for, and those opposing, the continuance of negotiations with the Methodist Episcopal Church. It said: "Knowing that there may be differences of opinion as to the details, we approve in principle the plan of unification by reorganization, wrought out by the Joint Commission and submitted to this General Conference."

A Commission of five bishops, ten traveling elders, and ten laymen was appointed

for the continuance of negotiations looking toward unification with the basic principles already agreed upon by the Joint Commission as feasible and desirable, or upon such other basis as our Commission may determine.

Instead of the joint convention proposed, we recommend a special session of the General Conference of our Church, when a plan of unification is endorsed by a two-thirds vote of each Commission, and approved by the General Conference of the Methodist Episcopal Church. Then our College of Bishops is empowered and instructed to call a special session of our General Conference.

The Commission was constituted as follows:

Bishops: Collins Denny, Edwin D. Mouzon, John M. Moore, W. F. McMurry, James Cannon, Jr.

Traveling Elders: Paul H. Linn, F. P. Culver, H. H. Sherman, D. H. Aston, Stonewall Anderson, N. M. Watson, W. E. Arnold, T. N. Ivey, J. T. Leggett, and T. D. Ellis.

Laymen: J. S. Candler, H. H. White, J. H. Reynolds, H. N. Snyder, R. S. Hyer, R. E. Cooper, J. W. Fristoe, W. H. Stockham, R. E. Blackwell, and G. T. Fitzhugh.

The Northern Commission was composed of:

Bishops: W. F. McDowell, W. F. Anderson, Edwin H. Hughes, F. J. McConnell, and W. P. Thirkield.

Ministers: J. W. Abel, E. P. Dennett, D. G. Downey, D. D. Forsyth, E. D. Kohlstedt, J. M. Melear, Archibald Moore, Frank Mason North, John H. Race, J. W. Van Cleve.

Laymen: Charles E. Allinger, E. H. Cherrington, W. A. Elliott, A. W. Harris, A. N. Jarvis, P. W. Kinchen, I. Garland Penn, James R. Joy, C. H. White, and Luren D. Dickinson of Michigan (later Governor of the State).

The changes in the personnel of the Commissions may well be noted. In the Northern Commission only Bishop McDowell, Dr. Downey, Dr. Van Cleve, Dr. Harris, Dr. Penn, and Dr. Joy were on the former Commission. In the Southern Commission Bishop Denny, Bishop Mouzon, Bishop Moore, Bishop Cannon, Dr. Ivey, Dr. Linn, Judge White, Dr. Snyder, Dr. Reynolds, Dr. Blackwell, and Dr. Hyer remained. The Southern Commission had as reserves Bishops Dickey and Dobbs; L. B. Elrod, D. M. McLeod, W. H. LaPrade, Jr., S. H. C. Burgin, and Plato Durham, ministers; and W. P. Few, L. D. Murrell, J. M. Rogers, T. M. Robinson, and C. C. Walsh, laymen.

The new Joint Commission brought new spirit, new courage, new determination, and new ideas to the new task. The sentiment in favor of union had continually increased in both Churches. The hope was everywhere expressed that a "way out" could be found.

SURVEYING A WAY

The Convention of Southern delegates that organized the Methodist Episcopal Church, South, in 1845 declared: "We shall always be ready, kindly and respectfully to entertain and duly and carefully consider any proposition or plan having for its object the union of the two great bodies, in the North and South, whether such proposed union be jurisdictional or connectional." It was a time to go back to the word "jurisdictional" and explore its possibility, and certain Southern Commissioners began to do it.

The Plan of Separation of 1844 to the Southern leaders carried the conception of one Church with two jurisdictions, separated by a permanent geographical line. The onrush of events kept them from maturing their conceptions and developing a governmental structure for the bi-jurisdictional Church. In the very beginning of the unification negotiations this jurisdictional conception was prominent, if not dominant.

Judge H. H. White of Louisiana at the Louisville meeting of the former Joint Commission, when it seemed no agreement could be reached upon the proposals under consideration, offered the following plan of unification by co-operation:

1. We suggest, as a plan of reorganization, the merging of the Methodist Episcopal Church and the Methodist Episcopal Church, South, into one Church, to be known as the Methodist Episcopal Church in America.

2. We suggest that this Church shall have throughout common Articles of Faith, common conditions of membership, a common hymnal, a common catechism, and a common ritual.

3. We suggest that the governing power of the reorganized Church be vested in the several General Conferences, of which it may be composed. We suggest that there be an Ecumenical Council to be composed of delegates from all the bodies of which the reorganized Church may be composed, which shall have no legislative power, but whose action shall be deemed in the highest degree advisory.

4. We suggest that the Mission Boards and other general Boards of the several General Conferences work in close harmony, and be jointly administered in so far as possible.

5. We suggest that overlapping and conflicting work in the limits of the respective General Conferences be eliminated as rapidly and as completely as may be.

6. The Ecumenical Council shall be composed *pro rata* of delegates from the several constituent General Conferences, as such General Conferences may determine.

This proposal was not discussed at that time nor any action concerning it taken. It, like other matters to which reference has been made, was studied as containing possible material for a new line of negotiations. Certain Southern Commissioners, after the action taken at Des Moines, pondered the possibilities of some bi-jurisdictional plan of union.

The Joint Commission met January 18-19, 1923, in Cincinnati. Dr. James R. Joy was seated in the place of Judge Alexander Simpson, resigned. Dr. S. H. C. Burgin was seated in the place of the Rev. D. H. Aston. Messrs. Allinger, Jarvis, and C. H. White, and Dr. Forsyth were absent. Dr. A. W. Harris paid high tribute to Dr. Frank M. Thomas, the able member and secretary of the Southern Commission, who had recently passed away. John M. Moore spoke in strong appreciation of Dr. John F. Goucher, educator, and distinguished and esteemed leader in his Church, and in the Commission, who had also gone recently to his reward.

Bishop McDowell, the chairman, reported that his Commission was under instructions "to act with the Commission of the Methodist Episcopal Church, South, either in arranging for the convention proposed, or in perfecting the plans already before the two Churches, or in working out new plans of unification for submission to the two Churches." Bishop Mouzon, the chairman, reported that his Commission had authority "to negotiate on such basis as our Commission may determine." The Joint Commission felt free of limitations and restrictions from either side, and at liberty to consider any proposals that might lead to an acceptable plan of union.

Dr. Downey read the following proposal from the Northern Commission:

Whereas, We hold ourselves to be essentially one Church, one in origin, in spirit, in belief, in polity, and in purpose, we propose, in order that this essential unity may become organic, the following plan of union:

1. That we hold a joint meeting of the two General Conferences composed as described by the Disciplines of the two Churches, and declare that they are united.

2. Every vote shall be taken by the two representations voting separately, and shall require a majority of each representation to make it effective.

3. Provide for the legal ratification of every act by a proper validating resolution on the part of said representations.

Dr. Downey said: "We simply believe that the way for us to get together is to get together, and once together, with the minorities protected, work out every problem as it comes."

The Southern Commission gave this proposal proper consideration, but respectfully responded that "no declaration of union would be practicable or advisable without some plan of union having been formulated and adopted upon which the declaration may be based."

John M. Moore in explanation stated:

We are not in position to say that we will come together in two General Conferences and say that we are united. We want a plan of union, something on which to unite. We are willing to unite on something that we agree to, but not willing to unite on something that we know nothing about. We are not ready simply to unite.

The Southern Commission said:

We propose that the Joint Commission on Unification enter upon the preparation of a plan of union based upon the principle of a united Church with two jurisdictions, each with its own governing body, with a common name, common Articles of Faith, common ritual, common hymnal, common general rules, common terms of memberships, common requirements and provisions for the ministry, common administrative boards and bodies wherever practicable, common judicial procedure, common constitution with a connecting federal body with such powers as may hereafter be agreed upon.

These suggestions called out many questions from both sides and the explanatory discussions prepared the way for a complete survey of the possibilities in the proposals from both Commissions.

Dr. T. D. Ellis, of Georgia, offered the following as a basis for action:

1. That a Church be organized by uniting the Methodist Episcopal Church and the Methodist Episcopal Church, South, under a constitution, with a General Conference and two Jurisdictional Conferences.

2. The name of the Church to be The Methodist Church.

3. Jurisdiction No. 1. To be composed of those Annual Conferences in America and the various mission fields now going to compose the Methodist Episcopal Church.

4. Jurisdiction No. 2. To be composed of those Annual Conferences in America and the various mission fields now going to compose the Methodist Episcopal Church, South.

5. Each Jurisdiction shall have a Jurisdictional Conference with the full powers now possessed by the General Conferences of the two Churches, except in so far as these powers are limited by the Constitution of the General Conference hereinafter provided for, and by such other powers as may be delegated to the General Conference by the Jurisdictional Conferences from time to time.

6. There shall be a General Conference composed of not less than two hundred nor more than five hundred delegates, each jurisdiction having an equal number of delegates.

7. The General Conference to have full power to legislate in reference to (a) the hymnal, the ritual, and the form of worship; (b) missions, schools, religious papers, etc.; (c) the transfer of ministers, churches, and conferences, upon the request of same, from one Jurisdiction to the other and the compensation to be paid by the Jurisdiction receiving the property; (d) to have unlimited powers of recommendation to the Jurisdictional Conferences.

This proposal by Dr. Ellis was first presented to the Southern Commission, and upon the request of Bishop James Cannon, Jr., that Commission asked that it be presented to the Joint Commission. The Commissioners of the Church North, upon hearing it, asked permission to study it overnight. The next morning they reported their willingness to proceed to construct a plan of union on the basis of the proposal by Dr. Ellis.

After further discussion, upon motion of Bishop Cannon, a

Committee of Ten was appointed to formulate and report some general statement of policy. The Chairman appointed John M. Moore, T. D. Ellis, P. H. Linn, R. S. Hyer, and Judge John S. Candler; Bishop W. F. Anderson, David G. Downey, Frank Mason North, E. H. Cherrington, and A. W. Harris.

On the next day the Committee made a partial report in which it presented a plan based largely upon the principles and provisions as outlined by Dr. Ellis. However, the report was too incomplete to warrant any action thereon. After some illuminating discussions the Commission voted to increase the committee to sixteen, by adding Bishop Mouzon, Bishop Mc-Dowell, Stonewall Anderson, H. H. White, Archibald Moore, and W. A. Elliott to develop the plan upon this basis, ad interim. The Commission then voted, after two days, to adjourn, to meet July 24, 1923, in Cleveland, Ohio.

The Committee of Sixteen acted promptly and was able to present to the Joint Commission at Cleveland a complete plan of union upon the basis of two jurisdictions. Two days were given to discussing, reviewing, and revising the proposed plan. It was finally edited by a committee composed of Bishop Hughes, Dr. Downey, and Dr. Harris; Bishop McMurry, Dr. Linn, and Dr. Snyder. Six members of the Northern Commission were absent and two from the Southern. Dr. Ivey had died in March preceding, and the Rev. L. B. Elrod had taken his place. The Hon. G. T. Fitzhugh of Memphis was absent, and Judge J. M. Rogers of Savannah took his place. On the motion to adopt the plan Bishop Collins Denny, the Rev. J. T. Leggett of Mississippi, and Judge Rogers voted No, while the other thirty-nine voted Aye.

I

THE PLAN ADOPTED BY THE JOINT COMMISSION ON UNIFICATION

TRANSMITTAL

We, the Commissions on the Unification of the Methodist Episcopal Church and the Methodist Episcopal Church, South, holding that these two Churches are essentially one Church—one in origin, in belief, in spirit, in purpose, and in polity—and desiring that this essential unity may be made actual in organization and administration throughout the world, do hereby propose and transmit to our respective General Conferences the following plan of unification and recommend its adoption by the two Churches by the processes which they respectively require.

ARTICLE I.   DECLARATION OF UNION

The Methodist Episcopal Church and the Methodist Episcopal Church, South, shall be united in one Church with two Jurisdictions, under a constitution, with a General Conference and two Jurisdictional Conferences.

ART. II.   NAME

The name of the Church shall be ———.

ART. III.   JURISDICTIONS

SECTION 1.   Jurisdiction Number One shall comprise all the Churches, Annual Conferences, Mission Conferences, and Missions now constituting the Methodist Episcopal Church, and any other such Conferences and Missions as may hereafter be organized by its Jurisdictional Conference with the approval of the General Conference.

SEC. 2.   Jurisdiction Number Two shall comprise all the Churches, Annual Conferences, Mission Conferences, and Missions now constituting the Methodist Episcopal Church, South, and any other such Conferences and Missions as may hereafter be organized by its Jurisdictional Conference with the approval of the General Conference.

ART. IV.   COMPOSITION OF GENERAL AND JURISDICTIONAL CONFERENCES

The General Conference and the Jurisdictional Conferences shall be composed of the same delegates. Said delegates shall be elected by and from the Annual Conferences, provided said General and Jurisdictional Conferences shall have not more than one ministerial delegate for every forty-five members of each Annual Conference and not less than one ministerial delegate for every one hundred and twenty members of each Annual Conference, and an equal number of lay delegates, chosen according to the regulations of each of the two Jurisdictions; but for a fraction of two-thirds or more of the number fixed by the General Conference as the ratio of representation, an Annual Conference shall be entitled to an additional ministerial and an additional lay delegate; and provided further that each Annual Conference shall be entitled to at least one ministerial and one lay delegate.

ART. V.   THE GENERAL CONFERENCE

SECTION 1.   *Voting.*—Every vote in the General Conference shall be by Jurisdictions and shall require the accepted majority vote of each Jurisdiction to be effective.

SEC. 2.   *Powers.*—Subject to the limitations and restrictions of the Constitution, the General Conference shall have full legislative power over all matters distinctly connectional, and in the exercise of said power shall have authority as follows:

1) To define and fix conditions, privileges, and duties of Church membership.

2) To define and fix the qualifications and duties of elders, deacons, local preachers, exhorters, and deaconesses.

3) To make provision for such organization of the work of the united Church outside the United States as may promptly consummate the unity of Episcopal Methodism in foreign lands.

4) To define and fix the powers, duties, and privileges of the episcopacy; to fix the number of bishops to be elected by the respective Jurisdictional Conferences and to provide, in harmony with the historic practice of Episcopal Methodism, for their consecration as bishops of the whole Church.

5) To alter and change the Hymnal and Ritual of the Church, and to regulate all matters relating to the form and mode of worship, subject to the limitations of the first Restrictive Rule.

6) To provide for a judicial system and for a method of judicial procedure for the Church, except as herein otherwise provided.

7) To govern any and all enterprises and activities which may be agreed upon as being of a connectional character.

8) To provide for the transfer of members, preachers, churches, pastoral charges, districts, Annual Conferences, Mission Conferences, and Missions, in the United States, from one Jurisdiction to the other, provided that no transfer shall be made without the consent of the member, preacher, church, pastoral charge, district, Annual Conference, Mission Conference, or Mission that it is proposed to transfer.

SEC. 3. *Restrictive Rules.*—In making rules and regulations for the Church, the General Conference shall be under the following limitations and restrictions:

1) The General Conference shall not revoke, alter, or change our Articles of Religion or establish any new standards or rules of doctrine contrary to our present existing and established standards of doctrine.

2) The General Conference shall not change or alter any part or rule of our government, so as to do away episcopacy, or destroy the plan of our itinerant general superintendency.

3) The General Conference shall not revoke or change the General Rules of the United Societies.

4) The General Conference shall not do away the privileges of our ministers or preachers of trial by a committee, and of an appeal; neither shall they do away the privileges of our members of trial before the Church, or by a committee, and of an appeal.

5) The General Conference shall not appropriate the produce of the Publishing House or of the Chartered Fund to any purpose other than for the benefit of the traveling, supernumerary, superannuated, and worn-out preachers, their wives, widows, and children.

ART. VI. BISHOPS

The bishops of the two Churches as at present constituted shall be bishops of the united Church without further action.

Immediately after the union shall have been consummated, the bishops shall meet and organize as one body, and shall arrange for the superintendence of the work of the Church.

A bishop may be assigned to administer in any part of the Church, provided that when he is assigned to administer within a Jurisdiction other than that by which he was elected, it shall be with the consent of the majority of the bishops of the Jurisdiction involved.

ART. VII. PRESIDENCY OF THE GENERAL CONFERENCE

The bishops shall select by a majority vote of the bishops of each Jurisdiction one or more of their number from each Jurisdiction to preside at the sessions of the General Conference.

ART. VIII. JURISDICTIONAL CONFERENCES

Each Jurisdiction shall have a Jurisdictional Conference possessing the full powers of the General Conference of the Church now constituting said Jurisdiction, except such powers as are herein vested in the General Conference, or which may hereafter from time to time be legally delegated to the General Conference by the Jurisdictional Conferences.

Each Jurisdictional Conference shall meet quadrennially where the General Conference is to assemble and immediately prior to its assembling, and when desirable may meet during the session of the General Conference, and at such other times and places as it may determine.

ART. IX. THE JUDICIAL COUNCIL

1. The General Conference shall, at its first session, provide for a Judicial Council, to be composed of an equal number of members elected by each Jurisdictional Conference, and the Judicial Council shall provide its own methods of procedure.

2. The Judicial Council shall be authorized to review, upon appeal of one-fifth of the members of the General Conference, or of either Jurisdictional Conference, or on the appeal of a majority of the bishops, on constitutional grounds, the acts of the General Conference and of the Jurisdictional Conferences; to hear and to determine all other appeals and matters coming to it in the course of legal procedure.

3. The Judicial Council shall have the right on its own motion, subject to such rules and regulations as shall be determined by the General Conference, to review the legislative acts of the General Conference or of either Jurisdictional Conference and to pass on the constitutionality of said acts.

4. The Judicial Council shall also have power to arrest an action of a connectional board or other connectional body when such action is brought before it by appeal by one-fifth of the members of said body, present and voting, or by a majority of the bishops.

5. All decisions of the Judicial Council shall be made by a majority of the total membership of the Council.

ART. X. AMENDMENTS

The General Conference shall at its first session provide, in harmony with the existing procedure of the two Churches, a method of amending the constitution; and until such method shall have been adopted, amendments shall be effected through the process now prevailing in the Churches, respectively.

ART. XI.   SCHEDULE

In all matters not specifically set forth in these Articles and until the General Conference by legal process shall otherwise ordain, the rules of government in the Disciplines of the respective Churches shall be in full force and effect and binding upon the Jurisdictions, respectively.

RECOMMENDATION

We recommend that financial support of the Colored Methodist Episcopal Church be continued by the Jurisdiction with which it is historically related and to such an extent as that Jurisdiction may deem wise.

II

The General Conference of the Methodist Episcopal Church met in May, 1924, at Springfield, Massachusetts, considered promptly the proposed plan of union, and adopted it by a vote of 802 to 13. That called for action in the South. The Southern General Conference of 1922 had said, "When a plan of unification is endorsed by a two-thirds vote of each Commission and approved by the General Conference of the Methodist Episcopal Church, then our College of Bishops is empowered and instructed to call a special session of our General Conference." The conditions had been met. Questions were raised at once by the opposition as to the constitutional right of the General Conference to instruct the Bishops to issue such a call.

The College of Bishops met in Nashville and on May 20, 1924, issued the call:

By order of a majority of the bishops of the Methodist Episcopal Church, South, a special session of the General Conference is hereby called to meet July 2, 1924, at 9:30 A.M., to consider the plan of unification recommended by the Joint Commission on Unification and approved by the General Conference of the Methodist Episcopal Church.

Bishops Warren A. Candler, Collins Denny, U. V. W. Darlington, and James E. Dickey dissented from the action of the majority—Bishops Mouzon, Moore, McMurry, Du Bose, Ainsworth,

Cannon, Beauchamp, Hay, and Boaz—and published their arguments against the legality of the call. The majority made prompt response. This controversy among the Bishops stirred the Church. There existed no authoritative body to which the question of the constitutional right of the General Conference to instruct the Bishops to issue the call could be appealed, and so the controversy could not be settled.

The dissenting Bishops delivered to the General Conference upon its assembling on July 2, 1924, in Chattanooga, the following statement:

We did not join in the call for the special session of the General Conference, because we were convinced that such call was illegal and contrary to the constitution of the General Conference and of the Church to which we pledge absolute fidelity. The grounds of our dissent have been published and we do not think it necessary to reiterate our reasons. We still entertain this view and, therefore, do not waive our previous dissent; but as a majority of the bishops have issued the call, and have assumed full responsibility for the legality of the Special Session, and are, equally with ourselves, entitled to their judgment, we are here to render such service as we can and to discharge every duty that rests upon us in connection with the momentous issues that confront our beloved Church.

Dr. A. J. Lamar of Alabama, one of the Publishing Agents of the Church, a man held in high esteem and great affection, a friend of unification, but an opponent of the proposed plan of unification, offered this resolution:

Resolved, That this General Conference request the bishops and all the Annual Conferences to join in a call for the General Conference to meet the first Wednesday in May, 1925, to vote on the adoption of the Plan of Unification of our Church and the Methodist Episcopal Church, submitted to this General Conference by the Commission on Unification.

This resolution brought on vigorous debate. Dr. Lamar, Dr. W. W. Scott of North Alabama, Judge Perry S. Rader of Missouri, and Judge W. L. Dean of Texas supported the resolution, while Judge John S. Candler, Judge H. H. White, Dr. Bascom Anthony, and Dr. T. D. Ellis opposed it. The resolution called for the affirmative action of all the Annual Conferences, and even one Conference, however small, could defeat the call of the General Conference and bring great delay, probable agitation, and possible postponement of unification. The resolution was voted down.

Upon the presentation of the majority report of the Joint Commission, which carried the plan of unification and the motion for its adoption, Bishop Denny was given the floor to read a dissenting report signed by himself, the Rev. J. T. Leggett, and Judge J. M. Rogers, the members of the Commission who voted against the approval and recommendation of the proposed plan of unification. This minority statement covers over twenty-four printed pages of the Journal of the General Conference. It reviewed the history of the separation, the attitude and position of the Southern delegates in 1844, the movement for fraternity by the bishops of both sides, the findings of the Cape May Commission, and the efforts at federation and the adjustment of conflicts between the Churches in the same territory. It claimed that the plan did not bring unification but disintegration and absorption, that it repealed the Plan of Separation, that it provided for the continuance and possible increase of the very troubles from which relief was sought, that the Church South would become a small province in a mighty empire, that the plan gave the members no voice in the destiny of their own Church, that the plan surrendered the liberty and independence of the Church, that the plan made the super-General Conference supreme and all-controlling, that it gave unrestrained powers to the Judicial Council, that it established a relation with the Negro race not best for him and not possible to us, that it surrendered what is vital to "us."

Dr. Lamar moved that this minority report be substituted for the majority report which transmitted the Plan of Unification, although the only part that could be classed as a report was the recommendation that the Commission as constituted be continued "to enter upon further negotiations with the view of perfecting a plan that will be more in harmony with the basic principles heretofore approved by the General Conference."

Judge John S. Candler, Dr. George R. Stuart, Dr. A. C. Millar, Dr. H. N. Snyder, Judge Perry S. Rader, and Mrs. J. H. McCoy spoke against the minority report and in favor of the Plan of Unification. Dr. A. J. Lamar, Dr. R. P. Shuler, and the Rev. W. H. Nelson spoke in favor of the minority report. Dr. T. D. Ellis was the floor leader for the Commission and performed his task with marked ability. He closed the debate with a forceful address. There were no dull moments that day. It was a time of great tension. The addresses were forceful, illuminating, and worthy of the great issue under discussion. The vote on the substitution of the minority for the majority report was 67 for and 275 against. The aye-and-no vote on the adoption of the proposed plan of unification was 298 for and 74 against.

III

The bishops were instructed to submit the Plan of Unification to the vote of the Annual Conferences meeting during the calendar year 1925. A resolution was adopted recommending that the vote by the members of the Annual Conferences be by ballot. At the end of three days the General Conference adjourned, the shortest and the most animated meeting of all the General Conferences ever held.

The opponents of unification and of the proposed plan became very active at once. Agitation spread throughout the Church, especially in the lower South. General, Annual Conference, and district organizations were formed to defeat the plan. Laymen in certain sections became active. Literature was published and circulated and speakers were sent out to expose what were regarded as defects and dangers of the plan. In some sections plebiscites were taken in the local congregations. The friends of unification and of the plan met the opponents in like fashion. From the close of the General Conference to the adjournment of the last Annual Conference in 1925 the Church was in the midst of great discussion and commotion. Much feeling was aroused.

The majority members of the Commission reviewed the positions and answered the arguments of the minority report in a pamphlet written largely by one man, as was the minority report, from which some statements are here presented:

The majority Commissioners deny that the address is in reality a minority report in nature or form, but rather a dissenting view of and a carefully prepared argument against the Plan of Unification, and a well-planned parliamentary effort to get before the Church in an official way the most plausible and forcible objections to unification and the plan proposed, that could be produced. Had it been a minority report, the common rule of procedure would have required that it be presented to both General Conferences, since they were under the necessity of passing upon the recommendation of the Joint Commission or any minority part thereof.

It should be said here that only in deference to its highly respected authors and those who hold similar views has this document been allowed to be discussed and acted upon as a minority report; but the friends of unification have had no desire to prevent by any technicality of procedure the fullest discussion of the great matter now before the Church. They are anxious that the plan be studied and viewed from every angle and therefore have welcomed criticism as well as commendation that its practicability and desirability, in which they so thoroughly believe, may be the more definitely and clearly brought out. The danger to unification, as to any great cause, is not in discussion and even in the severe arraignment by one who seriously questions its value, but in ungrounded prejudice, uninformed views of its provisions, and blind misconceptions as to what its application will bring about. . . . .

This report makes one thing quite evident: the minority want established a geographical line, hard and fast, drawn across the United States, that will make a real Southern and a real Northern Church, and each absolutely confined to its own territory. They want no real General Conference, governing the two Churches or jurisdictions, but rather a General Conference for each Church or jurisdiction, such as each Church has now, with perhaps some sort of a connecting advisory Council. . . . .

The minority report is an argument for the overthrow of the plan and a plea for the continuance of the existing state and relations of the two Churches. The majority are thoroughly convinced of the practicability and adequateness of the plan for the accomplishment of all the ends of a genuine union, and they firmly believe that its adoption will be of immeasurable benefit and service to all Methodism, to the nation, and to the Christian Church throughout the world.

The opposition gathered strength in some states. The Negro, "absorption of the South by the North," "Northern preachers will take our leading churches," "no protection of our property or our institutions," "no name," "no constitution," "modernism in the North" were made the rallying cries for inciting and developing discontent, distrust, and disaffection.

"We favor unification, but not the pending plan," was the claim of many persons, and they carried much influence in the Church. The friends of unification and of the plan could not say that it was complete and without deficiencies. But it was an excellent plan of co-operation, a partnership plan, that offered possibilities of growth into the full, complete, and adequate plan.

The Annual Conferences gave a vote of 4,528 for and 4,108 against the adoption of the plan proposed—a majority, but not the required three-fourths of all the votes cast. Thus the detour so well laid out failed to take Methodist union to its long-sought goal.

Chapter Ten

BACK TO THE MAIN ROAD

THE GENERAL CONFERENCE OF THE METHODIST EPISCOPAL CHURCH, South, met in May, 1926, in Memphis, Tennessee. The delegates had been elected in the midst of the unification agitation and they found themselves divided in spirit, and not altogether happy in their relations to each other. "Unification is dead!" said one group. "Unification will rise again," said the other. What should be done now?

The General Conference adopted a sensible resolution, recommended by its Committee on Church Relations:

1. That there be no agitation, discussion, or negotiation concerning unification during the ensuing quadrennium.

2. That a special Committee of Research and Investigation, composed of seven elders and seven laymen, be elected by the General Conference upon nomination of the Committee on Church Relation, whose duty it shall be to make a careful and scientific study of the whole question in its historic, economic, social, legal, and other aspects, and report their findings in detail to our next General Conference in 1930.

3. That the following be the members of this Committee: Franklin N. Parker, Andrew Sledd, J. W. Mills, Ivan Lee Holt, A. R. Kasey, V. C. Curtis, A. L. Moore, T. D. Samford, W. P. Few, M. E. Lawson, H. C. Stuart, J. M. Rogers, Nathan Newby, H. H. White.

The Commission on Exchange of Territory between the two Churches was continued with the following members: Bishop W. F. McMurry, Dr. W. A. Cooper, Dr. W. E. Arnold, Dr. Frank Barrett, Judge Nathan Newby, Dr. E. L. Woolf, and the Hon. W. E. Brock. The General Conference of the Methodist

180

Episcopal Church in 1928 appointed a Commission on Interdenominational Relations that could function with the Commission on Exchange of Territory. These two Commissions helped to restore good will, and they kept alive the eager desire of many for eventual unification.

The General Conference of the Church South met in May, 1930, in Dallas. The Episcopal Address expressed the faith "that the recent failure of plans looking toward unification was only temporary," and cherished "the hope that at some future time we shall be wise enough to find a way whereby a united Methodism may, with undivided energies and unwasted resources, deliver her full strength upon the common task of reforming the continent and spreading Scriptural holiness over these lands."

The Special Committee of Research and Investigation appointed in 1926, with Dr. Franklin N. Parker of Emory University as chairman, submitted a highly interesting and informing report on the movement for fraternal relations and union since the separation in 1844. It gave the history of the approaches made, commissions appointed, actions proposed, and actions taken. It made clear that great progress toward union had been made, but said:

While a satisfactory scheme of unification with the Methodist Episcopal Church may ultimately be legally adopted and carried out, yet it would not be wise at this time to attempt to outline the legal steps necessary to be taken to effectuate a plan of unification as a fact.

The General Conference created a Commission of fifteen members on Interdenominational Relations with instructions "to cultivate the spirit of fraternity with the Methodist Episcopal Church looking toward the ultimate union of these two great branches of Episcopal Methodism and the answer of Christ's prayer that all his disciples may be one." The duties of the Commission on Exchange of Territory were transferred to this

Commission. The Commission was constituted of Bishop W. F. McMurry, J. L. Decell, T. D. Ellis, F. P. Culver, John F. Caskey, C. D. Bulla, W. A. Stanbury, L. S. Barton, A. R. Kasey, and H. L. Clay, ministers; and J. H. Reynolds, L. P. McCord, Nathan Newby, J. T. Ellison, and Dice R. Anderson, laymen.

I

The General Conference of the Methodist Episcopal Church in 1928 appointed a Commission on Interdenominational Relations composed of Bishops W. F. McDowell, F. J. McConnell, F. D. Leete, Herbert Welch, E. G. Richardson, Charles L. Mead, and Robert E. Jones, and the following ministers: Robert Bagwell, R. N. Merrill, H. E. Woolever, L. C. Wright, J. H. Race, R. B. Stansell, E. M. Antrim, B. F. Abbott, Ray Allen, Paul W. Edwards, L. T. Guild, O. W. Auman, F. W. Court, F. W. Mueller, and R. A. Elliott.

The General Conference of the Methodist Protestant Church in 1928 appointed a Commission on Interdenominational Relations composed of President John C. Broomfield, Dr. Thomas H. Lewis, J. C. Williams, R. F. Day, L. E. Bee, F. W. Lineberry, S. W. Taylor, A. Norman Ward, and Charles Bragg, ministers; and Harry Shaw, W. C. Perkins, N. S. Williamson, P. M. Ellis, J. H. Baker, and J. Norman Wills, laymen. In June, 1929, Dr. Lewis died, and Dr. L. B. Smith was appointed to his place.

On July 1, 1930, the Commissions of the Methodist Episcopal Church and the Methodist Protestant Church met in Pittsburgh to explore the possibilities of union between those two Churches. Previously Bishop McDowell, Bishop Mead, and President Broomfield had had some conversations about the matter. The two Commissions decided to confine their work to mere discussions, without taking official action until such time as the Commission of the Church South could at least be present. On June 30, 1931, the two Commissions met in Chicago and continued their discussions. Bishop W. F. McMurry, Chairman of the Southern Commission, was present by invitation and stated emphatically that his Commission had no authority or power to discuss union, since its functions were limited to matters of comity and the exchange of property, churches, and Conferences.

During the meeting of the Ecumenical Conference in October, 1931, in Atlanta these two Commissions had their third meeting. It was during that Conference that Bishop McDowell, Bishop Herbert Welch, Bishop Charles L. Mead, Bishop F. D. Leete, and President J. C. Broomfield had an informal interview with John M. Moore in regard to the possibilities of new negotiations for union among the three Churches. There were two reasons for this inquiry. One was the doubt of possible new negotiations so soon after the heated discussions in the South of the Parternership Plan of 1924. Another was the feeling created by the action in 1928 of the General Conference of the Methodist Episcopal Church in adopting a resolution to the effect that the General Conference of that Church would go to only those places where the Negro delegates would be entertained upon the same basis as white delegates. The reaction to that resolution in the South was very strong. Bishop Edwin D. Mouzon gave out to the newspapers an interview upon this action, stating that it had postponed the union of the Church South and the Church North indefinitely. Bishop McDowell in the above-mentioned interview asked John M. Moore if, in view of Bishop Mouzon's statement, there was any probability, or even possibility, that the General Conference of the Church South in 1934 would endorse new negotiations on union. The reply was:

Yes, the General Conference, in my opinion, will in all probability appoint a Commission on Methodist Union to begin renewed negotiations at once. While such a resolution as that passed by the General Conference of the Methodist Episcopal Church would keep the General Conference of any united Church out of the South at least for many years, yet it would have to be passed by the General Conference of the united Church to become valid, and such a resolution will probably never be proposed. The resolution of 1928 on entertainment will not prevent the appointment of a Commission on Union.

This incident was personal, but it had to do with later actions and has some historic values.

The two Commissions met in Pittsburgh, January 13 and 14, 1932. Bishop Leete stated to the joint meeting that the Commission of the Methodist Episcopal Church felt "that before any definite action was taken one more effort should be made to secure the co-operation of the Commission of the Methodist Episcopal Church, South." A subcommittee, however, was appointed to formulate a basis or tentative plan of union of the Methodist Protestant Church and the Church North.

In 1932 the General Conferences of the Methodist Episcopal Church and the Methodist Protestant Church met. They received the report on union from the Commissions and appointed new Commissions. Further action was postponed until after the General Conference of the Church South, with the hope that its action would institute a new movement for the union of the three Churches. Their hopes were not disappointed.

These negotiations were the first in which the Methodist Protestant Church participated since the formulation of the historic "Suggestions" of 1911. Its leaders were strongly favorable to union, but they recognized that the real union required in American Methodism must first be achieved by the Church North and the Church South. They heartily supported the statement in the proposed basis of union that "the differences in the practice of democracy and in methods of administration which existed in 1830 have so changed through the processes of time that there no longer remains any sufficient justification for these two groups of Methodists to be other than one in organization as well as in spirit."

The proposed plan of union wrought out by the two Commissions recommended the name "The Methodist Church," a General Conference with full legislative powers over all matters distinctly connectional, subject to the restrictions of the constitution, the Restrictive Rules as existing in the Methodist Episcopal

Church, the Episcopacy as in the Methodist Episcopal Church, with the suggestion by the Methodist Protestant Church that a term of eight years for bishops be adopted by the first General Conference, the district superintendency as in the Northern Church, the lay representation of the local charge in the Annual Conference, the annual meeting of the local church as in the Methodist Protestant Church, the historic Articles of Religion with the attached publication of the statements of the Methodist Protestant Church on Sanctification and on the Resurrection and the Judgment. The plan provided for a convention of one hundred and ten members from each Church, to be held following its adoption by the constitutional votes of the two Churches, to complete the governmental structure for the operation of the United Church.

The union proposal was not fully acceptable to the membership of either Church. The Methodist Protestant people were in the South and Southwest, as well as in the North and Northeast. Those in the South preferred to be in the Church South, that they might have affiliation with the Methodists with whom they lived. That was especially true in North Carolina, where there were about 10,000 members. The union proposed would leave separating lines still in existence. To remove them would put part of the membership in the Church North and part in the Church South, and that was not acceptable. From the standpoint of the Church North the union would increase its membership in the South, and while that might be desirable in one way it could be a cause of new irritation, and prove a hindrance to negotiations for the union of the Northern and Southern Churches. For this reason the proposal did not have the sympathy and encouragement of the leaders in the Church South. Notwithstanding these states of mind in the three denominations there was still a very strong desire in the two negotiating Churches for union if it could be accomplished without injury to the general cause of Methodist union.

II

The Southern Commission on Interdenominational Relations, appointed in 1930, recommended to the General Conference of 1934 "the creation or continuation of Commissions authorized to begin at once after May, 1934, definite efforts on the part of the three Commissions to make and agree upon plans for the union of the three Churches, and others that may enter the negotiations upon invitation or with our approval."

The Bishops in their address said:

We have been looking toward union for a long time. We need to move toward it, and in a way that will effectively promote the interests of American Methodism. National life and creative church life call for unity and solidarity. Protestantism in this country greatly needs in this day the momentum of a great uniting movement in the mobilization of the ecclesiastical forces of the same origin, same policy, same belief, same spirit, and same purpose. The hope of the unity and union of all American Methodism should never be allowed to grow dim. It should flame forth until oneness is made complete. Union will not come in a day, but it can be promoted by the right attitude every day; and determined purpose, Christian patience, and loyal persuasive persistence will bring happy, joy-giving consummation of union in these United States.

This statement brought forth marked applause from the Conference. Unification was back in the thinking of the Church.

The report of the Commission and the statement in the Episcopal Message and memorials from seven Annual Conferences on the subject went to the Committee on Church Relations. That Committee, with T. D. Ellis as Chairman and M. T. Plyler as Secretary, and with such unification advocates as Ivan Lee Holt, Nolan B. Harmon, Jr., F. P. Culver, G. C. Emmons, J. N. R. Score, Frank C. Tucker, H. N. Snyder, J. H. Reynolds, and Nathan Newby as members, brought back a recommendation, that a Commission on Interdenominational Relations and Church Union be appointed composed of five bishops, ten other

ministers, and ten laymen, and that the Commission be directed
to confer with the similar Commissions of the other two
Churches as soon as possible, and endeavor to work out a plan
of union and submit the result to the next General Conference.

The General Conference adopted the report of the Committee, expressed its appreciation of the kindness and consideration of the Methodist Episcopal Church and the Methodist
Protestant Church in postponing their negotiations for union
until after this session of the General Conference, expressed the
hope that plans might be perfected which might result in the
union of American Methodism, and appointed as its Commissioners Bishops Edwin D. Mouzon, John M. Moore, W. N. Ainsworth, Paul B. Kern, and Arthur J. Moore; J. L. Decell, G. C.
Emmons, J. W. Moore, W. W. Peele, Paul W. Quillian, T. D.
Ellis, Ivan Lee Holt, F. N. Parker, Clare Purcell, and Charles C.
Selecman, ministers; and John W. Barton, John S. Candler, P.
D. Maddin, Daniel C. Roper, H. N. Snyder, W. E. Brock, Joseph
W. Lewis, J. H. Reynolds, John T. Scott, and H. H. White, laymen. The attitude and spirit of these chosen representatives of
the Church were an encouragement to action.

The Commission of the Methodist Episcopal Church appointed
by the General Conference of 1932 was composed of Bishops W.
F. McDowell, Edwin H. Hughes, Frederick D. Leete, Ernest G.
Richardson, and Robert E. Jones; J. S. Ladd Thomas, E. D.
Soper, Edward Hislop, F. W. Mueller, Edward Laird Mills,
Harry E. Woolever, E. J. Hammond, Robert B. Stansell, Willis
J. King, and Morris E. Swartz, ministers; and E. H. Cherrington,
James R. Joy, James A. James, Earl H. Conder, Vincent P.
Clarke, W. H. Spurgeon, W. H. Wilcox, W. W. Schweninger,
Clyde O. Law, and F. H. Trotter, laymen.

The Commission of the Methodist Protestant Church was composed of President John C. Broomfield, J. C. Williams, A. Norman Ward, Charles Bragg, Roby F. Day, L. E. Bee, F. W. Lineberry, S. W. Taylor, J. C. Weaver, L. B. Smith, ministers; and
W. C. Perkins, Henry Shaw, N. S. Williamson, J. H. Baker, P.

M. Ellis, J. Norman Mills, and F. B. Hanna, laymen. In 1935 Dr. Ward died suddenly. Dr. James H. Straughn succeeded him. In 1936 the following were added: E. A. Sexsmith, G. Charles Weaver, J. S. Eddins, and C. R. Green.

This Joint Commission, without haste but without waste of time, set about its serious task of producing a plan of union. The first meeting was held in Chicago, August 27-29, 1934. Bishop McDowell, Bishop Mouzon, and Dr. Broomfield were chosen the Chairmen, and Dr. Woolever, Dr. Decell, and Dr. Smith the Secretaries. The meeting was given over to explanations of past actions, clarifications of present positions, and exploration of future possibilities. The Methodist Protestant group had had no occasion to become entirely acquainted with the issues that kept the two Episcopal Methodisms apart, nor with their efforts to restore union and the bases upon which negotiations had proceeded, nor with the fundamental principles in their ecclesiastical polity and procedure. Very few of the other two groups were members of all the Commissions that had labored so strenuously and conscientiously to find a way of union. But all of all groups were thoroughly dedicated to the high purpose of producing a plan of union that would be adequate and satisfactory to the three Churches. That they were equal to their responsibility the results of their labors abundantly show.

What should be the procedure of the Joint Commission? What line of action should be taken? What manner of plan may be possible? It was readily agreed that a small Committee of survey, of creation, of formulation should be appointed. Those appointed were Bishops Edwin H. Hughes and John M. Moore; Messrs. Ellis, Quillian, Decell, Smith, Williams, Woolever, Mueller, and Hislop, ministers; Messrs. Cherrington, Joy, Perkins, Maddin, and Brock, laymen; and the three Chairmen.

This wise and exceedingly capable committee did not undertake to produce an entire plan before reporting to the Joint Commission. The main principles and features were first decided upon and carefully stated. Then, in accordance with these, certain sections of a plan were prepared, the Commission was convened, and its action taken. By this process the plan was completed, reviewed, revised, section by section, item by item, and finally adopted without a dissenting voice. Finer co-operative and constructive work was never done by a committee or commission. The Committee on Plan held four meetings, and the Commission met in Louisville, March 13-14, 1935, and in Evanston, Illinois, August 14-16, 1935, for its final session.

III

Unification had been the desire and purpose of the two Churches for a score of years. Strong Commissions of able men had labored arduously, faithfully, and conscientiously to produce a basis of union. They had done much in developing understanding, appreciation, and fraternal attitudes, but the twenty years of negotiations had not found a meeting plane of the Northern and Southern minds. They held conflicting ideas and demands of ecclesiastical polity and control. The North thought in terms of centralized authority with centralized agencies. The South thought of sufficient sectional control and agencies to ensure its protection against a dominant majority and to give latitude for its own expression. These ideologies had been very slightly mollified or modified by the three years of negotiations of the first Joint Commission, as the published debates will show. The Plan of Union of 1920 was not adopted by the Joint Commission, nor recommended; it was only submitted to the General Conferences. The Southern Commission was more favorable to it than the Northern, but even its approval was with mental reservations. The Southern criticism centered upon the General Conference and the Northern upon the Regional Conference. One saw the danger in "supreme centralization," the other in "division into six churches." The two minds had not met. That Plan of Union had no sponsor, and it went to the archives.

Can these two minds holding the conceptions of over fifty years be brought together? May not the strong, dominant elements in each conception, or ideology, be welded into a unity and a plan produced that will not only protect and promote the interests of all parties, but will also create a stronger and more substantial and serviceable ecclesiastical structure than either had ever possessed? These were the questions for which answers were sought by the Joint Commission of 1934. That affirmative answers were reached the facts of history forcibly testify.

The men who organized the Methodist Episcopal Church in 1784 were largely in their English origin monarchists in government and high-churchmen in their ecclesiastical thinking, and they very naturally made a General Conference of supreme centralized power. The South inherited this view as well as the North, and that is why its representatives in the early Commissions insisted that the Jurisdictional Conferences be virtually General Conferences, and opposed one General Conference for the entire Church. The South would not accept centralized power, and the North would not accept more than one General Conference with such power. The problem was the production of a system with distributed power.

That wa sthe problem of the Constitutional Convention of the United Colonies in 1787. They solved it by distributing power between the Federal Government and the States, and then distributing the Federal power between the executive, legislative, and judicial departments. That example was ever before the minds of the Commissioners on Union, and these principles had been deeply considered in the earlier studies of possible solutions.

This writer in the winter of 1910-1911 set aside three months for a careful and thorough study of the history of the Separation, of the debates and, acts of 1844, of the twenty-five years succeeding, of the divergent and obstructing issues that had developed, of the utterly incompatible and exclusive methods of union proposed by the two sides, of the approaches to each other that had been made in good will and righteous purpose, and he came to the deliberate and definite conclusion and conviction that the

form of the American government offered the best and most
nearly correct pattern for the governmental structure of a united
Methodist Church. Not all the features would be needed or desired, but the ideas and principles underlying and undergirding
the plan could be employed. This conviction was never shaken
by any later study or discussions. Patience was often drawn upon
heavily by the excursions of great and good men; but their fail-
ures, due to the conflicting views of other great and good men,
left the way open for creating renewed approaches to these early
convictions.

Those were master men of master minds who championed the
respective sides in the great era of 1916 to 1920. History ran
heavily in their blood. Each felt deeply the rightness and righteousness of his positions upon which compromise was not to be
entertained. Their seniority in years and rank and their superiority in statement and debate would have imperiled any
proposal which failed to contain or support their inclinations.
But time has its own way of changing the commanders in chief.
Fifteen to twenty years not only had effected these changes, but
had dissolved many issues, softened many attitudes, and altered
many viewpoints. Proposals were now possible without the danger of bayonets of preconceptions and time-honored prejudices.
Championship of the conclusions and convictions of twenty years
before seemed proper, and with determination it was entered
upon. From time to time completed drafts of every action, every
item, and every word, after long, tedious, intricate study and formulation, were presented to the Committee on Plan by its members. While the findings and formulations of 1920 were freely
drawn upon, wherever practicable, yet the proposals of this one
Commissioner were the unfoldings and formulations of what had
been embryonic in his mind since March, 1911, and what was
championed by Dr. Edgar Blake in 1916 in the Evanston Conference.

The members of the Committee on Plan were committed to
the jurisdictional system, and they all made from time to time

important proposals and valuable suggestions.   They exhibited unusual inventive and constructive genius in developing the formulations, and the subcommittees did their work with efficiency and marked dispatch.   The Commission received the reports of the Committee on Plan in a fine spirit of co-operation and entered heartily and understandingly into the critical work of perfecting the proposals and the formularies.   With such remarkable co-operation and intelligent participation the meetings at Louisville and Evanston were sufficient to bring to happy completion the work of the Commission.   The Plan of Union was unanimously adopted by the Commission and cordially recommended to the three uniting Churches.   Thus the main road was opened and Methodist union moved on.

IV

The Plan of Union places the governing power of The Methodist Church in five bodies: (1) the General Conference, (2) the Jurisdictional Conference, (3) the Annual Conference, (4) the Judicial Council, (5) the Council of Bishops.   The General Conference is the supreme legislative unit under the restrictions of the Constitution, with its duties and powers defined, beyond which its authority does not go.   The Jurisdictional Conference is the essential, vital, and principal administrative and promotional unit of the Church, with legislative power limited to regulations on regional affairs.   The Annual Conference has the final vote on all constitutional changes and elects the members of the General and Jurisdictional Conferences, and is the major unit in ministerial and local-church service.   The Judicial Council is the appellate tribunal of final authority in questions involving the constitutionality of legislative acts.   The Council of Bishops is the historic itinerant general superintendency, constitutionally established and protected, charged with the specific duty of placing the ministry, presiding over the Annual Conferences, and supervising and promoting the spiritual and temporal interests and affairs of the entire Church.

The Jurisdictional Conference is the key and core of the entire system. To it is assigned the duty and power to choose the bishops, not only for itself but for the entire Church, and to choose its proportion of the entire membership of all the General Boards. It is its duty—and a very grave duty it is, for which it must not be denied the power—to provide for the interests and institutions within its boundaries. It is its duty and power to establish and constitute Jurisdictional Conference Boards, and to carry them on efficiently and forcefully, auxiliary but not subordinate to the General Boards of the Church. It is its duty—and it must not be denied the power—"to promote the evangelistic, educational, missionary, and benevolent interests of the Church." It is its duty—and it is guaranteed the power—"to make rules and regulations for the administration of the work of the Church within its Jurisdiction." The Jurisdictional Conference that fails to do any and all of this has missed the meaning, purpose, and plan of the union.

The Plan of Union sets up a commonwealth of balancing bodies wherein no one shall be supreme, except in its own field, but all shall have responsibility, in co-operation and co-ordination, for the welfare of the entire Church. For anyone to usurp chief control or for anyone to become weak and ineffective in the discharge of its constitutionally assigned responsibility is to break down the governmental structure by which a nation-wide and world-wide Church can hope to function with its greatest efficiency, reach, and power. The Plan was adopted and recommended by the Commission to the Churches with confidence that it would bring union and unity and provide an ecclesiastical polity that would establish and maintain The Methodist Church in might and victorious movement for the Kingdom of God.

Chapter Eleven

UNION COMING IN

THE PLAN OF UNION MET WITH GENERALLY FAVORABLE RECEP-
tion throughout all the Churches. The General Conferences
of the Methodist Episcopal Church and the Methodist Protestant
Church met in May, 1936, and gave overwhelming constitutional majorities in favor of adoption. The vote of the former
was 470 for to 83 against; that of the latter, 142 for to 39 against.
Both General Conferences authorized the vote of the Annual
Conferences in the ensuing year. The vote of the members of
the Annual and Lay Conferences of the Methodist Episcopal
Church was 17,239 for and 1,862 against; that of the members of
the Annual Conferences of the Methodist Protestant Church was
1,265 for to 389 against. Twenty of the twenty-five Annual
Conferences of the latter Church were in the affirmative, which
was more than the two-thirds majority required for constitutional
adoption. These votes thrilled all Methodism.

Here it might be said that the Methodist Episcopal Church
from 1869 was aggressive in its advocacy of union, or reunion.
While it had its own conception of the basis of that union, yet
it was always willing and ready to go along with the Church
South in what finally was thought to be best. That was true in
the appointment of the Cape May Commission in 1876, and in
the historic declaration of the co-ordinate status of the two
Churches. It was true in the setting up of the Commission on
Federation in 1894 and 1896. It is true that it took no action
in 1912 on the 1911 "Suggestions," but in 1916 it adopted without change or reservation the Declaration of the Oklahoma General Conference of the Church South. In 1920 its General Con-

194

ference, after the most diligent and laborious consideration of the Plan, which the Joint Commission submitted but never adopted, by a large and able Committee, asked that the Plan be further considered by a joint convention, but expressed its readiness to "accept any equitable plan of union that shall be mutually satisfactory to the membership of both Churches." In 1922 it entered zealously into the production of the second plan, and in 1924 adopted it promptly with practically no opposition. In 1928 it appointed a Commission on Interdenominational Relations which stood ready to enter new negotiations at any time for union, and in 1932 it continued the same status.

It is true that it was slow in coming to the Jurisdictional Conference idea. But in the Joint Commission, in the very beginning in 1934, the Jurisdictional Conference was accepted unreservedly. The Plan of Union met very little opposition and was adopted promptly and overwhelmingly, and the Church committed itself enthusiastically to the regime of the new and greater American Methodism. Its seventy years of devotion to a great cause, the cause of Methodist unity and union, is worthy of the highest praise from the Methodists of the new day.

The Methodist Protestant Church has won the appreciation and admiration of all American Methodists. For fifty years and more it yearned for the fellowship of a united Methodism. Its battle for lay representation in all Conferences by all the Methodisms had been won. To live on by protests against "autocratic bishops and domineering presiding elders" was not altogether comfortable, especially when the "autocracy" and the "domineering" were not apparent. To criticize fine churches and worldly-minded church members and to exalt one's own religious virtues might be warranted, but it was not spiritually or ecclesiastically profitable. To protest, and ever to protest, is a hard role to maintain, even if one is in the right.

Strong convictions of able men brought the Methodist Protestant Church into existence, and these leaders had been succeeded by men of like force and views. But their objectives had been won. Men like Thomas H. Lewis saw that a Church of protest cannot be a Church of power. Positiveness is essential to aggressiveness. Dr. Lewis lifted a mighty voice for union. But what could be done? His Church was in the North and in the South. To unite with either of the other two Churches was to divide his own people and then fail to close the great breach. Nothing could be done from 1911 on for over twenty years. But when the union of all three appeared in the offing in the early 1930's the strong leadership of the Protestant Church rejoiced as those that wait for the morning. Their hope of fifty years seemed about to be realized. They entered heartily into the negotiations for union, and their General and Annual Conferences acted promptly and decisively. While the part in the negotiations of the Methodist Protestant Church was necessarily restricted by reason of the basis and status of separation in the other two Churches, yet its action throughout was enthusiastic and pronounced.

The Methodist Episcopal Church, South, never looked with any favor upon any proposal of reunion, or the restoration of the former status, and for the first sixty-six years of separation no other form of merger was proposed or considered. Contrary to the general supposition, it came very slowly to the Jurisdictional Conference idea, as ultimately adopted. The "Quadrennial Conferences" as proposed in the "Suggestions" were largely meant to be more or less regional General Conferences with ample self-determination, and that idea and desire was surrendered or modified reluctantly. But the interest in Methodist union came alive when the first steps were taken in 1910 looking toward the production of a new governmental structure, and the Church South co-operated fully in all the negotiations. The opposition was often very strong, especially against proposed provisions, and it continued strong up to the early 1930's, as this narrative indicates. However, this opposition served union well as it held in check any final action until the instrument of union had been brought to adequacy and completeness. Because of this opposition and the measures that had to be taken to give it satisfaction, much of this story has dealt with the doings in the Church South. But with the coming of the final and sturdy Plan of Union the opposition turned into support. Only praise and good will go out to those who held the Churches true to the high cause of a glorious Methodism.

In the fall of 1935, after the Plan of Union had been completed by the Joint Commission, Bishop William Fraser McDowell, that prince of men, that master of assemblies, that apostle of union, that untiring toiler in the creation of an acceptable and adequate plan of union, was called suddenly to his eternal reward. Bishop Edwin H. Hughes succeeded him as Chairman of the Northern Commission and Bishop Edgar Blake as a member of the Commission. The Southern Commission lost by death Mr. John Wynne Barton, a former Publishing Agent of the Church, and the Hon. Joseph W. Lewis, a prominent lawyer of St. Louis. In February, 1937, Bishop Edwin D. Mouzon, a great preacher, a superior leader, a forceful advocate of unification, a member of every Commission since 1916, was also called suddenly to his eternal reward. John M. Moore succeeded him as Chairman of the Southern Commission. "God buries His workmen, but carries on His work," said Mr. Wesley.

In 1935 Dr. Albert Norman Ward, of the Methodist Protestant Commission, suddenly went to his reward. He was the President of Western Maryland College. He was quiet in manner, thoughtful in expression, sound in judgment, considerate in his relations, and firmly committed to union. He stood high in the councils of the Joint Commission. He was succeeded by Dr. James H. Straughn, who was elected President of the General Conference in 1936, and then became Chairman of the Methodist Protestant Commission.

In December, 1936, the College of Bishops of the Church South received requests from twenty-five of the thirty-eight Annual Conferences in the United States to present to the Annual Conferences in the coming year the Plan of Union for their action.

The procedure that had been customarily followed in the vote on constitutional amendments was first the vote by the members of the General Conference and then the vote by the members of the Annual Conferences. However, the law as written gave precedence to the vote by the Annual Conferences, but allowed either to take the vote first. The Bishops acceded to the request of the twenty-five Annual Conferences and the question of the adoption of the Plan was presented to all the Annual Conferences during the Conference year of 1937. The result of the vote of their members was 7,650 for and 1,247 against the adoption of the Plan, which is more than the constitutionally required three-fourths majority. Only one Annual Conference, the North Mississippi, failed to give a majority in the affirmative.

The public discussion of the Plan of Union was not engaged in by the people of the South until after it had been voted upon by the Church North and the Protestant Church. In those two Churches there was not much discussion. Some Protestant Conferences were unfavorable to union, largely for doctrinal reasons. The strong adherents of the doctrine of sanctification, and especially of the belief in the imminent second coming of our Lord, contended that "Modernism" infected the other two Churches, and that "Socialism" was promoted by some of their leaders. The opposition in the North confined itself largely to the provision of a Jurisdictional Conference for the Negro Annual Conferences. Their argument was that this Jurisdictional Conference was racial, whereas the other five were geographical. The conclusion to be drawn from the argument was that they would have the Negro Conferences included in the Jurisdictional Conference in which they are geographically located. Since they are located largely in the South, the utter impracticability of such an arrangement would be quite glaring to those who know the South, its customs and its attitudes. This proposal would be an argument against union.

The antagonism to the Negro Jurisdictional Conference forcibly expressed by certain white leaders and violently stressed by certain Negro leaders, and the reasons which they gave for their antagonism, recruited considerably for a time the opposition in the South, especially in those sections where the membership of Negroes in the Church at all, and particularly in the General Conference, was strongly opposed. The Negro was made the chief obstacle to union by both groups, but for opposite reasons.

The opposition in the South based its criticism of union also upon the power of the General Conference, with its overwhelming majority from the former Methodist Episcopal Church, to control all legislation, policies, properties, and institutions; to elect all connectional officers through its majorities in the General Boards; to destroy the Jurisdictional Conferences at will by its constitutional majorities in the membership of the General and Annual Conferences; and to centralize government and Boards as it might desire.

The opposition in the South complained because a plebiscite vote was not taken in the local congregations by which certain argumentation and agitation could be carried on. They knew, of course, that such a vote had no legal value, as the law of the Church specified how the Plan of Union, with its constitutional content, was to be acted upon, and a plebiscite of local congregations had no place, and never did have any place, in any legal procedure in Methodism.

The leadership of the opposition centered its greatest strength upon an effort to invalidate union, and the vote on the Plan of Union, because the North Mississippi Conference voted 117 for and 125 against the adoption of the Plan of Union, giving a majority against adoption. They claimed that the adoption of the Plan required a majority vote of each and all the Annual Conferences, because, as they claimed, the Plan altered the Articles of Religion and altered the process for altering the Articles of Religion. They based their contention that the Articles of Religion were being affected upon the claim that the Church South had adopted the footnote to Article XXIII by the constitutional process, and consequently that it was a part of the

Articles of Religion. They laid much store by this argument, by which they expected to defeat adoption, or, failing in that, to defeat the final consummation of union.

The General Conference of the Church South came April 28, 1938, in Birmingham. The members of the Commission were fully aware that the vote would be overwhelmingly in the affirmative, but that the leadership of the opposition would test the legality of the action, and the constitutionality of the vote of the Annual Conferences. The Chairman of the Commission, upon the advice and co-operation of members of the Commission, with the special assistance of Dr. T. D. Ellis, sought the legal guidance of such distinguished lawyers as Judge W. H. Swiggart, the General Counsel of the Nashville Chattanooga and St. Louis Railroad and a former member of the Supreme Court of Tennessee; Judge J. Morgan Stevens, of Jackson, Mississippi, a former member of the Supreme Court of Mississippi; Judge Walter McElreath, of Atlanta; Judge Hugh A. Locke, of Birmingham; Judge J. T. Ellison, of Centerville, Alabama; and Judge Nathan Newby, of Los Angeles. Every motion made relating to adoption, and every authoritative statement and motion by the College of Bishops, was first carefully scrutinized by this committee of lawyers. No defects in fact or form were allowed to exist to give any aid to contrary action in the future.

April 29 was set apart for the discussion and action upon the Plan of Union. Dr. Ellis read a carefully prepared motion for its adoption. No advocate of adoption spoke except following one who opposed. This kept up until every person who desired to speak in opposition had spoken. Then Judge J. G. McGowan, of the opposition, moved the previous question, and that the vote be taken. Dr. Ellis, who represented the Chairman of the Commission, spoke briefly, and the Yea and Nay vote was taken, resulting in 434 for adoption and 26 against.

Upon the announcement of the vote the College of Bishops, in accordance with the law, declared that the adoption of the Plan of Union had been effected.

Then John M. Moore, the President of the College of Bishops, read the following request to the Judicial Council:

To the Judicial Council of the Methodist Episcopal Church, South: More than one-third of the College of Bishops hereby in writing, attested by the President and Secretary of the College of Bishops, request the Judicial Council to determine the legality of the act of the General Conference of the Methodist Episcopal Church, South, on the 29th day of April, 1938, and of all actions of the Annual Conferences of the Methodist Episcopal Church, South, in the ratification and adoption of the Plan of Union of the Methodist Episcopal Church, the Methodist Protestant Church, and the Methodist Episcopal Church, South, and the legality of the approval and authorization of the union of the Methodist Episcopal Church, South, with the Methodist Episcopal Church and the Methodist Protestant Church, and whether or not the said union and Plan of Union have been legally adopted, and union legally authorized.

Signed: John M. Moore, U. V. W. Darlington, H. M. Du Bose, W. N. Ainsworth, James Cannon, Jr., Arthur J. Moore, Paul B. Kern, A. Frank Smith, Collins Denny.

I

The Judicial Council was composed of Judge Martin E. Lawson, President, the Rev. J. Stewart French, D.D., Secretary, Dr. A. C. Millar, Dr. W. G. Henry, Dr. J. W. Johnson, Dr. A. J. Weeks, Professor R. L. Flowers, Judge Orville A. Park, and Judge M. A. Childers.

Bishop Collins Denny and his son, the Hon. Collins Denny, Jr., presented to the Council the arguments of the opposition, while John M. Moore, Dr. T. D. Ellis, Judge Hugh A. Locke, Judge Nathan Newby, Judge J. T. Ellison, and Judge Walter McElreath supported the legality of the adoption by the Church. The two sides were given an equal amount of time.

Bishop Denny and Mr. Denny, Jr., stated as a basis of appeal:

(1) Said plan of union cannot be adopted without revoking, altering, or changing the Articles of Religion of the Methodist Episcopal Church, South, and said Articles of Religion cannot

be revoked, altered, or changed without the joint recommendation of all the Annual Conferences and by a majority of two-
thirds of the General Conference succeeding.   (2) The adoption
of said plan of union would amend, alter, or change the procedure established for amending or altering the first restrictive
rule, and that procedure cannot be amended or altered without
the joint recommendation of all the Annual Conferences and a
majority of two-thirds of the General Conference succeeding.
(3) The North Mississippi Conference, by a vote of 125 to 117,
declined to approve said Plan of Union, and thereby withheld its
recommendation that the Articles of Religion be revoked, altered,
or changed in accordance with said plan, and thereby withheld
its recommendation that the procedure for altering or amending the first restrictive rule be itself changed in accordance with
the provisions of said plan of union.

The opposition was basing their contention upon a clause in
the following constitutional proviso whose legal validity was
being attacked by the unificationists:

Provided that upon the concurrent recommendation of three-
fourths of all the members of the several Annual Conferences,
who shall be present and vote on such recommendation, then a
majority of two-thirds of the General Conference succeeding
shall suffice to alter any of the above restrictions, excepting the
first article, which may be altered upon the joint recommendation of all the Annual Conferences by a majority of two-thirds of
the General Conference succeeding.

That clause following "excepting the first article" was never
in the law of the Methodist Episcopal Church, and not in that
of the Church South till 1906, when the General Conference,
acting alone, instructed the Editor of the Discipline to insert it,
although it was to be a vital amendment to the Constitution.
The unificationists contended that since it was not submitted to
the Annual Conferences it had not been constitutionally adopted
and legally inserted, that it was null and void, a dead law, and
that no action taken under it was valid.   Because action was
taken under it, the validity of that action was denied.

After the insertion of the clause was approved by the General Conference the footnote to Article of Religion XXIII was recast in form without any alteration in substance, adopted by the General Conference, and sent to the Annual Conferences for their vote, in order that the footnote might have constitutional standing as a part of Article XXIII. The vote of the Annual Conferences, because of oversight, was not completed till 1922. The contention of the opposition about the alteration of the Articles of Religion centered largely on this footnote. The fact is that the footnote was not changed by the Plan or the Uniting Conference, and it stands unchanged in the Discipline of The Methodist Church today. But the action taken to give it constitutional standing was null, even though it received the constitutional majorities in the Annual Conferences for its adoption.

Article of Religion XXIII is as follows:

The president, the congress, the general assemblies, the governors, and the councils of state, as the delegates of the people, are the rulers of the United States of America, according to the division of power made to them by the constitution of the United States, and by the constitutions of their respective states. And the said states are a sovereign and independent nation, and ought not to be subject to any foreign jurisdiction.

The footnote:

The Twenty-Third Article of Religion in the Disciplines of all our Churches in foreign lands shall read:

"XXIII. Of the Duty of Christians to the Civil Authority.

"It is the duty of all Christians, and especially of all Christian ministers, to observe and obey the laws and commands of the governing or supreme authority of the country of which they are citizens or subjects, or in which they reside, and to use all laudable means to encourage and enjoin obedience to the powers that be."

The footnote of 1820:

As far as it respects civil affairs we believe it the duty of Christians, and especially of all Christian ministers, to be subject to the supreme authority of the country where they may reside, and to use all laudable means to enjoin obedience to the powers that be; and therefore it is expected that all preachers and people, who may be under the British or any other government, will behave themselves as peaceable and orderly subjects.

The footnote of 1820 was never changed by the Methodist Episcopal Church, but the Methodist Episcopal Church, South, substituted the above footnote for it.

The author may here be allowed to state parenthetically a personal opinion. It is a grave question whether Article XXIII, notwithstanding its position and history, without any religious or theological content whatsoever, is in reality an Article of Religion at all; or whether any General Conference previous to 1812 could by its action have made it an Article of Religion; or whether any General Conference and the Annual Conferences since then could by the constitutional process have made or could make any such statement, or any such footnote, thereto, an Article of Religion. Articles of Religion are formulas of religious belief, and Article XXIII is not that. A charge of doctrinal heresy based upon any attitude of mind or spirit toward Article XXIII could scarcely be maintained in any competent court, civil or ecclesiastical. Nevertheless, Article XXIII has constitutional standing, and the footnote inserted by the Church South had constitutional recommendation by reason of the manner of its adoption. To say that Article XXIII is not an Article of Religion is to invite criticism; but to say that it is, is to dim the distinction that exalts religion and its sacred doctrines.

The proviso for making constitutional amendments was adopted in 1828-32, stopping with "excepting the first article," as a substitute for the proviso of 1808 which required the majority of each and all the Annual Conferences to make any constitutional change. The Rev. Collins Denny, later Bishop, was a member of a special committee of the General Conference of 1906 which reported that "excepting the first article" left implied what had been omitted by the Secretary or Editors of the 1832

Discipline—namely, that the old law held good for altering the first article; and consequently that the General Conference after seventy-four years had the right to make this interpretation and restore the clause. This committee's recommendation was adopted by the General Conference and the clause went into the law.

The unificationists pointed out that Nathan Bangs, Beverly Waugh, and Daniel Ostrander composed the Editorial Committee for the Discipline, and that their accuracy in such work could scarcely be questioned. No member of that General Conference of 1832 ever questioned the accuracy of the record. Nathan Bangs wrote a history of the Church in that era and reported the action, but no error. Robert Emory, son of John Emory, who was elected Bishop at that Conference, in his *History of the Discipline* says: "The former proviso, at the close of the Restrictive Rules, was struck out, and the following substituted." Robert Paine, later Bishop, a member of that Conference, reported the substitution, but indicated no error or implication.

The representatives of the unificationists presented arguments and briefs to the Judicial Council. They argued the illegality of the clause in question, the unfounded contention that the Articles of Religion would be affected by adopting the Plan of Union, and the power of the Church to change by the constitutional process the existing constitutional process for making any constitutional alteration.

The Judicial Council after three days rendered its decision, written largely by the Rev. Dr. J. Stewart French. The conclusion was that:

1) There has been no material or substantial change in the XXIII Article of Religion from that historically held in common by the three uniting Churches; and even had there been, the adoption of that which was for foreign countries, and is a footnote in our home *Discipline*, was not according to the legal method of making a constitutional change in the first Restrictive Rule, and therefore cannot be regarded as having the weight

of an Article of Religion, but only that of a non-constitutional pronouncement of General and Annual Conferences.

2)   The insertion in the Discipline of the phrase, "Which may be altered upon the joint recommendation of all the Annual Conferences by a majority of two-thirds of the General Conference succeeding," by the General Conference of 1906, was clearly illegal. If it was meant as a part of the Constitution, it would have had to go the rounds of the Annual Conferences, and have come back to the General Conference of 1910. It was never submitted to them.

3) The General Conferences of 1828-32 and the Annual Conferences of that quadrennium, eliminated the Annual Conference as a constitutional unit and substituted therefor the members of the several Annual Conferences. The fact that one, or more, Annual Conferences should give a majority against a proposed constitutional amendment would avail nothing to prevent the change if three-fourths of the members of the several Annual Conferences, present and voting, followed by two-thirds of the members of the succeeding General Conference were in favor of and voted for it.

4) The General Conference of 1832 made it impossible to change the first Restrictive Rule, unless and until, by constitutional process, the phrase "excepting the first article" should be stricken from the constitution by direct repeal or by substituting for it some method of amending the said Rule.

The Judicial Council decided that:

(1) The actions of the members of the several Annual Conferences in approving the Plan of Union and authorizing its adoption, as reported to the General Conference, were and are legal; (2) the action of the General Conference in ratifying and adopting the Plan of Union was and is legal; (3) the union of the three Churches and the Plan of Union have been legally adopted, and the union has been legally authorized in accordance with the Plan of Union.

This decision of the Judicial Council has contributed incalculably to the solidity of union and the permanency of the Plan of Union. It became authoritative for the Church before any civil courts of the land in any litigation that may seek to destroy or impair the union of the three Churches. The illuminating review of the facts, issues, and evidence involved supporting the opinion and decision have given to the Church a legal document that will be historic. The decision was the final act in the adoption of the Plan of Union by the three uniting Churches.

II

Unification is a process in which there are many steps. There are more things to be accomplished than simply the union of the Churches. Many able lawyers have expressed the opinion that the General Conferences had the power to unit the Churches as the General Conference of 1844, as declared by the Supreme Court of the United States, had the power to divide the Church, without the concurrence of the Annual Conferences. But whether or not the opinion is valid, no one wanted union without a constitutional basis of that union, and consequently a Plan of Union had to be produced and the constitutional processes of the Churches employed to adopt it. But even with the constitution adopted, union could not function until a detailed governmental structure was built. This Methodist union implied basically that the governmental structure should be built of the material found in the three uniting Churches. How best could this structure be produced?

The Plan of Union embraced a plan of procedure which the Joint Commission had carefully worked out, and that called for a Uniting Conference to be held within twelve months of the adoption of the Plan of Union, and the continuation by the General Conference of the Joint Commission with such changes in personnel as might be necessary or desired, up to the Uniting Conference. The entire structure of the Uniting Conference was worked out early in the negotiations after much study, and passed to a sub-committee of which Bishop Mouzon was Chairman, and it came to final adoption with very slight changes.

The Joint Commission of 1920 suggested a first General Conference of four hundred delegates from each Church, to be chosen as the respective General Conferences might determine. The three Methodist Churches of Great Britain consummated their union in 1932 in London by a Uniting Conference. From these two actions came the suggestion of the name, the size, and the equality basis of this Conference, with General Conference power, but with restrictions to the use of only the materials in the three prevailing Disciplines.

The Methodist Episcopal Church had brought Bishop Edgar Blake, a very valuable man, into the Commission in the place of Bishop McDowell. The Methodist Protestant General Conference had elected the Rev. James H. Straughn, D.D., its President in 1936, and made him chairman of the Commission. The Church South General Conference in 1938 elected Ivan Lee Holt, W. W. Peele, Clare Purcell and J. L. Decell to the episcopacy. Bishop Arthur J. Moore was assigned very heavy duties in foreign lands. Bishop Holt took Bishop Arthur J. Moore's place in the Commission, and Bishops Decell and Peele were made alternates. B. P. Taylor, W. M. Alexander, W. G. Cram, J. Emerson Ford, and H. H. Sherman were elected to the vacancies; and Mrs. J. W. Perry and Harry Denman succeeded Mr. Barton and Mr. Lewis, deceased.

The General Conference of the Church South requested its Commission to elect John M. Moore chairman and "to make such financial provisions for him as that he may be free to take whatever steps that he may deem necessary in the performance of this responsibility; this amount to be paid out of the Episcopal Fund." It was a year that heavily taxed mind, body, and spirit to the utmost, by day and by night.

The Joint Commission faced grave responsibility and arduous labors in preparing the prospectus of the Discipline. A meeting was held June 30, 1938, in Evanston, and the two hundred members of the Special Committee specified in the plan of the Uniting Conference were appointed, and their duties indicated. All members of the Joint Commission were given assignments to some one of the Committees. These eight Committees held two and three meetings each, and they were exacting, laborious meetings. The Disciplines were divided into eight sections, and each Committee was required to prepare one section of the prospectus of the new Discipline. Their work was carefully and efficiently done. The Committees reported the results of their labors to the Joint Commission, which met in Jackson, Mississippi, January 24, 1939, for a week's session. Every page of every report was carefully reviewed, revised, and passed upon by the Commission. The amended reports were printed in a volume immediately, and the *Prospectus of the Discipline,* by March 15, 1939, was in the hands of every delegate to the Uniting Conference, which was to meet in Kansas City, Missouri, April 26, 1939. When the Uniting Conference met, the delegates had the material in hand and had some acquaintance with it; and each delegate had his assignment to one of the eight Standing Committees, and was ready to go forward with the work of preparing the Discipline for The Methodist Church.

Bishop Edwin H. Hughes, Dr. James H. Straughn, and John M. Moore, the three Chairmen of the Joint Commissions, had been incessant in labors, great labors, for the entire preceding year. Bishop Hughes was an ambassador of good will all through the South; and his great addresses and stirring sermons inspired confidence, built up bonds of respect and regard, and released new streams of mutual affection between the leaders of the two great sections. His service in the Commission, in the Committee on Plan, in the Committees on Syllabi, and on Prospective Sections of the Discipline, and in the guidance of the Uniting Conference was statesmanlike, eminent, and magnanimous. His spirit, wisdom, and devotion brought calmness, confidence, courage, and capability into all the work of the Commission and the Conference.

Dr. Straughn represented his Commission in preparing for and conducting the Uniting Conference with remarkable ability, adaptability, geniality, and co-operative insight. Dr. Broomfield had rendered splendid service in producing the Plan of Union.

Dr. Straughn entered into his labors without the loss of a step. These two men merit the high esteem in which they were held by their Church of yesterday and are now held by their Church of today. When on the second day of the Uniting Conference, in pursuance of the Plan of Union, the delegates from the Annual Conferences of the Methodist Protestant Church assembled apart for the purpose of electing two ministers of that Church to the office of bishop in the united Church, their choice appropriately fell upon Dr. Straughn and Dr. Broomfield.

III

The Uniting Conference was a marvel of efficiency, dispatch, and conscientious labor. It was able to transact all its business, complete the Discipline of the Church, pass the necessary enabling acts for completing actions that required considerable time, and adjourn on the fifteenth day with two Sundays of intervening worship. Without the previous preparation of the Prospectus of the Discipline by and through the Joint Commission the time required would not have been less than six weeks. The wisdom of the Joint Commission in all its preparatory labors was abundantly justified by the results.

The Committee on Program, Public Meetings, and Addresses, of which Bishop Ivan Lee Holt was the Chairman, won high praise for the many attractive and commendable features which were daily presented. The Director of Music, Professor James R. Houghton, of the Boston School of Theology, a master of music in knowledge, voice, and leadership, by his rare service brought excellence and variety into the music of the Conference. Dr. Oscar T. Olson and Bishop Holt prepared all the fine liturgical exercises used in the various periods of worship. Bishop Ernest L. Waldorf and Bishop Holt appointed the leaders and speakers for the morning worship of each day. Bishop Charles C. Selecman and Bishop Ralph S. Cushman supervised the morning watch and the afternoon evangelistic addresses, with Dr. Harry Denman giving constant aid and direction. Bishop Adna W.

Leonard, by the appointment of the Council of Bishops, preached the sermon at the ordination of Bishop Straughn and Bishop Broomfield, on Sunday, April 30. Every speaker and participant made high contribution to the excellence of the programs.

The Conference was honored by the stimulating presence and able addresses of distinguished fraternal messengers from the British Methodist Church. They were the Rev. Robert Bond, D.D., the President of the Conference, and the Right Honorable Isaac Foote, a member of the King's Privy Council and eminent church leader. Only a half-dozen years had passed since a Uniting Conference in that country brought into union its three Methodist bodies. Such bonds of unity and brotherhood represented by men of such distinction and ability create good will and kinship between our two great nations. By the unity of men shall come the Kingdom of God.

The program of the first morning and last night was in the hands of the three Chairmen. The fifty bishops and the nine hundred delegates before going to the auditorium on the first day celebrated the Sacrament of the Lord's Supper in the nearby Cathedral of the Protestant Episcopal Church, and marched in procession to the auditorium. Bishop Hughes presided. After brief devotional exercises the roll was called, the plan of organization and the rules that had been previously prepared were presented and adopted. The Rev. Lud H. Estes, of the Memphis Conference, was elected Secretary and his nominations of assistants were approved. The three Chairmen then read the official statements of the action of their Churches in the adoption of the Plan of Union. Dr. Harry E. Woolever, one of the secretaries of the Joint Commission, presented to the Uniting Conference for the secretaries the report of the Joint Commission, the adopted Plan of Union, and the Prospectus of the Discipline of The Methodist Church, which had been prepared under the supervision of and by the Commission as required under the Plan of Union. The address of the Bishops of the two Churches and the President of the General Conference of the Methodist Protestant Church was read by John M. Moore.

IV

The final act of the Conference was, as it was to be, the adoption of the Declaration of Union. This Declaration was one of the most carefully prepared statements that was ever produced for any ecclesiastical body. The first draft, in memorandum, was made by Dr. T. D. Ellis in the fall of 1938. He turned it over to John M. Moore, who wrote it out in full. Judge W. H. Swiggart, of Nashville, a former member of the Supreme Court of Tennessee, then gave it review and revision in the interest of legal accuracy and force. Then Judge J. Morgan Stevens, of Jackson, Mississippi, a former member of the Supreme Court of Mississippi, gave it scrutiny and added some suggestions. Other lawyers were consulted, even down to the mid days of the Conference. The manner of the adoption of the Declaration was wrought out by this writer in August, 1938, at Lake Junaluska, North Carolina, but kept unrevealed until the program of the closing session was being arranged. The adoption of the Declaration of Union did not create union; that was done by the General and Annual Conferences, but it brought into operation The Methodist Church.

The nine hundred delegates and the fifty bishops, after fifteen crowded, arduous high days, had come to the final consummation of their great and glorious labors. It was night, and the capacious auditorium was packed with fourteen thousand persons, mostly Methodists, from all parts of the country. Dr. Houghton, the Conference Director of Music; Professor J. Max Kruwell, the Conference organist; and Professor Powell Weaver, the director of the special chorus of three hundred voices, were in their places. The organ pealed forth its majestic strains. The nine hundred delegates came in and took their seats. Then the bishops marched in, and to the platform, led by the three Chairmen of the Joint Commission, Bishops Edwin H. Hughes,

James H. Straughn, and John M. Moore, who took the seats at the chairman's desk. The scene portrayed grandeur and majesty and the crowning glory of historic achievement.

John M. Moore called the Conference to order. The rich worship service which was followed had been prepared by Dr. Oscar T. Olson of Cleveland at the request of Bishop Ivan Lee Holt and President H. L. Freeman, his associates on the Conference Committee on Worship. Bishop Holt announced the opening hymn, "The Church's One Foundation." Bishop Ernest G. Richardson gave the Call to Worship, the Invocation, and the Collect. Bishop Robert E. Jones announced the hymn, "O for a Thousand Tongues to Sing." Bishop Arthur J. Moore led in prayer, and read the second Collect. The Doxology was sung, the Canticle of the Church was led by Bishop Frederick D. Leete, and the Gloria Patri was sung. Bishop Paul B. Kern read the Scripture lesson from the Gospel according to John, seventeenth chapter. Bishop John C. Broomfield announced the Litany Hymn, "Jesus, with Thy Church Abide." The Bishops participating were members of the Joint Commission.

Bishop Edgar Blake here gave the profoundly impressive commemoration of the faithful: "We shall look upon the faces of six heroes of Methodist Union who rest from their labors in the Divine Land." As he announced their names, their photographs were thrown upon the screen to be seen by the vast audience. He gave a beautiful and faithful literary portraiture of each.

Albert Norman Ward, faithful, quiet, persuasive member of the Methodist Protestant Church.

Thomas Hamilton Lewis, eloquent and prophetic President of the Methodist Protestant Conference.

Eugene Russell Hendrix, Bishop of the Church South, early effective advocate of Methodist Union, a prince of the Church.

Bishop Edwin Du Bose Mouzon, a man of impressive and commanding personality, a leader in the movement for Methodist Union.

Bishop Earl Cranston, a far-visioned leader of the Church he loved, who labored to the end of his days for the merging of American Methodism and whose pioneering spirit has long been recognized as a chief factor in achieving the union which we here consummate this night.

Bishop William Fraser McDowell, until the day of his sudden death, Chairman of the Commission of the Methodist Episcopal Church, a princely servant of God, whose persuasive influence was a determining factor in the progress of union and whose wisdom helped to guide the movement to its successful end.

The great audience was deeply affected by this touching commemoration.

Here the Chairman introduced Bishop Hughes—"the man we delight to honor, whom we hold in great affection, the speaker of this hour, the leader of the hosts of Methodism, Bishop Hughes."

The address of Bishop Hughes, with the refrain, "The Methodists Are One People," was delivered with impassioned eloquence and deep religious appeal, and it moved profoundly the immense audience. Only three days beforehand he had been notified by the other two Chairmen that he was to speak, but of all his great addresses this stands at the summit and will ever be outstanding in the minds of that vast audience.

The climax of the occasion was the never-to-be forgotten Declaration of Union. The people all stood. Bishop Straughn read the Preamble. Bishop Hughes read the Affirmation. Serious stillness came upon the audience. John M. Moore read the five Declarations, and after each the nine hundred members of the Conference and the fifty bishops, standing, lifted their right hands and said in a stupendous chorus, "We do so declare." The sixth declaration was read in unison by all the bishops and delegates. The people were then seated, and they bowed devoutly and engaged in the following liturgical prayer of Consecration led by Bishop A. Frank Smith:

THE BISHOP: In the name of the Father, our God, by whose favor we live in this heritage of faith:

To the honor of Jesus Christ, the Son of the living God, our Lord and Saviour;

To the praise of the Holy Spirit, source of light and power: We consecrate this communion of faith that is The Methodist Church.

THE PEOPLE: Holy, holy, holy, Lord God of Hosts; heaven and earth are full of thy glory. Glory be to thee, O Lord most high.

THE BISHOP: We consecrate this Church
For the worship of God in praise and prayer;
For the ministry of the Word;
For celebration of the Holy Sacraments.

THE PEOPLE: God is a Spirit, and they that worship him must worship him in spirit and in truth.

THE BISHOP: We consecrate this Church
For the guidance of childhood;
For the sanctification of the family;
For the training of youth in faith and knowledge.

THE PEOPLE: Remember now thy Creator in the days of thy youth.

THE BISHOP: We consecrate this Church
For the edifying of the body of Christ;
For the cure of souls that doubt;
For the persuasion of those who have not yet believed;
For the evangelization of the world;
For the promotion of righteousness, Christian unity, and good will.

THE PEOPLE: All souls are mine, saith the Lord. Inasmuch as ye did it unto the least of these my brethren, ye did it unto me.

THE BISHOP: We consecrate this Church
For the redemption of character;
For brotherhood with all men;
For the ennobling of this life and the deepening of the assurance of the life eternal.

THE PEOPLE: The ransomed of the Lord shall come to Zion with songs and everlasting joy.

THE BISHOP: We consecrate this Church
In grateful remembrance of all who have loved and served the cause that is here consummated;

In loving memory of those who have fared forth from this
earthly habitation;
In high hope for those who shall share in this heritage of faith
in days to come.
THE PEOPLE: Holy, holy, holy, Lord God of hosts! Heaven and
earth are full of thee. Heaven and earth are praising thee,
O Lord most high!
THE BISHOP AND PEOPLE: Having part among the people of God
and the Church Universal in the inheritance of apostles and
prophets, fathers and teachers, martyrs and evangelists; we
give thanks unto the Father who hath made us meet to be
partakers of the inheritance of the saints in light. Com-
passed about by so great a cloud of witnesses, we do here and
now consecrate The Methodist Church to the worship of
God and the establishment of His Kingdom among men
everywhere, through Jesus Christ our Lord. Amen.

The presiding Chairman then recognized Judge H. H. White,
of Louisiana, a Southern Commissioner in all the negotiations
for union since 1916, and he said, "I consider it a high privilege
and honor to move that the Declaration of Union, which has
been adopted section by section, be now adopted as a whole."

Dr. James R. Joy, of Newark, New Jersey, long-time Editor
of the *Christian Advocate* (New York), who had been a member
of every Commission since 1916, was recognized, and he said,
"I have the honor to second the motion of Judge White."

Judge Harry Shaw, of West Virginia, a Commissioner of the
Methodist Protestant Commission, was recognized and he also
seconded Judge White's motion.

The Chairman then asked all the delegates who favored the
motion to adopt the Declaration of Union as a whole to stand
with uplifted right hand. They were then seated.

The Chairman then asked those who opposed the adoption of
the Declaration of Union to stand with uplifted right hand. A
heavy silence ensued.

The Chair then declared: "No one stands in opposition. . . . .
The Declaration of Union has been adopted. The Methodist

Church now is! Long live The Methodist Church!" It was
8:59 P.M., May 10, 1939.

The immense audience in smiles and tears spontaneously
sprang to their feet and engaged in tremendous and prolonged
applause. The great chorus at the peal of the organ broke forth
in Handel's "Hallelujah Chorus," from *The Messiah.* Deep
religious emotion and spiritual power came like a Pentecost upon
the people. The star of Methodism had risen to its zenith.

Bishop Hughes was then given the chair to close the Conference.

Bishop U. V. W. Darlington, the senior Bishop of the Methodist Episcopal Church, South, read the exhortation and the
ascription of praise, and announced the closing hymn, "O God,
Our Help in Ages Past."

The Chair recognized Dr. T. D. Ellis, of the South Georgia
Conference, a prominent member of the Joint Commission, to
make the motion to adjourn; and Dr. E. H. Cherrington, another
prominent Commissioner, to second the motion. The motion
being carried, Bishop John L. Nuelsen, the senior Bishop of the
Methodist Episcopal Church, gave the benediction.

With that apostolic benediction the greatest Conference ever
held in American Methodism came to its triumphant end. The
Methodist Church on that memorable night went forth in
majesty and power to do the will of God and to establish the
Kingdom of the Lord Jesus Christ on earth.

Chapter Twelve

WAYSIDE OBSERVATIONS

THE AUTHOR HAS FINISHED HIS TASK OF TRACING THE LONG AND difficult road over which Methodist Union has come and of telling the story of the delicate, intricate, and arduous negotiations of the seventy years from 1869 to 1939 in which the leaders of the Churches were almost continually engaged. The efforts at understanding and reconciliation, made by both sides at different times, were always commendable, but often they did not get far. Something had happened in 1830 when Protestant Methodism went apart, which men did not forget. Even greater things happened in 1844 when Episcopal Methodism was torn asunder. Not only had Separation been effected, but living principles had been enunciated and immovable landmarks established which could not be disregarded, much less discarded. The journey toward union could not begin until the Pact of 1844 was recognized and its principles and provisions respected. From these old roots, by sympathetic nurture and skillful grafting, a new life and organism were produced and the Churches were lifted into a beautiful and fruitful unity.

The Plan of Union is not a Southern plan nor a Northern plan. Neither side can claim its exclusive authorship, and each side made large contributions to it. Neither side alone could have produced such a plan. It is a joint plan developed by steps and degrees, by joint action, from the source elements and principles contained in the manifesto of the protesting group in 1828, and in the historic act of the undivided General Conference in 1844, and also from the joint thinking of leaders of both sides who sought to adjust American Methodism to the new

218

era of American life. Unification by reorganization, the guiding
and controlling principle set up by the Commission of Federation
in 1911, has produced The Methodist Church of today.

That the Plan of Union which has been adopted will give
permanent and productive union is reasonably and confidently
believed. However, it is also confidently believed that to attain
the high ends for which union was consummated the Plan in
letter and spirit must be loyally and faithfully carried out. To
emphasize this opinion the author may be allowed the liberty of
adding to the historical sketch some personal observations, interpretations, and suggestions.

The unification of the Methodist Episcopal Church, the Methodist Episcopal Church, South, and the Methodist Protestant
Church was hailed by many substantial citizens of the country,
in the churches and out, as a notable and meritorious achievement. It was regarded as a commendable example for the action
of other denominations of a common faith, and it gave impetus
to the cause of general denominational fraternity and approach-
ment and of the unity, if not union, of related Protestant bodies
in America. To be sure, much of this had no basis beyond sentiment and friendly impulse, but even that has atmospheric value.

The union met with very little opposition from the membership of the three uniting bodies. However, there were small
withdrawals in some sections. The largest groups withdrawing
were of persons who held to belief in the imminent second coming, or in second-blessing sanctification, upon the plea that
modernism controlled the united Church. Some of the opponents found extreme socialism among some of the leaders of the
new organization as a cause for their rejection of union, while
others objected to the membership of the Negro in the united
Church. A "Layman's Organization for the Preservation of the
Southern Methodist Church" was formed, and promoted by a
semimonthly bulletin. In South Carolina some eighteen to
twenty small village or rural congregations declared themselves
still churches of the Methodist Episcopal Church, South, ejected

their pastors who were loyal to The Methodist Church, and transferred the church property to independent trustees. These churches went so far as to organize the South Carolina Conference of the Methodist Episcopal Church, South. These actions brought on suits of injunction in the State courts through the Bishops in charge, with well-chosen, able attorneys as counsel. The opposition had also able attorneys. The chief element in the controversy became necessarily the question of the validity of the union and the legality of the adoption of the Plan of Union. The decisions so far have held that the adoption of the union and the Plan of Union was legal and valid. Appeals have been made to the higher courts. The case has also gone into the Federal Courts. Final decision may be delayed for some years. In the meantime the united Church goes confidently on, while the opposition does not increase its size, influence, or power. Methodist union will not probably be imperiled by the opposition.

The danger lies, if there should be any, with the lack of knowledge and appreciation of the conditions and conceptions out of which union came. There are too many of our people, many of them leaders, ministerial and lay, who have given too little study to the background of Methodist union to understand what was and is involved. Even after union was consummated, many Methodists failed to bring their understanding up to their sentimental approval. They have not acquainted themselves with the underlying essential principles and aims in the unification. As a consequence, they held tenaciously to their old conceptions of polity and practice and seem unable or unwilling to recognize that a new governmental structure has been set up with new principles and new procedure.

The union of the three Churches was not merely to remove overlappings, divisions, barriers, frictions, and sectional thinking, feeling, willing, and action. To be sure, to do that is greatly worth while, as far as it has been achieved. But it must be recognized that sectional thinking, feeling, willing, and action will be with us a very long time in this country, on both sides and all sides of the country, even with all the causes held in common to draw us together. The union was not merely to make a big church, multitudinous in members, extensive and encompassing in territory, rich in resources, powerful in action, and capable of possessing the land, and of being a major world church. That can be regarded as having real value, but its appeal is hardly in keeping with the highest and finest in Christian thinking. Bigness can prove to be a disadvantage, and even a disaster. Union has not of itself destroyed the possibilities of ecclesiastical unwieldiness nor driven sectionalism from the motives of control, but it can sustain both.

Methodist union is set to a high objective far beyond the removal of divisions and the quieting of delayed sentiments and unwholesome ambitions. The positive controlling purpose of this slowly constructed union is to conserve, preserve, and promote the substantial and demonstrable vital, social, moral, and religious values of Methodism in the United States of America, and to make of The Methodist Church the most efficient religious organization and force of which it is, or can be made, capable.

When union was adopted, Methodism in some sections was only marking time, in some was retreating, and in none had extraordinary vigor and valor. There was too much living on the past, if not *in* the past, and too little reaching for the future. Of the nineteen divisions of American Methodism a very large majority had shown no noticeable increase in twenty years. They had spent much time and energy building divisional fences for self-preservation, or in side-line activities to meet social and community demands. The spirit, the devotion, the sacrifice, and the service that made Methodism had subsided. The time had come to make new alignments, proper realignments, essential structural adjustments, and to create new molds for the new run of Methodism. In the language of the industries, American

Methodism needed retooling. Unification had for its chief purpose the inauguration of just such a movement.

The Methodist Church is not a massed aggregation of three Churches; it is a well-developed organism for three Churches, possessing and expressing the characteristic elements of each, but having a distinct originality and quality of its own. It is legally, ecclesiastically, doctrinally, and religiously the successor of the Methodist Episcopal Church, the Methodist Episcopal Church, South, and the Methodist Protestant Church; and in it they henceforth shall live, move, and have their being. Their names, their traditions, and their history shall ever be a sacred heritage, a treasured possession never to be surrendered, always to be honored and kept inviolate. The Methodist Church, however, came into being not by a reunion or a merger but by a creation. It will live and grow only as its originality and distinctiveness are recognized, appreciated, asserted, and cultivated. The stream of its activities has, and must ever have, a channel of its own that is broader and deeper than that of any one of its tributaries. To press it into the thought, polity, and plans of any one of the three is to restrict its service, cramp is activities, and limit its reach. The Methodist Church began in 1939—and not in 1844, or in 1828, or in 1784. Those who think for it, plan for it, and build for it must acquire its genius, catch its vision, realize its responsibility, and create its encompassing strategy.

Six Distinct Factors

The constitution of the United Church was set forth in the Plan of Union. A thorough knowledge of that constitution is essential to a competent understanding of the basic encompassing strategy of the Church. Failure here makes confusion in the application of church law and in the conceptions of possible administrative actions. Ministers and laymen should know thoroughly the constitution, that they may be delivered from the controlling conceptions of the preunion era.

The constitution sets up six very distinct factors of government with carefully defined powers and duties which cannot be added to or subtracted from except by the constitutional process. These are the General Conference, the Jurisdictional Conference, the Central Conference, the Annual Conference, the Judicial Council, and the Episcopacy. What they can do, and what only they can do, is plainly put down. They have no right or authority to go beyond or fall behind what is specified. When powers and duties are defined, that which is not included is excluded. That is an accepted and well-known principle of law.

Once the General Conference was considered supreme, especially in the Church North, and more or less so in the Church South. But it is not so, nor can it be so, in the united Church. Subject to the Restrictive Rules and the Constitution, the General Conference has "full legislative power over all matters distinctively connectional," which are definitely set out, nor does it have any other. To exercise any other power would be a usurpation. The members of a General Conference may pass any resolution which they approve on any social or economic question or issue, but in doing so they act personally and they cannot bind the Church by their action. Legislation is their only province, and legislation has to do only with adopting rules and regulations for the governmental policy and procedure of the Church as indicated in the Constitution. The General Conference cannot make a law outside of its limited legislative power. To be sure, because of the character and quality of the members of the General Conference, their pronouncement on any social, moral, and religious subject or issue would and should have great influence and force in the Church, but without the binding power of law.

The General Conference, as in the Churches before union, shares with the Annual Conference the power to make constitutional alterations and to express the particular will of the entire Church. The power to pass upon the constitutionality of the legislative acts of the General Conference is now vested in the Judicial Council with final authority. The Judicial Council is an appellate body only, with jurisdiction limited to appeals from Conferences, Boards, and the Council of Bishops, all under prescribed conditions. Appeals from individuals cannot be heard. It has no power to interpret any law except as that law affects the constitution, or in affirming or denying the decisions of Bishops made in the presidency of Conferences. The Judicial Council is not and cannot properly be a Judiciary Committee for the General Conference, even should it be requested to act as such. The reasons are: first, that a committee for a legislative body in good parliamentary procedure is a committee from that body; second, that since the Judicial Council may be required to pass upon the constitutionality of the very act in question, it should not give an opinion until it sits legally in its appellate responsibility. Besides, the General Conference is capable, or should be, of interpreting the statutory laws of the Church or of altering them so it and its constituency can interpret them.

THE JURISDICTIONAL CONFERENCE

The distribution of the power held by the General Conference in its period of supremacy was further largely effected by the creation of the Jurisdictional Conference. The legislative powers of the Jurisdictional Conference are not extensive, but they are sufficiently comprehensive to enable it to meet its constitutional responsibility as a promotional and administrative body. The Jurisdictional Conference has not only the power but the duty—

1. To elect the Bishops.

2. To elect all the members of the General Boards, each Jurisdictional Conference electing the quota of representatives as determined by the General Conference.

3. To provide for interests and institutions within its boundaries.

4. To promote the evangelistic, educational, missionary, and benevolent interests of the Church and to establish and consti-

tute Jurisdictional Conference Boards auxiliary to the General Boards, for discharging this responsibility.

5. To appoint a Committee on Appeals to hear and determine the appeal of a traveling preacher of that Jurisdiction from the decision of a Trial Committee.

Very evidently the Plan of Union has assigned the Jurisdictional Conference duties very great, very important, and very definite, and has not merely bestowed privileges. Behind these duties is not a "may," but a "must." With the duties was conferred the power, adequate and undisputed, to discharge these duties. These duties and powers should be diligently and thoroughly studied.

The constitutional rights, duties, and powers of the Jurisdictional Conference have not yet been fully recognized, respected, and provided for by either the General Conference or the Jurisdictional Conferences themselves. This may be accounted for by the fact that in 1940 the membership of the Church had not had time to think thoroughly through the provisions, specifications, and implications of the Plan of Union nor to come to a complete understanding of the genius of union itself. Old conceptions, old methods, old regional and area devices and processes were still in mind. The Jurisdictional idea of boards, benevolences, movements, systems, cultivation, and promotion as set forth in the Plan had not taken hold fully on the Church. But that should not now be true. The Plan of Union is explicit; its letter and spirit are known, and they invite, if not require, faithful, scrupulous, conscientious observance by the General and Jurisdictional Conferences, and by all officers, agents, and agencies of the Church. The Plan is a pledge as well as a process.

There are problems that yet remain unsolved, and among them is the administration of the great connectional interests of the Church. We have been in the midst of a period of experimentation and adaptation. While the general results have not been wholly unsatisfactory, there is no reason to conclude that they have been as effective as the situation demands and our resources in money and personnel make possible. There seems no reason to group all our connectional boards under one rigid policy. The work of certain boards is national and international and that of certain other boards is essentially jurisdictional. For example, the Board of Foreign Missions in its administration deals with problems lying largely outside of the United States, whereas home missions deals with problems that are domestic, and that vary with the differing conditions, social and economic, moral and religious, to be discovered in different parts of the United States. Another example is the work of Temperance and Education. The former by its nature is on the national level, while the latter has its roots in local and regional conditions and interests. Such problems and others quite similar lie for solution within the range of the Plan adopted.

The plan and purpose of union contemplate an expanded and expanding horizon of a great new American Methodist Church. That Church must fit into every nook and corner of this country, into every class and classification of people, and into every type of regional and community thought and civilization. The United States has a great variety of thinking, feeling, willing, and action, and the Church that satisfies and serves such a population and citizenship must find many and varied ways of domesticating itself among the people. Back of the Jurisdictional Conference System of interest and institutions, administration and promotion, boards and agencies, is a very sound philosophy which churchmen more and more are recognizing.

There is still a North and a South in this country, and there is an East and a West, and they are not merely geographical. They are social, economic, ethnic, cultural, civilizational, ideological. To be sure, they are not so extremely so as to be divisional, but they are sufficiently distinct to create varied human characteristics and values. Each of these great sections has produced values that should be conserved and promoted. New

England is a storehouse of great American treasures. From its western border through a half-dozen great states lie the major industrial regions with immense populations with continental European backgrounds, ideas, and ideals. Then there is the Middle West, largely agricultural, with a commercial outlook, and with ideas and attitudes of its own. The vast Northwest, reaching to the Pacific Ocean, has another very different outlook on life. Then there is the Old South extending from Virginia to the Gulf and out to the Mississippi with a marvelous homogeneity, and a civilization that is rooted in settled thought and fine culture that defy the ravages of change, and with a proud people who are devoted to their history and traditions and loyal to their country and its fundamental idealism. Then comes the broad Southwest of independent thought and action, progressive in spirit and creative of a new civilization. The Church that wins and serves these great sections must fit into them and must have respect and regard for them and their distinctive social, political, economic, and cultural views. Not to do so is to invite gradual deterioration and decay of the Church.

In producing an ecclesiastical structure for an American Methodism that would establish an acceptable and binding unity of all these sections it was necessary to provide for variety in expression in administration and in promotion. The Plan of Union was built with that in view. Provision was made to protect and promote regional rights, regional thought, regional ingenuity and resourcefulness, regional distribution, regional cultivation, regional responsibility, regional control, and the development of regional interest, loyalty, and action. That is the meaning and purpose of the Jurisdictional Conference. Its possibilities for the stimulation, development, aggressiveness, and growth of Methodism are immeasurable.

The early and old contention that six strong, vigorous, well-organized Jurisdictional Conferences would make six Churches instead of one now has little standing with those who have thought the matter through and know the durability and power of the constitutional connectional bonds of this Methodist union. To hold such a contention is to discount and discredit the General Conference, having as it does the only connectional legislative powers, the constitutionally intrenched general superintendency, the common ministry, common membership, common doctrine, ritual, spirit, purpose, and procedure in the entire Church, as bonds of permanence and power. The Jurisdictional Conference has no voice on any of these unifying bonds, nor even a vote on any connectional legislative or constitutional question and alteration. When it is seen how impregnable is the solidarity of congregationally governed and diocesanly administered denominations, the fear of a strong, vigorous Jurisdictional Conference can be forever banished.

Dr. Lynn Harold Hough, Dean of Drew Theological Seminary, in his book, *The Christian Criticism of Life,* wisely says:

There is a false passion for unity which leads inevitably to the blurring of the very distinctions which give significance to life. . . . . The passion for unity may become an all-devouring passion, destroying these distinctions upon which the validity and the permanent meaning of human experience depend. Where the mind reaches principles by whose means alone it is possible to understand and interpret life and then, driven by a false desire for unity, destroys these very distinctions, one has a kind of false abdication of the critical intelligence. The desire to rise from heterogenous diversity to harmonious unity is of course a necessary and right desire. But it is one thing to seek the unity which preserves the necessary distinctions. And it is quite another thing to lose oneself in the unity which destroys the necessary distinctions. In the latter case the passion for unity has become a false and destructive thing.

The Jurisdictional Conference has to win its standing against several obstacles before coming into full recognition, cordial appreciation, and loyal support from a great part of the Church's constituency. In the first place, it is new, a new administrative and promotional unit in American Methodism; and new measures are generally received with suspicion, or at least with hesitancy. This has been so with the Jurisdictional Conference. It is feared by some almost as much as a divider of the Church into sections as embraced by others as the only safe and sane bond of substantial union. In the second place, instead of being accepted as a co-ordinate, which it is, it is being regarded by many as a subordinate, which it is not. The General Conference, constituted as formerly, very naturally could be inclined, because of its history, to assume the right to dictate to the Jurisdictional Conference what it should do, and how it should do it, in the fields of responsibility which have been assigned constitutionally to the Jurisdictional Conference.

In the third place, if the General Boards are allowed or ordered by General Conference action to monopolize all the funds raised in the general budget, the Jurisdictional Conference will be denied the necessary resources for carrying on the work of its constitutionally required Boards. If after that the Jurisdictional Conferences are encouraged, if not instructed, not to lay an assessment of their own, the breakdown of the plan of union as it relates to the Jurisdictional Conference is inevitable. Death by starvation would be inescapable.

This creates a state of centralization in the Church which the Jurisdictional Conference was constituted to prevent. The promotional work of the Church in all departments was meant to be done by the Jurisdictional Conference Board and not by the General Boards. The responsibility of the Jurisdictional Conference for the "interests and institutions within its own boundaries" requires that the administration of these matters shall not be in some far-away General Board, but in the Jurisdictional Conference Board which will observe the policies of the General Board.

In the fourth place, those who were reared in the atmosphere and thought of a supreme General Conference, who have always thought of centralization as indispensable to unification, who have considered distribution of power as disparaging if not destructive to unity, who have regarded the Jurisdictional Conference as a temporary expedient for getting union and not as the permanent and essential basis for an indissoluble union, will be inclined to allow it to become ineffective, and to be drawn more and more under the influence and control of the General Conference and the General Boards. This attitude is very hurtful.

The Jurisdictional Conference strong, vigorous, courageous, and full of force is the hope of a great Methodist Church in the United States, and in every part of this country. Its prescribed duties and powers look to the intensive cultivation of all the field, to the earnest promotion of all the causes, to the intimate supervision of all the varied interests, and to an intelligent administration of all the affairs of the Church. A Church of 8,000,000 members covering 3,000,000 square miles of territory with varying regions of homogeneity requires just such Jurisdictional Conferences as the Plan of Union has constituted and established.

Union will not be endangered by the vigor, the aggressiveness, and the effectiveness of the Jurisdictional Conference in the discharge of its constitutionally assigned duties and powers. The danger to union will be elsewhere. It will always be where there is inefficiency. It can arise from disregard for the values, possibilities, and leadership of any section, or from the failure to maintain proper regional constituency balance in the officers of the Boards, Commissions, and agencies, and in the chairmanships of committees in the General and other Conferences. It can come from the unwieldiness in the Boards and in Annual, Jurisdictional, and General Conferences which limit, if not destroy, intelligent fellowship and efficiency, and which may develop discontent and criticism and create longings for other days and conditions. It can come from the far-away-ness of headquarters of the few centralized controlling boards and the foreignness of their officers because of lack of acquaintance with them. It can come from centralization of benevolences to be directed only to General Boards and Commissions to the entire disregard and neglect of Jurisdictional Conference interests and institutions. World Service limps when home service is ignored. But all these signals of possible danger to union, as light is thrown on them and correction is made, will not continue long. Union is thoroughly intrenched in the mind, heart, and purpose of American Methodism, and it will endure.

THE CENTRAL CONFERENCE

The Central Conference was not new in the Methodist economy. The Methodist Episcopal Church established Central Conferences in 1920, and they were made the norm for the Central Conference in the united Church. They are established for the work of the Church outside the United States of America. They are given provisions very similar to those of the Jurisdictional Conference. They are constitutionally given the powers and duties to promote the evangelistic, educational, missionary, and benevolent interests and institutions within their boundaries; to elect the bishops for their respective Central Conferences; to establish and constitute Central Conference Boards and elect their administrative officers; to determine the boundaries of the Annual Conferences within their areas; to appoint a Committee on Appeals and to make the necessary rules and regulations for the administration of the work within their boundaries, subject to the powers vested in the General Conference. Their bishops are members of the Council of Bishops, but their vote is restricted to interests of their own Central Conferences or to those common to all Central Conferences.

The Central Conference is the best provision so far devised for the administration of the work of the young national Church that has been developed under missionary service. A better name for it might be possible and may yet be adopted. It gives the largest possible self-determination and self-control without an estranging autonomy and separating independence. It maintains vital relations with the strong, sympathetic, supporting mother Church and receives not only material assistance and personal missionary aid but also the vigorous religious and ecclesiastical life of the Church developed through a long Christian history.   Independence casts away all this and puts the young Church upon the backgrounds and resources of its own nation.   The Central Conference living up to its powers and duties will become more and more the strong, versatile, and vital agency in the growth of Methodisms outside the United States.

THE NEGRO METHODISTS

The Negro population of the United States is about 12,000,000. The Negro membership of The Methodist Church is about 325,000.   The combined membership of the three independent Negro Methodist denominations—the African Methodist Episcopal Church, the African Methodist Episcopal Zion Church, and the Colored Methodist Episcopal Church—is about 1,800,000. The membership of the one Negro Baptist Denomination, the National Baptist Church, is 3,500,000 to 4,000,000.   Accurate and exact statistics on all these churches are not available. Thirty years ago, when all the Negro Baptist denominations united into one, the total Methodist membership and the total Baptist membership were about equal.   The Methodists have kept up their divisions, their competitions, and their self-preservation methods and have had only small increase in all that time, while the united Baptists have given themselves to vigorous, aggressive, enthusiastic propagation, and their number has about doubled. Facts are telling arguments.

The Commissioners of the Methodist Episcopal Church, South, from the beginning advocated a united Negro Methodist Church in the United States.   This recommendation was inserted in the Oklahoma declaration of the General Conference of 1914.   But it became more and more clear that such an act of union must rest necessarily with the Negro Methodists themselves.   It rests there today, and it will rest there as long as they desire it so. They are fully capable in their leadership to determine their own course and action.

This author in his first article on a Plan of Methodist Union,

published in March, 1911, in the *Christian Advocate* (Nashville),
said:

The union of the American Methodists of the Negro race is
just as desirable and as important, if not more so, as the union
of the white Methodists. There is no satisfactory reason, and
practically no excuse, for the existence of four groups of Negro
Episcopal Methodists, since there are no doctrinal, political, or
sectional differences, past or present, to keep them separate. Do
not the leaders among the white Methodists owe it to the Negro
Methodists to use their friendly offices in bringing about this
great desired union? Union of white Methodists and Negro
Methodists into one Church, however large or small the Negro
element, would not be desirable or scarcely possible, at this
period of our social, political, and religious life. Any negotiations for union should proceed upon the plan of having a
united Negro Methodism as well as a united white Methodism.

This same position was taken by this author in an address in
Evanston, Illinois, February 15-17, 1916, on "A Suggested Working Plan of Methodist Union."

A quarter of a century passed, and the noble, stalwart, able,
honored leaders of the Church South of that day, whose lives
were rooted in the experiences, history, sentiments, and traditions of the first fifty years of separation, had been gathered to
their fathers. Their successors in service, while approving their
judgment and wisdom as to the union of all Negro Methodist
groups, yet saw that the union of the three negotiating Churches,
if and when effected, must include the entire membership of the
three Churches, and that only, and that other unions must be
left to the future. With that conviction reached they set about
the one task of producing a plan upon which the three Churches
could and should unite. The final result was the provision of a
Negro Jurisdictional Methodist Conference for the Negro Annual
Conferences and Missions of the Church North and the Protestant Church of the same status as the white Jurisdictional Conferences.

The Joint Commission on Union from the very beginning in

1916 took cognizance of the close relation of the Colored Methodist Episcopal Church, with a membership of about 450,000, to the Church South. That Church was set off and set up by the Church South in 1870 at the request of its Negro membership. It has been fostered by the Church South from its beginning. It was one of the interests in the general benevolences of the Church South to the amount of $74,000 annually. Assistance was given to it also in the building of churches and schools, not only officially but by private donors. In the Plan of Union of 1920, and of 1924, there was a recommendation that financial support be given that Church by the Southern sections of the United Church. In the Plan of Union which was overwhelmingly adopted by all three Churches is this recommendation: "We recommend that financial support of the Colored Methodist Episcopal Church be continued by those jurisdictional divisions with which said Church is historically related, and to such an extent as those Jurisdictions may deem wise." That is a binding recommendation.

What has happened? That overwhelmingly endorsed recommendation has been entirely ignored. The two Southern Jurisdictional Conferences, at their very first meetings, did nothing, proposed nothing. The first General Conference did nothing, proposed nothing. However, the General Conference did advise, if not instruct, the Jurisdictional Conferences not to lay any assessments for anything, after it had laid a general assessment upon the Conferences for all that it was thought they would bear. It is hardly thinkable that this treatment of such a recommendation will be allowed to be continued. To do so is to estrange from The Methodist Church in the South the Negro people who have the largest and best access to the Methodists of the South. Union has not brought the Negro membership of the united Methodist Church any closer to the Methodists of the South, except officially, than they were before union. To cut off the Colored Methodist Episcopal Church is to destroy not only the historic but the strongest bond with the Negro people which exists in the South.

It has been suggested that the Colored Methodist Episcopal Church be invited to join The Methodist Church and become a part of the Negro Jurisdictional Conference. It must be recognized that there are difficulties in the way of that action. In the first place, that Church, with its autonomy, independence, self-control, and self-determination, with its own bishops, boards, and complete organization, would be slow in surrendering all this to enter a union in which it will be only half of a minority group with its limited voice and influence. In the second place, their entering The Methodist Church would not produce nor even promote the union of Negro Methodists, which is the highly desired end in any further unions. In the third place, the other great historic Negro Methodist bodies, because of their history and attitude, would not be inclined to any union with a Church which will always necessarily be governed ulteriorly by white Methodists. In the fourth place, the Methodists of the South would not look with any degree of favor upon a greatly increased proportion of Negro representatives in the General Conference and in the General Boards. In the fifth place, a united Negro Methodist Church with the three Negro denominations as constituent units would mobilize and solidify great autonomous, self-determining forces for a positive, forceful, aggressive movement and service among the Negro people and also would be in position to join The Methodist Church in forming a strong, effective Inter-Church Council through which the two Churches could be of mutual assistance, and united in advancing the causes of evangelism, education, and social benefits and the Christian life for the Negro population of the country. To that consummation all Methodism should earnestly and sympathetically look.

The Methodist Church begins its career with three distinct, vital lines of definite responsibility and major service to the Negro Methodists of the United States which should be pursued with intelligence, diligence, devotion, and vigor. They are: (1) to render every possible assistance to the bishops, ministry, and members of the Central Jurisdictional Conference in their courageous, sacrificial efforts to advance Methodism and Christianity among the Negro people; (2) to carry out to the letter the recommendation, if not commitment, in the Plan of Union to furnish financial support to the Colored Methodist Episcopal Church through the two Southern Jurisdictional Conferences in keeping with what was being done before union by the Methodist Episcopal Church, South; (3) to give continued hearty sympathy and furthering support to any and all movements and negotiations for bringing together into one strong aggressive Negro Methodist body the African Methodist Episcopal Church, the African Methodist Episcopal Zion Church, and the Colored Methodist Episcopal Church. To most Methodists to do these things will be a joyous privilege; to all it will be a sacred obligation.

FINAL WORD

These wayside observations indicate that, to this writer at least, while union is now in operation, it is yet not complete. All the terms, prescriptions, and demands of the Plan of Union have not yet been put into full effect. It has to be recognized and appreciated that union is a process as well as an act, and it may be a long process. There has not been time enough for the transition in thinking from the old state of things in the three Churches to the new status in the one Church. Time will be required for the Church to come to a full understanding of all the constitutional provisions. It is also true that many adjustments in methods and administration of many kinds—legal, social, and regional—require time for the process. But patience and persistence, loyalty and labor, intelligence and conscience will bring the eventual reward. Faithful observance of the Plan of Union by all persons on all sides, proper respect and regard for the rights, responsibilities, and rewards of all sections for all sections, and the faithful loyalty to our ecclesiastical posterity equal to our allegiance to our ecclesiastical ancestry will give union its permanence and power and Methodism its advance and triumph.

The Methodist Church is in position to assume an exceedingly responsible place among the religious forces of this country and of the world. But to do so The Methodist Church must be The Methodist Church. It must have a mind, a voice, a will, a thought, a strategy, and an end of its own. Its catholicity, its tolerance, and its fraternity, great as they are and should be, must not dim or diminish its positiveness of doctrine, its robustness of polity, or its aggressiveness of life and labor. Bigness may command space, but it does not secure position and power. The Methodist Church will never be much of a world Church, unless and until it has content, substance, force, and mastery as an American Church. Its power will be and must be American power, in and through the organisms, agencies, and people that create power. Vitality centers in the heart, whether of the human body, the government, or the Church. The heart of each must be kept with diligence if the extending body shall be maintained in health and strength. This is decidedly true with The Methodist Church.

The Methodist Church today is the powerful heir of the accumulated values and forces of 150 years of American Methodist life and labor. The past has been illustrious with achievement and renowned for the eminence and ability of its master workmen whatever their place or position. Differences in their views at times brought divergences in action, but Methodism never deviated from its mission and its divinely directed way. We of today have only honor and praise for them all. They followed their convictions in their own way, but gave Methodism their best life and strength. They are all ours now, and in our hearts they shall all live forevermore.

The road to Methodist union has been very long, very difficult, and over many cuts and streams, and through many dark valleys and over rough ranges. But there has always been someone who took up the precious load when others fell by the way. Many honorable names have been carved on the monuments that mark the wayside. These noble and great men could not see alike, especially when they looked back, but in mutual confidence and respect they toiled on together. They might toil in different groups and on different sides of the roadbed, but at nightfall they found that they had somehow extended the road. What they really accomplished they never knew. But when we of this day drove down the spike of gold at the end of the road, somehow we heard a shout all along the way that reached clear back to the beginning. Well done! Honor to each and all! May their names be indelibly inscribed upon Methodism's scroll of everlasting remembrance. Well done! The long road is finished and Methodist union has arrived in beauty and majesty. May The Methodist Church live long and well!

Index

239